THE
SECRET TEMPLE

THE
SECRET TEMPLE

Masons,
Mysteries,
and the
Founding of America

PETER LEVENDA

continuum

NEW YORK • LONDON

2009

The Continuum International Publishing Group Inc
80 Maiden Lane, New York, NY 10038

The Continuum International Publishing Group Ltd
The Tower Building, 11 York Road, London SE1 7NX

www.continuumbooks.com

Printed in the United States of America

9780826430007

Library of Congress Cataloging-in-Publication Data
Levenda, Peter.
 The secret temple : masons, mysteries, and the founding of America / Peter Levenda.
   p. cm.
 Includes bibliographical references and index.
 ISBN-13: 978-0-8264-3000-7 (pbk. : alk. paper)
  ISBN-10: 0-8264-3000-7 (pbk. : alk. paper) 1. Freemasons—United States—History. 2. Freemasonry—United States—History. 3. Secret societies—United States—History. I. Title.

HS515.L48 2009
366'.10973—dc22

                              2008045810

To my brother, Leonard

Contents

Acknowledgments

I HAVE ALWAYS RESISTED JOINING THE MASONS, and probably that was a good thing, for it allowed me to write this book with no oaths or secrets to restrict me. During the 2004 presidential election the reader may remember that both John Kerry and George W. Bush were asked by Tim Russert on the NBC News Program *Meet the Press* to describe their membership in another secret society, Skull and Bones. Even though the election of the leader of the Free World was at stake, both men refused to discuss it. For a researcher or journalist, that kind of obligation can only be a frustrating obstacle.

So I can honestly say that no Masons of my acquaintance were asked any embarrassing questions. The result of my inquiries of them was usually to be sent in the direction of a good book or the address of a public archive. Whatever conclusions I have come to in the course of this work are, then, entirely mine.

I would like to mention in this place the editorial and support teams at Continuum who have made this process as painless as possible. I especially would like to thank David Barker, John Mark Bolling, Gabriella Page-Fort, Katie Gallof, Burke Gerstenschlager, and Elizabeth White.

In addition, my discussions with James Wasserman on the theme of Masonic brotherhood proved stimulating, and his book on Masonic sites in Washington, D.C., is a useful reference.

Sophie Kaye proved a charming and generous friend, as did her somewhat reserved associate Newman.

We do not realize that there is an America without and an America which extends within.

—A. E. Waite, Introduction to *The Works of Thomas Vaughan*

INTRODUCTION

"I have abstained from becoming a member of them, that I might not have my tongue tied or my pen restrained by the engagements I must have made on entering the chapter or encampment."

—Godfrey Higgins, quoted in A. E. Waite,
The Real History of the Rosicrucians

THE AVAILABLE LITERATURE on the Freemasons tends to fall into two categories: books by non-Masons and books by Masons. The books by non-Masons are either scholarly works concentrating on a specific aspect of the group—its history, its influence on specific political events, and so on—or they are nonacademic works intended for a popular audience that claim to unveil the mysteries of Freemasonry and as such may be pro-Masonic or anti-Masonic in nature.

The books by Masons are either works that were written for other Masons and for those involved in esoteric studies, or they are scholarly works that discuss Masonic history and practice. The problem with all Masonic literature is that there is very little that can be accepted as representing the official position of Freemasonry; texts written by Freemasons can run the gamut from Albert Pike's rather pious *Morals and Dogma*—a work that could be considered part of the Masonic "canon" if such existed—to the works by Robert Lomas that claim to have uncovered the deepest secrets of Freemasonry through studies of Egyptian history, Jewish religion, the Crusades, and the Shroud of Turin.

Another problem area consists of the organizational structure of Masonry itself. There is no Masonic "pope," no one hierarch who determines what Masons should or should not believe. There is a code of conduct, a set of oaths and rituals, and little else unless one wants to spend the time and effort necessary to actually study the old books and become expert in the esoteric side of the group. To complicate things further, there are Masonic groups that are considered irregular by the mainstream Lodges: groups such as Co-Masonry, *Le Droit Humaine*, and the Rites of Memphis and Mizraim. These latter tend to be more overtly esoteric in nature and have their origins not in the United Grand Lodge of England but on the Continent, in France and Italy.

And then, of course, there is the Illuminati: more properly called the *Illuminaten Orden*, or Order of the Illuminates, a group that began in Germany in the late eighteenth century in an atmosphere of revolt against monarchical regimes. Founded by law professor Adam Weishaupt at the University of Ingolstadt, Bavaria, in 1776, the Illuminati had nurtured close associations with the Freemasons until the former were suppressed for their political intrigues. Quite often, the history—and legends—of the Illuminati are confabulated with Masonic history to the extent that the two societies seem inextricable when in reality nothing could be further from the truth.

So, when we begin to study Freemasonry and most especially the influence of Freemasonry on the United States, we have to wade through a large volume of literature written by people with their own agendas. Thus, it is fashionable in some circles to equate Freemasonry with the idea of a global conspiracy. The source of this concept can frankly be laid at the doorstep of the Masonic temple itself; for although Freemasons famously describe their organization as "not a secret society but as a society with secrets," this clandestine, esoteric character naturally leads to all sorts of fanciful imaginings. One only needs to remember how the CIA was characterized during the Cold War as an all-powerful secret society bent on world domination to understand how people (and groups) who openly admit they have secrets can be assumed to be up to no good. It is unfortunately a truism in our world that people are rarely out to secretly loan money, secretly heal illness, or secretly remove obstacles from one's path in life. People and groups remain secret so that their work can continue unimpeded—by laws civil or religious, by government oversight and action, or by society in general; the implication being that their work would not be condoned or even understood.

This is the environment in which we now find ourselves, for Freemasonry was born in secret and is concerned with a secret that even some Freemasons themselves admit has possibly been lost to them forever. The secret is so important, so potentially devastating, that the outward form, rituals, and appearances of a secret society must be maintained in the event that the secret is, eventually, revealed either through accident or design. The secret nature of Freemasonry—as well as the famous stipulations of brotherhood, decency, and moral living—may actually be the vehicle or vessel for this missing piece of the puzzle. Its rituals may be nothing more than an elaborate system of codes pointing to this secret.

In fact, as we shall see, the story of Freemasonry may be nothing less than the secret history of Western civilization itself.

There are three different ways of approaching Freemasonry. The most popular one by far begins with the assumption that Freemasons are part of a worldwide conspiracy and are, in effect, the secret rulers of the governments of the world. It combines conspiracy theories about assassinations and revolutions with the image of the Freemason as a member of a secret society that practices initiations in the dead of night with terrible oaths and equally terrible penalties for breaking them.

Another approach is the purely academic one. It is based on documentation, much of it produced by the Freemasons themselves, going back to the fourteenth century. It consists of tracing the influence of Masons on the political events of the day and is thus inextricably linked to politics, much as the conspiracy theorists would have it. There is virtually no academic history of the Masons that consists only of internal—that is, purely Masonic—history because that history is seen as myth and legend. Masonic history is always described with reference to contemporary political (and sometimes cultural) events. In the United States, as an example, the most famous Freemasons are presidents and politicians. Freemasons are usually not famous simply by being Freemasons. It's their influence on the world around them that provides them with fame; their membership in a Masonic lodge is usually seen as a detail, and a relatively unimportant one at that.

The third approach is less popular and somewhat less conventionally academic. This is the attempt to understand Masonry on spiritual grounds. Of what do the initiations consist? What do they mean? What are their purpose? How do we decode Masonic symbolism? Is it possible to understand Masonry without being a Mason?

There are two ways of answering that last question. We might say that it is impossible to understand any group, any culture, or any religion without being a member of it. Conversely, we may say that only an outside observer can bring a totally unbiased perspective. Neither answer is sufficient, of course. Quantum theory tells us that the observer changes the event observed. While this is true for waves and particles, many will object that one cannot "port" quantum theory to historical observation. However, as recent anthropological research has shown, it is quite difficult to come away from six months or a year of living among preindustrial aboriginal peoples with a comfortable sense of having understood or "known" those peoples, since the very alien presence of the anthropologist in that setting of necessity changes the environment around her. People react to her differently, will say things designed to elicit a certain response, will hide ancestral secrets, will disguise their motivations and, if possible, their actions. Surface events will be observed, but without knowledge of the deeper connective tissue that binds them together, that organizes them around an unspoken center, the events will be misunderstood or mischaracterized.

The Masons are a group that has made a virtue of secrecy. While their organization is certainly not secret—there are Masonic temples throughout the world, easily identifiable as such—their practices are secret. Generally, non-Masons may not "sit in" on an initiation as interested observers. And the secrecy of the initiations surrounds an even deeper secret, an essential mystery, as we shall see.

Thus, this book is an attempt by an outside observer—albeit one with decades of experience in observing secret societies around the world—to explore the relationship between Freemasonry and the American experience, in the hope that this examination will reveal some essential truths about both Freemasonry and the revolutionary dream of the founding fathers. In order to do this, we will divide our inquiry into two parts. In the first, we will begin with a discussion of the legends and Biblical traditions that formed the intellectual environment for the first Masonic lodges. In the second part, we will look at historical Freemasonry basing our research on the available texts and on researches by other scholars in the field. We will move to the colonies for an idea of how deeply Freemasonry and the hermetic arts were entrenched there before the American Revolution. At the same time, we will look at revolutionary movements in Europe that were influenced by Freemasonry. After that, it is essential to investigate the anti-Masonic movement of early-nineteenth-century America, and the subsequent adoption of Masonic ideas and designs by the prophet of the Church of Jesus Christ of Latter-Day Saints, Joseph Smith Jr.

Throughout, our inquiry will be devoted to a more interior examination of Masonic groups, ideas, and symbols. The idea of the Masonic temple will be explored in an effort to understand the roots of the concept, whether in Solomon's Temple or the Pyramids of Egypt. This research will take us to some fascinating areas of world history, with reference to everything from the Dead Sea Scrolls to the alignment of Egyptian monuments with the stars. The idea of a temple as "sacred space" and the importance of sacred architecture to the Masons will be examined for the insights it will give us to the meaning of the temple and its associated initiations. This will lead us to an investigation of the sacred geometry that was said to have influenced the design of America's capitol: Washington, D.C.

Finally, we will take a good, hard look at the conspiracy theories that have plagued the study of Freemasonry for almost two hundred years—with, perhaps, some surprising results. From the *Protocols of the Elders of Zion* to the *Propaganda Due* lodge of Italy, we will try to separate the wheat from the chaff.

Americans live with a basic dilemma. They place a high value on their personal privacy, perhaps more so than most people; this may be due to the much-advertised dissolution of the American nuclear family with its associated emphasis on the individual over the group. At the same time, they expect perfect transparency in their government. It has been the (sometimes pointless) secrecy of American government institutions that has contributed to the paranoia and cynicism of the conspiracy theorists. One suspects that if something is being kept secret, then that secret is evidence of guilt, of culpability. That sentiment is what has colored much of the anxiety concerning the most famous secret organization of all, the Freemasons. The author is not a Freemason. He has never joined any occult order or secret society. He has no horse in this race. Thus, the result of his labors will be untainted by personal agenda. It is possible that the conclusions drawn in this study will be rejected by Freemasons themselves, or even provide a new perspective on the old Craft; but at the very least they may provide talking points for future conversations on the role of a secret society in this most public and least private of global communities: the United States of America.

Peter Levenda
Miami 2008

PART ONE

VEILED IN ALLEGORY

CHAPTER ONE

Who Are the Masons?

The modern fraternity of Free and Accepted Masons, or the Freemasons, has existed officially since St. John's Day in London in June 1717, but its true origins are clouded in the obscurity of time, mystery and bad record-keeping.

—Christopher Hodapp, *Solomon's Builders*

THIS IS THE CRUX OF THE PROBLEM. First, the Freemasons have an "official" date that has nothing really to do with the origins of the group but is a convenient starting point for any historical analysis; and going forward is relatively easier than going backward from that date. Second, this statement by Hodapp is a qualified one in another respect: it refers to "the modern fraternity of Free and Accepted Masons" which is not identical to the other Masonic groups that also claim valid "lines of succession."

And, third, the remark about "bad record-keeping" is sadly one of the facts that confronts any serious attempt to write the definitive history of the society.

We must also be certain to separate the mundane history of the society from the legends and myths contained in their own rituals and other writings, for the latter speak of origins in ancient Egypt and Jerusalem and there is no way to determine the truth or falsity of these allegations. Indeed, the Masons themselves insist that these references are purely allegorical. However, it is possible to trace the origins of Masonry back to the guilds that were responsible for building the great Gothic cathedrals of France. The Gothic cathedrals themselves were—directly or indirectly—the result of the activities of the military orders in Jerusalem, including the Knights Templar, an order of knights that was based at the site of King Solomon's Temple. When we realize that Solomon's Temple is a central

3

concept in the initiation rituals of the Freemasons, then we have something to work with, for at this point the mundane history and the allegorical history merge, but perhaps not in the way intended by the creators of the rituals.

A further wrinkle is alluded to in Hodapp's humorous (but slightly disingenuous) statement about "bad record-keeping." There is an awful lot we do know about the history of the eighteenth century, when the Freemasons officially began; there is also a lot we know about the seventeenth and sixteenth centuries. It is only when we confront the case of the Freemasons that we suddenly find ourselves adrift in an ocean of mystery without a paddle or a rudder. Although archival records do exist of Masonic groups and even Masonic initiations from the seventeenth and sixteenth centuries, they are sparse and open to a great deal of interpretation. The reason for this is simple, of course. The Masons were—and are—a secret society (or, to use their phrase, a "society with secrets"). The modern version of this society was born in an era of religious and political turmoil, both in the British Isles and on the Continent. Protestants were fighting Catholics; Puritans were fighting Anglicans. The Templars had been suppressed by the Church and the French king on October 13, 1307; it is less than a century later—in 1390—that the first recorded Masonic "charges" can be reliably dated.

Opponents of the Templar-Mason theory point to the vast distance in time between the suppression of the Knights Templar in 1307 and the founding of the Grand Lodge of England in 1717: more than four hundred years. They insist that the Templars could not have survived underground for that length of time, only to resurface centuries later as the Free and Accepted Masons. That is a reasonable objection to make, if you stick to 1717 as the year the first Masonic lodge was created. However, as we will see, between the suppression of the Templars and the first *known* Masonic "Charges" is a space of only eighty-three years. Add to this the fact that the Masons (at least in France and, to a certain extent, in England) were guilds that developed around the building of the Gothic cathedrals—that, in effect, they were employees of the wealthy and powerful military orders— indicates a connection that is definite but no less mysterious.

OPERATIVE VERSUS SPECULATIVE MASONRY

One of the first issues to be confronted when approaching the subject of Freemasonry is the difference between Operative Masonry and Speculative Masonry. *Operative Masonry* is the term used to refer to actual masons: those individuals who built the great cathedrals, castles and guild halls of Europe. *Speculative Masonry* refers to what we know today as Freemasonry: a fraternity composed of secret initiations and meetings behind closed doors. Unfortunately, the term *speculative* has become a term of opprobrium among scholars and academics, so that anything that calls itself "speculative" immediately evokes a standard reaction. *Speculation* is not knowledge, nor science. It is a term roughly equivalent to "imagination," or even "guessing." It is used in this case to describe men who call themselves Masons yet who never laid a single stone or cemented a single brick. In this case, then, they are "speculative" in that they have no direct knowledge of the arts of architecture and construction but instead attempt to use the basis of these arts—geometry—in an attempt to understand the workings of the natural world and to improve their own spirituality.

Freemasons are quick to assure outsiders that their society is not a religion. You will find that assertion again and again on their websites and in books written by Masons. It is virtually impossible, however, for an outsider to understand how a group can use elaborate religious symbolism—from the building of Solomon's Temple to the image of Jacob's Ladder, the Book of the Law, and the Holy of Holies—without being itself religious. In fact, Freemasons may be accused of being slightly disingenuous on this point. No matter how often or how firmly they insist that they are not a religion, the fact of their rituals and spiritual allegories argues strongly in favor of a different point of view. To advance spiritually—as a Mason might say, "morally"—through the experience of ritual initiations is, if not religious, at least hermetic or occult. Add to this the wealth of literature written by Masons on the more esoteric aspects of the Craft, and we are left with the unmistakeable impression that Freemasonry shares a great deal in common with the rites of Mithra or Eleusis, mystery cults of the ancient world.

So, in order to provide a basic context for what we mean by Freemasonry, it will be useful at this point to provide an overview of the Masonic degree system. This will give us a set of symbols and terms—a mutual language—for interpreting what comes next.

THE MASONIC DEGREE RITUALS

Although much has been made of the so-called higher degrees of Freemasonry—such as the thirty-third degree—there are actually only three degrees that are the bedrock of the Craft and which constitute what is known as Blue Lodge Masonry. These are the degrees of Entered Apprentice, Fellow Craft, and Master Mason.

Originally there were only two degrees, those of Entered Apprentice and Fellow Craft. However, by the time of the creation of the Grand Lodge in 1717, a third degree had been added. Technically, the new degree was the second degree, but the name was retained. Thus, the new—second—degree had the name Fellow Craft but had nothing to do with the original Fellow Craft degree, which was now the Master Mason degree.

In order to understand Freemasonry it is necessary to begin with a discussion of these three degrees. The other degrees—associated with the appendant orders, such as the York Rite and the Scottish Rite—are not considered superior to the original three but amplifications or clarifications of them, developed by Master Masons who felt that the first three degrees required additional knowledge in order to be fully appreciated.

The descriptions of the degree rituals that follow are based on published accounts, both in standard reference works on Masonry such as *Duncan's Masonic Ritual* and on popular accounts written by Masons such as Robert Lomas.[1] Recourse was also had to some of the earliest published accounts of Masonic initiations published in the eighteenth century and that differ both from each other and from modern versions in an effort to disentangle some of the biblical, historical, and hermetic references.[2] I have relied upon factual accounts—such as the rubrics and details of the rituals—rather than "initiated" interpretations where possible. Lomas is included because he describes how the initiation rituals are conducted in modern-day

Great Britain, and thereby provides a point of comparison with some of the earlier versions. Copies of the Masonic "tracing boards," which are two-dimensional illustrations of the degree work, were also useful. There is a great body of work on Freemasonry and its rituals, but due to the problematic nature of Freemasonry and its secrets I have decided that if I must err it should be on the side of caution in describing Masonic initiations.

THE FIRST DEGREE, OR ENTERED APPRENTICE

The name of the first degree is self-explanatory. It refers to the lowest grade of guild worker, the unskilled laborer who begins at the bottom and learns his craft from the master stonemasons through a long and demanding internship. In Freemasonry, all men are "unskilled labor" in the spiritual sense: they are the rough stone, or *ashlar* (a term from the rituals), from the great quarry of humanity, a stone that has not been shaped or dressed. Becoming initiated in the order is the first step toward finding the dressed stone that is hidden within the shapeless mass. It is, in a sense, an attempt to bring order to chaos: an expression of humanity's dominion over the earth by taking a lump of rock and shaping it into something at once beautiful and useful. A sculptor does much the same, and the stonemasons who built the great Gothic cathedrals were also involved in the carving of the statues that adorned them. A sculptor will tell you that the sculpture is hidden within the stone, waiting to be released. The first-degree initiation of Freemasonry is designed to do the same. It is the beginning of a process that culminates in the final, third-degree ceremony with its overtones of death and resurrection.

The space in which the initiations takes place is the lodge. A lodge is both the physical building or room where Masons meet and perform their rituals and conduct the business of Masonry, and it is also a term used to refer to the group of members themselves. Members of the lodge are lodge brothers; there are no women permitted to join Masonry in its orthodox version, although Co-Masonry does allow women to become initiates. Co-Masonry is not officially recognized by the United Grand Lodge, however. The UGL is considered the spiritual head of organized Masonry, although it has no temporal power over any of the lodges, which operate pretty much autonomously as long as they maintain the traditions. This disconnect between Masonry and Co-Masonry may be a moot point to an outsider, since Co-Masonry is an important manifestation of Masonic practice and ideals, especially from a more hermetic or occult viewpoint (about which more later).

"Every Lodge is a Temple," writes Albert Pike in his massive and influential *Morals and Dogma*. "The room or place in which [Freemasons] meet, representing some part of King Solomon's Temple, is also called the Lodge. . . . "[3] King Solomon's Temple, or KST as it is often abbreviated in the shorthand of the rituals, is a central fact of Freemasonry. KST is viewed as representative of the universe, a microcosm of the macrocosm. Thus, the decorations of the Masonic temple often indicate this relationship. By imitating the design of the KST, the Masonic temple also imitates the design of the cosmos. It is a telescoping of the greater world outside the initiate into the sacred space of the temple, which then becomes interiorized in the initiate himself, thus ideally bringing him into alignment with the universe and hence with the perceived plan of the Great Architect, or God.

The temple itself is furnished with several items that bear examining before we get to the ritual itself. While each lodge will have its own design and arrangement—no two are identical—there are a few basic requirements that are kept from lodge to lodge.

Ideally, the physical footprint of the lodge consists of a rectangle that is composed of two squares end to end. The rectangle's length is from east to west, and its breadth from north to south. The ostensible meaning of this is to replicate how the ancient peoples thought of the earth, as a large rectangle with the sun rising in the east and setting in the west, thus marking the length of the rectangle on the earth. However, some architectural impressions of King Solomon's Temple do show a rectangle with this orientation.

On the ceiling of the lodge may be seen any one of a variety of symbols—the sun, the moon, the zodiac—but the All-Seeing Eye will usually be found directly above. This symbol famously has been duplicated on the back of the U.S. dollar bill as well as upon the Mormon Temple in Salt Lake City. Often, the eye will be seen in the middle of a pentagram—in this case, a five-pointed blazing star. In other cases, the Eye may be replaced with the letter *G*.

The letter *G* is said to stand for the English word *God*, but is also said to refer to *geometry*. Geometry is the liberal art revered above all others in Masonry, and it comes from the Greek original meaning "to measure the earth." One of the many Masonic interpreters—J. S. M. Ward—suggests that the letter *G* was not the original symbol, but a type of mason's square known as a gallows square.[4] This instrument is shaped like an upside-down letter *L*, with the horizontal bar shorter than the vertical leg. Later Masons—either not understanding it as a gallows square or wishing to conceal its meaning—confused this symbol with the Greek letter gamma, which they then translated as *G*. It is a creative solution, but the evidence to support this interpretation is thin.

The All-Seeing Eye—or the letter *G*—is often drawn within an equilateral triangle, which is also of Masonic significance. (Again, reference may be made to the dollar bill, which depicts the Eye within a triangle atop a Pyramid.) The triangle symbolizes strength, but the number of its sides is also suggestive. For instance, there are three degrees in Masonry, and three sides to a triangle.

At St. Paul's Chapel on Church Street in lower Manhattan—the oldest building in continuous public use in the city, having been built in 1766—we find over the altar a depiction of a triangle and within it the sacred name of God in Hebrew letters: the famous Tetragrammaton, YHVH. This was George Washington's church on the day of his inauguration, April 30, 1789; an original oil painting of the Great Seal of the United States dating to the eighteenth century is in a frame there. St. Paul's is a chapel of Trinity Church on Wall Street, and the cemetery there has several ancient tombstones with Masonic symbols engraved upon them. (Trinity Church was the centerpiece of the 2004 film *National Treasure*, a fictional account of secret codes hidden on the back of the Declaration of Independence by America's founding fathers.)

In some lodges, the sun may be painted or otherwise shown on the south side of the temple (perhaps as a lighted candle), indicating the sun at its zenith, or highest point, at noon. The moon would be in the west, as if it was setting (represented also as a candle).

At the western end of the lodge as one enters, there may be two pillars, representing the two pillars that stood at either side of the great entrance to Solomon's Temple. These are called by the names Jachin and Boaz, on the right and left respectively. These Hebrew words are usually translated as "He shall establish" for Jachin, and "In it is strength" for Boaz.

At the eastern end of the lodge can be found the throne. The Masonic official known as the Worshipful Master sits here, and participates in the initiation at various points, normally to give information on the meaning of the ritual. There are also three pillars representing the Ionic, Doric, and Corinthian styles. These columns or pillars have philosophical significance, as does everything to be found in a Masonic temple. The three pillars are often arranged as candles or lamps in a specific manner around a central desk or what appears to be an altar as it is sometimes called.

On this table one will find the VSL, or Volume of Sacred Law. Among Christians, this would be the Bible; it could as easily be the Qur'an, the Tanakh, or any other sacred scripture appropriate to the person being initiated. The prime requirement to become a Mason is that one should believe in God, and this requirement is reinforced by the presence of a written scripture. Along with the VSL, depending on the ritual being performed, there may be a square and a compass or compasses. For different degree rituals, different instruments appear alongside or on top of the VSL.

The meaning of the square and the compasses has been interpreted by virtually every Masonic commentator, but (briefly) the square represents the measurement of straight lines, perpendiculars and sharp angles and the compasses that of the circle and its arcs. Together—square for earth and circle for the heavens—they represent the cosmos as a kind of geometric duality. Both the square and the circle contain exactly 360 degrees, yet their geometric shapes are different. Different, but equal, they can represent any number of such dualities to the Masonic candidate. Together, the VSL, the square, and the compasses constitute the Three Greater Lights.

Depending on the size of the lodge there will usually be chairs, benches, or pews arranged on the long north and south walls of the temple area. Other Masons—and only Masons—will occupy those seats. Only those who have achieved the third degree of Master Mason can attend all the ceremonies. Thus, an Entered Apprentice cannot observe the passing or raising of higher-degree Masons. There will be a light above or behind the Worshipful Master's throne, symbolizing the light coming from the east. The backrest of the throne will have small pillars, one on each side, built into it symbolizing the twin pillars of Jachin and Boaz which are crucial to some parts of the Masonic ceremonial. These are the two pillars that formed the entrance to King Solomon's Temple. From a Kabbalistic perspective, they would represent the twin pillars of Severity and Mercy on the Sephirotic Tree. Together, the sun at noon, the setting moon, and the backlit Worshipful Master constitute the Three Lesser Lights.[5]

In addition, the floor of the temple may be constructed or decorated in a checkerboard pattern of black and white squares, a motif that is found on many Masonic documents, tracing boards, and other illustrations. The checkerboard pattern has a long and illustrious pedigree, calling to mind instantly the game of chess and its origins as a sacred game between the forces of light and darkness. Today, it might be interpreted as a grid, a group of cells called a *matrix*— from the Latin *mater* for mother, from which we get the words *matter*, *material*, and even *Demeter*, the goddess of corn (which is also an important Masonic symbol). The *prima materia* is an alchemical term indicating the base material of the Philosopher's Stone. All of these meanings would be relevant to the Temple's design, since—as a replica of KST—the temple represents the universe; not the universe in a chaotic state but as an ordered cosmos, created and designed by the Great Architect.

In the first-degree ritual, the lodge is opened by the assembled Masons—according to tradition there must be at least seven present, including the WM or Worshipful Master—and the applicant for initiation must wait in a special room outside where he is divested of most of his clothing and everything made of metal, such as his jewelry, watch, and the like. The lodge at this time is said to represent the first floor of Solomon's Temple.

The applicant is then dressed in a coarse white garment, and portions of his body are laid bare: a breast, a knee, an arm, and the heel of his foot. He is blindfolded, and led to the entrance of the lodge room or temple by a man carrying a sword, accompanied by two others.

After a series of knocks (usually three) on the door and an exchange of words the door is opened and the prospective initiate is led inside, across the threshhold, and suddenly feels the sharp point of a sword against his chest. He is still blindfolded, cannot know how many people there are watching him, and has no idea what to do next. In every case, he will be prompted by a voice at his shoulder as to how to respond to the questions that are asked of him.

He is led, still blindfolded, to the cushion in front of the altar in the center of the room. He is made to kneel, and then is asked a series of questions. He is prompted how to answer. Then he is raised from the kneeling position and made to walk around the temple—a ceremonial journey known as circumambulation—stopping at each of the cardinal directions and always walking clockwise, the path of the Sun. After he has passed all the cardinal points, he will be required to assume various awkward physical positions, and more questions will be asked and more lectures will be given to him. All the while he remains blindfolded and in a state of physical and psychological disorientation. In this, the initiation ritual mimics those of the great mystery religions of the ancient Middle East—in particular, what we know of the Mithra cult.

The initiate is then asked to take various oaths, under penalty of fates worse than death. These oaths are to keep secret certain elements of Masonic practice, and are usually only those of the passwords and grips by which one Mason recognizes another. However, their application is greater than it appears.

If someone who claims to be a Mason does not know these simple gestures and familiar words, they cannot gain entrance to the temple. By keeping these things secret, the Mason protects the Secret Temple itself. In ritual practice, there is a man who stands outside the temple entrance, carrying a sword. He is known as the Tyler, and it is he who knocks on the door to admit the initiate. A lowly position, it would seem, but on a symbolic level it is the equivalent of the Guardian at a Threshhold. A concept character familiar to so many mystical sects the world over, and one who makes an appearance in

Mozart's Masonic opera *The Magic Flute*, the Guardian is an obstacle that must be passed in order to reach higher states of consciousness or spiritual enlightenment. In practical terms, the Tyler has an important job to do in keeping curiosity-seekers and other unqualified persons from disrupting the rituals. He must examine the credentials of anyone claiming to be a Mason before he is permitted to enter. Further, if an initiation to the third degree—for instance—was taking place, and an Entered Apprentice wished to sit in the lodge and observe, he would not be permitted to do so by the Tyler. Often, the position of Tyler is taken by a past Master of the Lodge, thus reinforcing its symbolic significance.

Finally, once all the information has been imparted in the form of long speeches replete with arcane references that the candidate cannot possibly understand completely on first hearing, and after the candidate has taken the appropriate oaths, the blindfold is removed and, blinking, the new initiate realizes he is facing a man sitting on a throne with a light behind him. This may be the only light in the room, or the strongest one.

The effect would be impressive, a subtle shock to the nervous system after all the wandering around in the dark—which is, after all, what the initiation represents. The candidate is referred to as a traveler in the dark, seeking the light; as a man from the West, going to the East. The ritual of the Entered Apprentice initiation is a reminder to the candidate of his spiritual status in life. Once reminded, the candidate is urged to continue his journey through the other two degrees so that this new knowledge and self-awareness may not be lost and the initiate sink back into the darkness from whence he came.

The proper position of the Entered Apprentice (EA) in the temple is in the northeast, between the WM in the east and the place of darkness in the north. This is for two reasons.

In the first and most obvious case, the new initiate is halfway between darkness and light; standing in that section of the temple, he cannot help but be reminded of that fact.

In the second case, the cornerstone of a building was often—though not always—set in the northeast corner. By assuming a position in the northeast—by identifying with the cornerstone—a Jewish or Christian Mason may be reminded of the Biblical text, "The stone the builders rejected has become the cornerstone" (Psalms 118:22), a sentiment that is repeated throughout the New Testament in relation to Jesus.[6] This would not be an orthodox interpretation, however, with its implied criticism of the builders—that is, the stonemasons themselves! Yet, the placement of the EA in the northeast is an obvious identification of the new member with the cornerstone: he who had been rejected or passed over in life prior to his initiation—a wanderer in the darkness—has now become an integral part of the lodge.

He is shown the secrets of the lodge, which consist of a secret sign, a grip, and a password, and then he is given an apron. For the different degrees, the apron is arranged differently, but in appearance it is like an envelope with a triangular flap. For the EA degree, the flap is arranged so it is pointing upward. The EA is then brought to the northeast corner, where he receives another long instruction, and is then brought to the north, where he receives the instruments peculiar to his degree: a hammer, a chisel, and a twenty-four-inch foldable ruler. These are typical stonecutter's tools, of course, but they also have moral and spiritual analogues in the Masonic environment. A twenty-four-inch ruler may refer to the twenty-four hours in the day. It is usually folded into thirds, so every eight inches equals the eight hours that are appropriate to some activity: work, sleep, and so on. The hammer and chisel are tools to work the stone, to make it ready for use: they smooth out the edges, so to speak, and can represent consciousness or even the initiate's conscience as he removes the unwanted traits in himself in search of that which is more valuable and reliable.

After all of this is shown the new initiate, he is invited to sit down and become a member of the lodge. Another dialogue ensues, in which some standard ritual questions are asked of the initiate, and he gives the standard answers.

In some of the older EA rituals that have been published, these are suggestive of the perceived tradition and heritage of the order. In Samuel Prichard's *Masonry Dissected*, published in London in 1730, we are shown the following exchange in the initiation of an Entered Apprentice:

Q. Are you a Mason?

A. I am so taken and Accepted to be amongst Brothers and Fellows.

Q. How shall I know that you are a Mason?

A. By Signs and Tokens and perfect Points of my Entrance.

Q. What are Signs?

A. All Squares, Angles and Perpendiculars.

Q. What are Tokens?

A. Certain Regular and Brotherly Gripes [*sic*].

In William Finch's *Masonic Treatise* of 1802, we have another exchange:

1. Bro. SW as Free and Accepted Masons where did you and I first meet,

   Upon the Square,

2. Where hope to part,

   Upon the Level,

3. Why so,

   As Masons we ought always so to do with all mankind, but more particularly as obligated Brother Masons.

4. From whence came you,

   From the west,

5. Where going,

   To the east.

6. What induced you to leave the west to go to the east,

   In search of a Master and of him to gain instruction.

7. Who are you that want instruction,

   A Free and Accepted Mason,

8. What kind of a man ought Free and Accepted Masons to be,

   A free Man born of a free Woman, brother to a King, and companion to a beggar if a Mason.

These are only brief excerpts from lengthy ritual dialogues, and the intention is to give some idea of the flavor and of the ritual language that is employed. The west is the place of the setting sun, and the initiate walks toward the east in search of light. Most Catholic churches—and many other Christian churches—have their main entrance to the west and the altar to the east, so this is an idea consistent with European architecture that is, itself, consistent with more ancient forms of religious expression (in particular, any religion that used the sun as an object of worship or as a symbol of resurrection).

In further exchanges, the EA is questioned as to the appearance of the lodge or temple; this serves to both remind the EA of the arrangement of the ritual space and all its details, but also could conceivably have been used to test an unknown Mason. The Entered Apprentice would have known about the furnishings of the lodge and to a certain extent what they signified, but not the deeper mysteries. If the EA could accurately describe what was in a lodge, then he obviously had been initiated to that degree if none higher.

To those who claim that the initiation rituals of the Freemasons are morality plays, or instructions on how to live a better life, this brief and admittedly inadequate description of the first degree should go a long way toward dispelling that idea. There is clearly more going on than moral exhortations. By reminding the candidate of darkness, he is reminded that the world he lives in is full of mystery and, at the same time, a subtle and reliable order. The order can be used to penetrate the mystery; the mystery can be used to discover the order.

If Freemasonry was only an institution designed to teach moral law, then it would have disappeared long ago, its protestations that it is not a religion proven false. If one has been born and raised in a religious—i.e., moral—tradition, then what need could there possibly be for a secret society that teaches what any scripture provides? It should be obvious that Freemasonry satisfies a quite different (though perhaps complementary) need.

THE SECOND DEGREE, OR FELLOW CRAFT

This degree has been subject to some controversy—as have all the other, later degrees—because it did not exist in the earliest known forms of Freemasonry but was part of the original First Degree.

The lodge room for this degree is said to represent the "middle chamber" of King Solomon's Temple, and the central icon of this degree is the Winding Staircase.

The Entered Apprentice is now dressed again in the same white garment as he wore at his initiation, only this time different parts of the body are laid bare. He is not blindfolded, since he has already seen the lodge and its members at his initiation. He is led to the door, another battery of knocks is given, and he is allowed inside. Brought before the WM in the east, another series of questions and answers transpires and he is shown a new set of grips and given a new password. He must demonstrate these to various officers around the lodge, at each of the cardinal points of the compass. When everyone has been satisfied that the new aspirant has learned the proper recognition signals, the next part of the ceremony begins.

The EA is then instructed in a strange and awkward method of walking, raising his feet high with each step, and progressing from the west to the east in this fashion. After this, the EA is made to kneel and hold the VSL—the Bible or another appropriate scripture—and made to swear another series of oaths with terrible penalties for breaking them. He is shown new signs, grips, and passwords and commanded to keep them secret. He is given a new apron, folded in a different manner. He is then brought to the southeast corner of the temple—not the northeast, as in the EA initiation—and told that he is standing at the point of sunrise on the winter solstice (whereas the northeast is the point of sunrise on the summer solstice). These solstices mark two of the four "quarter days" of the year, the other two being the vernal and autumnal equinoxes. But they have other meanings for Masons, who hold that the feast days of the two Saints John—John the Baptist, and John the Evangelist—are the most sacred in their calendar. The feast day of John the Baptist is June 24 (the summer solstice), and that of John the Evangelist is December 27 (the winter solstice). Oddly, there is no explanation of the choice

of Freemasonry for these two saints as their patrons. In some of the
earliest recorded initiation rituals, an aspiring Mason would be asked
from whence he came and would reply "from the Lodge of Holy Saint
John," so the usage goes back at least to the seventeenth century, if
not earlier. Critics have been quick to point out that there existed in
the Middle East a certain heresy, known as the Johannite heresy,
which claimed that John the Baptist was the true Prophet and that
Jesus did not die on the cross. The Mandaeans held that belief, and
still do today. It has been suggested that the Masons got their ideas
concerning John the Baptist from this sect, by way of the Crusaders
and most especially the Knights Templar. We will look at this later, in
the chapter on the Knights Templar, but for the moment let's say that
this theory—while attractive—has certain flaws and cannot be
proven with any degree of certainty.

Eventually, during the second degree ceremony, the initiate is
shown a different set of tools: the square, the level, and the plumb
line or plumb rule. (This latter is a wooden frame that holds a plumb
bob, used for determining whether something is straight and level.)
He is given general philosophical meanings for these tools, which are
of course stonemason's tools. The square teaches morality, the level
that all men are created equal, and the plumb rule to encourage
"upright" action.

The initiate is encouraged to study the seven Liberal Arts: geometry, rhetoric, grammar, astronomy, logic, arithmetic, and music. The
emphasis, of course, is upon geometry.

Eventually, the ritual comes to a close and the newly made Fellow
Craft member has "passed," in Masonic terminology.

The explanation usually given for the strange, exaggerated walk
mentioned above is that it represents the path that all must take in
life, since life does not provide us with straight lines but is constantly
pushing us off balance in one direction or another. That would be the
outward, exoteric explanation.

However, as I describe in my previous work,[7] there is a shamanistic dance known to ancient cultures all over the world that involves
a kind of limping walk. In China, this is known as the Pace of Yu, and
is used by Chinese alchemists "to walk" on the stars of the Big Dipper
and approach the Garden of the Immortals. In the rituals of these

Daoists, the four cardinal directions are saluted and then the alchemist or magician must engage in this exaggerated prance in a carefully prescribed fashion as he slowly advances toward the Pole Star. As the overhead canopy or ceiling of a Masonic temple includes the depiction of Ursa Major and Ursa Minor as well as the Pole Star, there is an odd and inexplicable consistency between the two forms of spiritual technology.

As a Fellow Craft Mason, there only remains one more degree to be attained, but it is the most deeply impressive. It involves a murder, a secret burial, King Solomon's Temple, and a resurrection.

THE THIRD DEGREE, OR MASTER MASON

It is a curious thing that at the heart of many Western religious and occult mysteries there is a scene of violent death. The biblical story of Cain and Abel records the first murder; Abraham is ordered to sacrifice his son, Isaac; Moses kills a man in Egypt; and warfare and bloodshed stain the pages of the Old Testament until its literal apotheosis in the Crucifixion of the New Testament.

The mystical murder of a king and his entourage is the centerpiece of the seventeenth-century Rosicrucian tale *The Chymical Wedding of Christian Rosenkreutz*. In ancient Egyptian religion, Osiris is slain by his brother, Set. Murder is sacralized in the Western mystery traditions, and the third-degree initiation ceremony of Freemasonry is no different. Perhaps one day a study will be made of this phenomenon in an effort to understand why murder should be such a focal point or, conversely, what this focus has contributed to the Western cultural experience in terms of the popularity of true-crime television programs; the romanticism attached to the cowboy, the serial killer, the gangster; and the glorification of war. Until then, however, we have the example of the Master Mason degree before us and whatever message we can extract from its somber and darkly beautiful ritual.

The Lodge is now understood to be the third and top floor of Solomon's Temple. The Fellow Craft Mason to be initiated to the third degree—or "raised," in Masonic terminology—is dressed in ritual garments once again after having given a series of passwords and grips. Different parts of the body are bared. Within, the temple is ablaze in light, but the door is briefly closed. When it opens again, the temple is now in almost complete darkness.

The candidate is led inside, up to the VSL, whereupon he takes more serious oaths with severer penalties. He makes another circumambulation of the temple, stopping at each quarter to demonstrate his knowledge of the new grip and password appropriate to the degree. He has already been given a separate grip and word that signifies the bridge between the Second Degree and the Third. His proper position within the temple now is in the northwest quadrant, which is the equivalent of the vernal equinox, the first day of Spring.

However, at this stage, a new development takes place. Whereas previously the rituals had been largely instructional lectures interspersed with grips and circumambulations, and odd postures to be maintained for sometimes excruciatingly long periods of time, this is now replaced with the ritual reenactment of the murder of Hiram Abiff.

This feature is probably the single most obvious clue that the Masonic legends and rituals represent something more ancient and do not derive directly from the medieval stonemason guilds, as has been suggested. There is no logical reason why the degrees of any of the medieval guilds—which normally consisted of apprentice, journeyman, and master ranks—should include the reenactment of a murder. The Master Mason degree ritual could be a clue as to the origins of Freemasonry precisely where Chevalier Ramsay—a Mason of the eighteenth century who is largely credited with creating the Scottish Rite—said to look for them: in the execution of Jacques deMolay, the Grand Master of the Knights Templar, by the Catholic Church.

In the Masonic ceremony—and there are several variations but the main procedure is the same—the initiate listens to the story of the architect of Solomon's Temple, Hiram Abiff, as it is enacted with the initiate himself in the role of Abiff.

The building of the Temple of Solomon involved two main personalities: Hiram, the King of Tyre, and Solomon himself. Hiram had been a friend of King David and then of David's son Solomon, and when the time came to build the famous temple it was Hiram who offered assistance in terms of materials, labor, and even design. By allowing Jewish ships to use Tyrian ports, Hiram allowed Solomon to import many choice materials for the temple and the temple service. There was another Hiram—Hiram Abiff, in the Masonic legend—who was a craftsman in bronze for the temple. This Hiram is mentioned several times in the first Book of Kings,[8] and is described as the son of a widow who was put in charge of the bronze casting of the two pillars Jachin and Boaz and many other temple objects. There has also been speculation that the Adoniram mentioned in 1 Kings 5:14 as the one in charge of all construction labor at the temple was this same Hiram, and that the name Adoniram is actually a portmanteau of two words: Adonai Hiram, or Lord Hiram. Whatever the personalities involved, the skill of the craftsmen impressed the Jews greatly. All of the stonecutting and other stonework was accomplished at the quarry so that when the stones of the Temple were finally laid there was no sound or sign of hammers or other construction tools, and no metal at all. The stones were laid perfectly and joined seamlessly together on site.[9] The fact that no metal was seen or heard at the construction site of the temple may be the reason why the candidate for the Entered Apprentice degree must remove all metal from his person before entering the lodge. As we have seen, the EA becomes, after all, the cornerstone.

There is no mention in the Bible of the murder of Adoniram, Hiram of Tyre, or Hiram the widow's son.

Yet the legend as told in the Master Mason initiation ceremony is specific if allegorical in nature. Only Hiram Abiff was in possession of the word of the Master Mason—the "Mason Word," as it has been called since the seventeenth century. Other versions of the story say that Hiram Abiff was in possession of another kind of secret that he would not reveal. In any case, Hiram had knowledge that the others did not and they wanted it and would kill to get it.

Some commentators have said that the Lost Word was the password necessary to release the wages of the construction workers; this is certainly a mundane solution to the problem but one that bears the aura of truth. A Lost Word, however, is central to much Jewish mysticism concerning the priesthood and the temple service. The correct pronounciation of the unutterable Name of God—to be pronounced only by the high priest, and only in the Holy of Holies and only on certain days—*has* been lost, and was lost when the temple was destroyed by the Babylonian armies four hundred years after it was built and the priesthood scattered, taken into captivity, or killed.

The initiate is "attacked" during the ritual, struck with a variety of weapons, weapons that are workmen's tools. After the first and second attack, the initiate is still standing, but the third attack—by a large hammer to the center of the forehead—lays him low. He is lowered to the floor by his fellow Masons and he is arranged as if dead, a corpse with his hands crossed over his breast, and a sheet laid over him as if in burial.

Several attempts are made to raise him from his grave. The first attempt uses the grips of the Entered Apprentice degree; the second attempt uses those of the Fellow Craft degree. Failing this, the Worshipful Master then lifts up the initiate from his grave by using the five points of fellowship.

This posture is illustrated in some books on Masonry, and it is obviously a close embrace. Five points on the initiate's body come into contact with those on the Worshipful Master's. The initiate has been raised from the dead, and sees on the burial cloth behind him a skull and crossbones that has been laid over it. This is the symbol of the third degree.

After this, the rest of the ritual is denouement. More postures, more secret grips and passwords; a new apron; new tools; and a reference to a Morning Star rising in the east.

That the Morning Star is probably not the Sun is provocative of a host of interpretations. In ancient parlance, the Morning Star was Venus as it rose just before or just after the Sun. The Evening Star was Venus setting with the Sun. Venus, in the Phoenician religion practiced by Hiram, King of Tyre, was Astarte. According to Josephus,[10] Hiram had a temple built to Astarte during his lifetime. Thus, during the same period as Hiram was helping Solomon build his Temple to the Jewish God he was also engaged in building a Temple to his own goddess Astarte. The parallel between the two construction efforts is remarkable, made even more so because some of the design elements that went into the building of Solomon's Temple were copies of elements used in the Tyrian temples, including bulls, lions, cherubim, and the tall bronze or brass pillars that adorned the entrances.

In a related discussion, the modern secret society known as the Hermetic Order of the Golden Dawn believed itself to be ruled by Venus.[11] The Golden Dawn was created by Masons as a vehicle for the study of Kabbalah and ceremonial magic, and thus shares some similarities with Masonic legends and initiations.[12]

The ritual of third-degree initiation concludes with the usual cryptic dialogue. The Fellow Craft candidate becomes a Master Mason because he is "seeking that which was lost," and hoped to find it in a lodge of fellow Masons. It is clear that one does not find it immediately upon becoming initiated. The word *initiation* itself signifies a beginning, not an end, and the experience of death and resurrection in the Master Mason ritual is just that: a ceremonial rebirth and a new beginning. The newly minted Master Mason is exhorted to study, to learn, to find his own path to the light—and to use all the metaphorical tools provided to him to do so. Being morally upright and using intellect to control the passions is a core teaching—all those squares and rulers and plumb lines and compasses—but this is all prologue. These characteristics are necessary if one wishes to penetrate the sacred mysteries in most religions or mystical societies. They signify the preparation of the candidate, not the ultimate attainment. A Master Mason is a work in progress.

Yet what work is it?

CHAPTER TWO

The Prehistory of Masonry

Masonry is regarded as the direct descendant, or as a survival of the mysteries . . .
of Isis and Osiris in Egypt.

—Robert Freke Gould, *History of Freemasonry*

What time that the children of Israel dwelt in Egypt they learned the craft of masonry.

—*The Cooke Manuscript*

SOME WRITERS ON THE HISTORY of the Freemasons have been
criticized for gullibility or wishful thinking by placing the origins of
the order somewhere in the distant past, most especially in ancient
Egypt as the above citation from one of the oldest of Masonic texts,
the *Cooke Manuscript*, implies. The *Cooke Manuscript* dates from
about 1450, and thus almost three hundred years before the formal
creation of the Grand Lodge of England in 1717 and, with the even
older *Regius Manuscript*, forms one of the few links between modern
Freemasonry and its more ancient forms. There is no documentation
that would support a case for Masonry's Egyptian origins, however, if
we identify what we know as Masonry with its verifiable historical
roots. Instead, we can reliably place the "Egyptian phase" of Freemasonry in eighteenth-century Europe, about sixty years *after* the formal organization of the Grand Lodge. This Egyptian phase was due
to several factors, most notably among them Napoleon Bonaparte's
expedition to Egypt in 1798 on the one hand, and the appearance on
the Masonic scene of the mysterious Count Alessandro di Cagliostro
on the other. It was Napoleon's invasion that led to a flurry of mania
in Europe as far as ancient Egyptian culture, religion, and designs
were concerned. It was Cagliostro who introduced a controversial
"Egyptian" form of Freemasonry to the lodges in France and Italy.

However, there is an element of truth in the contention that Freemasonry has its ideological (if not its historical) origins in ancient Egypt, and recent excavations at the site of the Great Pyramid have revealed that work crews involved in the erection of Egypt's most famous monument were organized into teams—called *phylae* in Greek, or *za* in Egyptian—with colorful names. These were work groups, evidently of free men and not slaves as originally thought, with totemlike identifications. The word *za* implies "tribe," which is an interesting idea, for this (and other evidence found at the sites) indicates that these groups enjoyed a high level of social cohesion and were not mere work gangs. While there is no trace of initiation rituals or similar practices among the *za*, these first construction teams—social units organized around the erection of stone monuments for the honor and glory of the state and its religious ideas and rites—were the ancestors of the voluntary associations and trade guilds of the Greco-Roman world and the later masonic societies of medieval Europe. Indeed, there is probably no more blatant a symbol of Masonic ideas than the pyramids of Egypt.

As representative of the stonemason's art, the pyramids offer an astounding example of the application of geometry to sacred space. Although no architect's instruments have so far been found in the excavations at Giza—instead only some very basic copper tools that seem, on first inspection, to be inadequate to the task of cutting stone—the basic elements that we will encounter in later manifestations of Masonic symbology had to have been employed. We know, for instance, that the pharaoh participated in the laying out of the dimensions and orientation of the temple using a stretched cord. A priestess of the goddess Seshat was involved in this process, and images of Seshat show a headdress composed of what appears to be a measuring device shaped much like a pair of compasses (said by some writers to be an inverted crescent moon, by others an inverted pair of horns), a seven-pointed star (which could also be a stylized form of the papyrus plant, sacred to Seshat in her aspect as a goddess of writing), and a line that stretches straight down from the star—that is, like a plumb line. The use of some form of level, square, and plumb line—all instruments that are used during the degree rituals of the modern Masonic Lodge—was essential to the erection of the huge stones of the pyramids: stones that were cut, dressed, and laid with great precision. In the rituals of Freemasonry, reference is constantly made to the *ashlar*, a Middle English word for "stone" that appears in two forms, as the *rough ashlar* and the *perfect ashlar*. The rough ashlar, or stone, is that which has been found in the quarry before it has been measured, weighed, cut, and dressed. It is a basic lump of inert matter. The perfect ashlar is the stone that has been made ready for use in the construction (of the pyramid, the temple, the lodge). The symbolism is obvious, of course: the rough ashlar is the candidate for Masonic initiation, and the perfect ashlar is the Mason who has achieved a high level of spiritual integration and perfection.

More than this, however, is the idea that the pyramids were huge constructions, involving the labor of many people, that were designed for sacred use. In other words, the geometry employed in their construction was geometry invented or perfected by a priesthood. The pyramids perhaps represent for us the first instance of the use of sacred geometry in history.

While the outward appearance of the pyramid seems to have virtually nothing in common with the Gothic cathedrals of the twelfth and thirteenth centuries CE, there is one essential similarity in concept and function that bears examination. The pyramids and the cathedrals were designed with an identical motive: they are sacred spaces used for rituals involving the death of a king . . . and his resurrection.

In the case of ancient Egypt and the pyramids, the king—the pharaoh—was mummified in an elaborate ceremony designed to ensure that he would be welcomed in the afterlife as an Osiris, a risen god. Perhaps the oldest religious scriptures in existence are the Pyramid Texts, hieroglyphic scripts found written in columns on the walls of the pyramid of Unas at Saqqara that date to the third millennium BCE. They consist of spells and prayers to ensure the safety of the pharaoh in the afterlife, as he ascends on a "stairway to heaven" from the earth to the stars.

In the case of the cathedrals, the death and resurrection of Jesus Christ is celebrated daily. The form of the crucified Jesus is usually the dominant figure one sees upon entering a church; the sacrifice of the Mass is a reenactment of the Last Supper and the entire ceremony is a reminder of Christ's death and resurrection. The events leading up to his crucifixion are depicted—in Catholic churches—in the form of the fourteen Stations of the Cross, which run around the perimeter of the interior of the church. (Oddly, the body of Osiris—the slain god who represented the possibility of resurrection to the Egyptians—was dismembered by his evil brother Set into fourteen pieces, before being reassembled by Osiris's wife and sister, Isis, in order to conceive the avenging son Horus.)

One may object that this idea of resurrection and survival after death does not form part of the Masonic rituals, but this objection would miss the point. In order to become a Mason, one must express belief in one god—monotheism—as well as a belief in life after death. No precise reasons are given for these requirements, and we don't know why a belief in survival after death should be a requirement for initiation into a fraternal order whose ostensible emphasis is on leading a moral life. Further, the third-degree initiation ritual of the Master Mason is itself an allegory of life after death and resurrection: the candidate is ceremonially slain and buried, and then brought back to life in a reenactment of the legendary murder of Hiram Abiff, the man in charge of the construction of King Solomon's Temple. Symbolically, the rough stone of the first-degree Mason has become a perfect stone. The Masons call this initiation *raised*. One attaining the first degree is said to be *initiated*; the second degree, *passed*; and the third degree, *raised*—as if from the dead.

Of course, this is an impression of Masonry that is obtained by reading the published rituals and informed by some previous research in ancient religions. It would not be embraced by all Masons, or perhaps by any Masons. This is the unsteady ground on which we find ourselves. What we can say with some authority, however, is that there is a tradition of sacred construction—involving an "initiated" understanding of geometry and proportion—that begins with the building of the pyramids and extends through the period of the Gothic cathedrals. In Asia, there exists a parallel understanding of the importance of sacred geometry and temple construction that we find expressed in India (*vaastu*) and China (*feng shui*), and as well in the magnificent temple complexes of Angkor Wat (in Cambodia) and Borobudur (in Java). It finds its form and function in ideas of proportion analogous to musical intervals (in other words, geometric intervals as pleasing to the eye as certain musical intervals are pleasing to the ear), and in arrangements that are oriented to topographical and geospatial phenomena such as the rising and setting of the sun, moon, and various stars on specific days of the year, and including a special orientation to the Pole Star.

The Masonic lodge reflects this concern with orientation, and the lodge officers take up physical positions around the lodge space that are very specific to their roles. The four cardinal directions are represented, of course, as well as some intermediate points on the compass, such as the northeast, which is especially important as the place where the cornerstone of a building is traditionally laid. During rituals, one is required to walk clockwise—imitating the path of the sun—even if walking counterclockwise would be the shorter route. There are other aspects of lodge design that are consistent with some basic ideas of sacred geometry, but the most obvious one is the letter G, which occupies a central place in most Masonic lodges.

One will find the letter G prominently displayed on Masonic literature and in many lodges. Often it appears within the compass-and-square design as an element of the most familiar Masonic symbol in the world. It has been thought by many to represent the word God, but actually stands for Geometer, a way of speaking of the Great Architect of the Universe, a phrase name that is usually abbreviated in Masonic writings as G.A.O.T.U. To the Masons—at least, in their rituals and other writings—geometry is the fairest of the seven liberal arts, the cornerstone of them all. In fact, geometry is spoken of so many times within the context of Masonic lore and ritual that it would be foolish to dismiss notions of sacred geometry and architecture as not being central to understanding the secrets of Freemasonry. The use of the compasses, square, plumb line, and other implements of the architect and builder are so blatant in Masonic iconography that we are forced to consider that the order is exactly what some of its apologists have claimed: a survival of the masons' lodges that were essential to the building of the great cathedrals of Europe and hence privy to the secrets of sacred architecture. In fact, one Masonic writer—the mystic J. S. M. Ward—has written that the letter G in Masonry is actually the architect's square.[1] Originally—

according to Ward—this instrument (called a "gallows square" due to its appearance) had one leg shorter than the other, forming an inverted letter *L*. This inverted *L* is the Greek for *G*, the letter gamma. Its appearance as the Latin letter *G* in modern lodges represents a kind of degeneration of the original concept, blurring its primary significance as a symbol of measurement (or a blind to confuse the initiate who is not worthy of the higher mysteries: this idea has its champions in Masonic literature as well).

Virtually everything one finds in a Masonic temple—and among the instruments used during the initiation ceremonies—is either linked directly to architecture and construction, or to a specific legend concerning the building of King Solomon's Temple. Geometry—sacred geometry—is the common denominator; for what we mean by "sacred geometry" is much more than a sacerdotal version of the Pythagorean Theorem that everyone learns in secondary school. The sacred geometry of the Freemasons is a survival of a complex cosmological and liturgical system that reached its full flower during the age of the Gothic cathedral but had been developing for thousands of years before that. This is the crux of the problem we confront when we try to establish the historical lineage of Freemasonry, for we are forced to contemplate two different types of history. The first is the kind of history that is the comfort zone of academics and scholars, the history of documents and dates, of events that can be verified and set into a simple chronology. The second is the history of ideas, and this type of history is not as amenable to measurement and quantification as the first. Thus, we would be remiss if we were to ignore, for instance, the general influence of the Florentine Academy of the fifteenth and sixteenth centuries and its fascination with Hermeticism, a school of thought that originated in Egypt.

Prompted by the discovery of an ancient text known as the Emerald Tablet of Hermes as well as by the *Corpus Hermeticum*—a compilation of writings on mystical subjects—the occult and magical interests of such leading lights of the academy as Pico della Mirandola and Marsilio Ficino exerted a tremendous fascination over the intelligentsia of the day (even as they were suppressed by the church). The study of the newly discovered Jewish Kabbalah was combined with this Egyptian mystical philosophy; the result was an explosion of occult writings and practices. The historian Frances Yates has identified Egypt as the origin of these ideas,[2] and their principle proponent as the doomed Giordano Bruno.

Hermes was the Greek name given to the god of wisdom, a Hellenized form of the Egyptian Thoth. A discussion of Hermeticism, therefore, is a discussion of Greco-Egyptian mysticism and occult practice, a discussion that includes alchemy: the art of transformation (of base metals into gold, i.e., of "rough" stones into "perfect" ones). The cities of Thebes and Alexandria were major centers of the Hermetic schools, and the discovery of their writings in the fifteenth century instigated a massive search into the surviving documents of Neoplatonism, Hermeticism, and the Kabbalah. This was not seen as a rejection of traditional Christian teachings, however, but as a means to verify and even vindicate Christian theology by using the tools of the Kabbalist and the Hermeticist to explain, clarify, and expand on the original themes of the Trinity, heaven and hell, the creation of the world, and the redemption promised by the death and resurrection of Christ. Regardless of this innocent intention, the church viewed the study of these documents as dangerous. Having recently come out of the suppression of the Knights Templar and the Inquisition against the heretical Cathar movement—both taking place in the fourteenth century— this new ideology was seen as another threat to ecclesiastical hegemony, another attack on the church's sovereignty in matters both secular and sacred. Kabbalah and Hermeticism became, in effect, "rejected knowledge."

This did not stop Bruno—a Catholic monk and sometime spy— from preaching Hermetic doctrines and writing at length on Hermetic and occult topics, before he was finally arrested by the ecclesiastical authorities and burned at the stake for his beliefs in the year 1600. Thus, thoughts of Egypt and its mystical and religious ideas and practices were already being felt in Europe at least three hundred years before the appearance of Cagliostro or the invasion of Egypt by Napoleon.

Therefore, we are required to employ the tools of the philosopher as well as of the historian, for only then can we be certain of solving one of the thorniest puzzles of modern times: the origin and true nature of Freemasonry. Egypt has given us our first clue, since many Masons themselves find comfort in the idea that their order began in the Giza Plateau or perhaps in the Valley of the Kings—or in the Hermetic academies of Alexandria, Florence, or Paris. Our second clue is more to the point; it is the holy city of Jerusalem and the Temple of King Solomon itself.

JERUSALEM

This ancient site—and its associated legends—are of prime importance to Masonry, and includes both Jerusalem and its complex of ideas concerning King Solomon's Temple (usually abbreviated as KST in Masonic texts). While the Pyramid Texts of ancient Egypt date to the third millennium BCE, the Temple of Solomon is much later and dates to the first millennium BCE, representing a more complicated legacy of Semitic and Mesopotamian ideas of sacred space as well as some Egyptian influences. It is a magnet for religious and mystical ideas of almost every stripe. Not limited in importance to the Jewish religion, Jerusalem and its temple are also sacred to Christianity and Islam. While Egypt gave us the first glimpse of sacred geometry, Jerusalem and the Temple will give us a much more articulated vision of the critical relevance of sacred space and sacred time to religious and mystical thought and experience.

There are at least two sets of legends concerning the building of the Temple. One, of course, is contained in the Bible; but other legends were commonplace in the Middle East, not only among the Jews but among their pagan neighbors, and involved the assistance of demonic forces, legends that would become enshrined in the Qur'an as well. The name of Solomon became synonymous with magic, demonic and angelic evocations, and supernatural power and knowledge. To the pious, there were always rationales for this behavior. Solomon was the archetypal magician whose command of spiritual forces was believed to be directly related to his divinely inspired wisdom. His reputation was such that a large number of grimoires—medieval sorcerers' workbooks—bear references to Solomon and in some cases are even named after him, purporting to be the very books Solomon used in his occult workings.

Thus, there is a dual nature to the story of King Solomon and his famous Temple. At the time the Masonic society was being formed out of the guilds of Western Europe, both of these ideas concerning Solomon were commonplace, the obverse and reverse of a single coin. We will investigate this in more depth a little later on in this chapter, but for now let us examine the history of Jerusalem and the Temple more carefully since it will bear on our study of the design of the U.S. capital, Washington, D.C.

Jerusalem was established as the capital of the new Jewish kingdom by King David, but the Temple was not built until his son—Solomon—became king and started its construction. The purpose of the Temple was to house the Ark of the Covenant and some associated objects, such as the Rod of Aaron and the Urim and Thummim. The Ark itself was said to contain the Tablets of the Law. In other words, the sacred objects that would be placed in the innermost chamber of the temple—in the Holy of Holies—were objects that were connected to the flight of the Jews out of Egypt and their subsequent wandering in the desert of Sinai. The Tablets of the Law—the famous Ten Commandments—were received by Moses on the top of Mount Sinai. The Rod of Aaron was used much in the way of a "magic wand" to combat the sorcerers of Egypt. In Exodus, we read that Aaron threw down his rod and it became a serpent. When the Egyptian magicians threw down their rods, which also became serpents, Aaron's serpent devoured them. Thus, the Rod of Aaron is a magical implement. The Urim and Thummim constitute a mystery: they seemed to have been used as a kind of divinatory apparatus, and are believed to represent the breastplate of Aaron, which had twelve precious stones embedded in it, one for each of the tribes of Israel.

Aaron, as Moses' older brother, was the spokesman for the Jews while they were in Egyptian captivity. Later, the role of high priest of the Jews was conferred on Aaron and the hereditary priesthood was passed down from father to son, eventually to become enshrined in the lineage of Zadok, from which we get the Zadokite priesthood and finally the Sadducees of the Second Temple period.

Thus, when a connection is made between King Solomon's Temple and the Egyptian captivity, there is some truth to the idea.

The Ark of the Covenant was the repository of objects that were intimately connected with Egypt and the flight from Egypt, and with the two men who had made it possible: Moses and Aaron. That the Jews had been thoroughly influenced by Egyptian religion is proved by the story of the Golden Calf (Exodus 32). When Moses had gone up the mountain to speak with God, his people became restless, thinking God had abandoned them. So Aaron led them in making an effigy, the Golden Calf, and began to worship it. It was the sight of this idol that enraged Moses and led to the first set of tablets being broken. This Golden Calf was most likely an effigy of the Egyptian god Apis, whose worship had been popular in Egypt since the Second Dynasty (early third millennium BCE), and particularly in Memphis. Therefore, the people Moses and Aaron brought to the Holy Land, the land of Canaan, were Jews who had lived their whole lives as slaves in Egypt. Yet Moses himself was raised not as a Jewish slave but as a member of the Pharaoh's household, adopted by an Egyptian princess, giving further credence to the idea that Moses had learned more of Egyptian religion and culture during his youth than Jewish monotheism.

It would be another five hundred years, however, before the erection of Solomon's Temple. Until that time, the Ark of the Covenant was a portable affair. It was a large box or chest, with poles that were slid through rings on either side of it so that porters could lift it and carry it. On top of the Ark were two cherubim, angelic figures with wings whose origins are obscure but were probably inspired by similar winged beings in Egyptian religious iconography. The poles and the Ark itself were made of the wood of the acacia (called *settim* in the biblical accounts), a wild thorn bush that grows in desert places and has hallucinogenic properties. Acacia will be found in Masonic literature as well, as a symbol of immortality for it is virtually indestructible.

This period before the establishment of Jerusalem is not well documented. We know that the Ark was for a time at the city of Silo before it was captured by the Philistines. The Ark exchanged hands and eventually wound up back with the Israelites, where we find it at Bethel. Later, about the year 1000 BCE, Jerusalem had been firmly established as the capital of the Israelite state and work on the Temple had begun. It is said that Solomon took seven years to complete work on the Temple, but seven may have been a symbolic number as it occurs repeatedly in Jewish and Christian mysticism. The date for its completion varies from authority to authority, but had to have occurred sometime in the period between 1000 BCE and 960 BCE.

The purpose for the Temple was simple: it was a permanent dwelling, a house, for the Ark of the Covenant. The area of the Temple known as the Holy of Holies was dedicated to this purpose, and the Ark was kept inside this small room, which was accessible by only one doorway, and this by no one except the high priest.

The location of the Temple proper was the top of Mount Moriah. There is a rock on this site that is said to be the rock where Abraham nearly sacrificed his son Isaac until the voice of God stopped him (Genesis 22). Today, this rock is under Muslim control as part of the Dome of the Rock, a hotly contested area since it sits atop the ruins of Solomon's Temple. (In actuality, this site is probably *not* the place where Abraham went to obey God's command. Instead, it would have been a site closer to the city of Shechem and Mount Gerizim, the mountain sacred to the Samaritans, and far north of Jerusalem.)

The selection of this particular site is pregnant with meaning. Abraham is the father of the three religions that claim him as their ancestor: Judaism, Christianity, and Islam. It is a sacrificial site, and as such was used by the Jews during the Temple period. What is most odd, however, is that the Rock is a place where a human sacrifice *almost* took place, but did not. Abraham's hand was stayed at the last moment, just as he was prepared to drive a knife into his son. Instead, he sacrificed a ram that had been caught in a thicket, killing it atop a pile of wood that had been laid on the altar stone, the same wood that had been intended for the sacrifice of Isaac. (It is interesting to note that Genesis omits one particular point in this story. It states that "Abraham returned to his servants, and they set off together for Beersheba" [Genesis 22:19], but no mention is made of Isaac returning with him. How and when Isaac made it down the mountain after the sacrifice of the ram is something of a mystery.[3]) The essential point to remember for the sake of this discussion, however, is the fact that the site of Solomon's Temple—the building held sacred in Masonic legend and ceremony—was considered to be a place of bloody sacrifice long before the birth of David and Solomon. Regardless of whether or not the Temple Mount is the actual place where Abraham was sent to sacrifice Isaac, the insistence of Jewish scripture and legend (as well as Islamic scripture) is important for an understanding of this particular mythologem, or pattern of mythological ideas.

The identification of ideas of sacrifice—human and animal, that is, blood sacrifice—with sanctity and contact with the divine is to be found in many of the world's religions, including its most ancient and "primitive." There is evidence to show that human sacrifice was considered the most acceptable to the gods, and that animal sacrifice was a later development, a "substitution" sacrifice. The Aztecs most famously conducted human sacrifice on a massive scale. Practices involving the sacrifice of human beings can be found in India, Scandinavia (in the case of the sacrificial victims discovered in peat bogs), and elsewhere around the world, in various places and at various times. The Jews did not practice human sacrifice but instead substituted the sacrifice of animals, an operation that was conducted on a massive scale during the Second Temple period. Thus, the crucifixion of Jesus in Jerusalem took on elements of human sacrifice that were redeemed by the idea of resurrection: a motif that we find in the third-degree initiation ritual of the Masons.

THE TEMPLE MYSTERIES

After the destruction of Solomon's Temple, the concept of the Temple became increasingly idealized. This process began with Ezekiel, who describes a future Temple in very precise terms. Ezekiel was a hereditary priest of Solomon's Temple who had been taken into exile in Babylon at a time when the Temple had not yet been destroyed. Thus, the process of idealizing the Temple began when it was still standing. This is an important point, because it implies that the "real" Temple was not something of stone and mortar.

After the Temple had been destroyed—only a few years after Ezekiel's vision—and the people of Israel allowed to return to Jerusalem, there was an intermediary Temple constructed on the ruins of Solomon's edifice. This was known as the Temple of

Zerubbabel, the Temple that would be rebuilt by Herod in the first century BCE. Zerubbabel's Temple was larger in size than Solomon's by about one-third, but not in any way similar to the sumptuousness of the original design. Herod would later tear down Zerubbabel's Temple completely and build his own more massive and impressive version on top of the original Zerubbabel foundations, which were themselves atop the much earlier Solomon foundations. In other words, the original site selected by David at about 1000 BCE remained the sacred site recognized by David and Solomon's descendants a millennium later. The fact that Herod's Temple was so much larger meant that the original foundations and footprint of Solomon's Temple were contained within its walls. The entire edifice was erected atop Mount Moriah, a site that may have been sacred to earlier tribes who lived in the area before the arrival of the Israelites.

None of this mattered to a sect that lived not far from Jerusalem geographically, but a world away ideologically. These were members of a group who opposed the Temple priesthood that had been estab-lished by the Maccabees and supported by Herod. The Jewish priest-hood had been hereditary since the time of Moses and Aaron, but since the Maccabbean revolt that honor had been bestowed as a kind of reward on members of other bloodlines, those who were not of the priestly class. A dissident sect of priests from the traditional Zadokite line seemed to have been among those occupying the site of Qumran on the Dead Sea. They opposed the priesthood and the practices of Herod's Temple in Jerusalem, and set themselves up in a kind of opposition to the Temple. Their rituals involved a compli-cated cycle of visualizations of an ideal Temple, a celestial Temple, that were discovered only in 1947 as part of the famous Dead Sea Scrolls, although mystical practices associated with a visualized Tem-ple were part of an ancient Jewish tradition known as *merkavah* or *hekhalot* mysticism.

During this practice, which was relatively unknown outside Hasidic circles until Gershom Scholem wrote about it in the 1940s, a mystic enters into a trance and visits the seven (or sometimes nine) "palaces" (*hekhalot*) or "chariots" (*merkavot*) in turn until he comes face-to-face with the divine Throne at the seventh (or ninth) level, in the Chamber of Chambers. While the number of palaces, chambers, or chariots varied from text to text, the use of the number seven was overwhelming.[4] This is consistent with the Qumran text known as the Song of the Sabbath Sacrifice, in which the number seven is repeated almost endlessly in association with angels, thrones, heavens, and so on.

What is impressive about this scenario is the tradition of Temple visualization whose traces we can discover in Masonic literature as well as in seventeenth-century English documents such as *Solomon's Temple Visualiz'd* by John Bunyan, the author of *The Pilgrim's Progress*. In the former work Bunyan devotes more than 150 pages to a minute description of the Temple taken strictly from the various books of the Bible and performs a kind of Kabbalistic exegesis on it, using biblical references as proof texts to show that King Solomon's Temple was a key to understanding the life of Christ and the Christian message. The problem with Bunyan's work is that he conflates the description of the Temple given in Kings with the one he finds in Ezekiel: clearly Ezekiel is not referencing the actual Temple of Solomon but a visualized one that he saw in a prophetic trance while a captive on the banks of the Chebar River in Babylon.

Yet why should a building have such tremendous influence over the dreams and aspirations—political, religious, and mystical—of millennia of Jewish thinkers and Kabbalists? Further, why should it have cast such a long shadow over the builders of the Christian cathedrals as well as upon the Masonic societies that were said to have developed from them? Why does St. Peter's Basilica, for instance, not enjoy the same (or even similar) prestige? Most writers on this subject take it for granted: the glory of Solomon's Temple is reported in the Bible, and the reputation of Solomon as a man of wisdom and power is noted in both the Tanakh (the Jewish scriptures) as well as in the New Testament of Christianity, as well as in the Qu'ran. There are crucial elements of the Temple histories and legends, however, that contain clues as to why it should be so revered and how the very idea of the Temple was able to find itself in the center of generations of occultists, mystics, Kabbalists, and esoteric societies of every stripe. The complex of Temple ideas, iconographies, and mystical practices and Masonic initiation rituals refers to a tradition of sacred geometry whose elements are all but lost to modern ways of thinking, if not to modern scholarship.

The Temple was conceived as a sacred space whose sacrality was increased at certain times of the year, particularly on the day of the New Year when the High Priest would enter the Holy of Holies and talk directly to God. Thus, it was a bridge between space and time: a place where the normal laws of the four dimensions were abrogated. The cubit—the unit of measurement employed in the building of the temple—was itself a sacred measurement, an echo of that used in Egypt by the pharaohs. Its orientation was specific, and meaningful, providing a bridge between the geography of the earth and the map of the heavens. More important, it contained the legacy of the flight from Egypt in the pot of manna and the Rod of Aaron. And, most important, it contained the tablets on which the Law had been written by the hand of God. Thus, the Temple—and especially its most secret chamber, the Holy of Holies containing the Ark of the Covenant—was a direct connection to history and to the divine. By building it atop the mountain where it was believed Abraham had almost sacrificed his son on the order of God, it was like putting a key into a lock.

The Romans would destroy the Temple during the Jewish Revolt, a few decades after the death of Jesus. The Ark and all its contents had already been missing since its first destruction by the Babylonians. Now all was lost. The Jewish people had to rethink and reimagine their entire faith, a faith that would have to survive without a building that had been the center of its religious life for a thousand years.

And a thousand years later, a mysterious band of Christian monks would find themselves at the same site and a new legend would be born.

CHAPTER THREE

The Knights Templar

Romantics like to see connections between the two, but there were none: no fabulous treasure passed on to the Templars after the fall of the Cathar fortress of Montsegur in 1244, no shared anti-Christian beliefs pervaded by esoteric cults, no Grail hidden in a mountain cave on behalf of a secret alliance.

—Malcolm Barber, *The Cathars: Dualistic Heretics in Languedoc in the High Middle Ages*

The rustic's proverb says that many a thing is despised that is worth much more than is supposed. Therefore he does well who makes the most of whatever intelligence he may possess. For he who neglects this concern may likely omit to say something which would subsequently give great pleasure.

—Chrétien de Troyes, *Erec et Enide*

SOMETIMES IT IS NOT THE FACTS THEMSELVES whose traces we must seek in the legends and rituals of the secret societies, but the interpretations, speculations, and convictions that gave rise to them. That some groups of Freemasons—particularly those that claim their lineage through Chevalier Michael Ramsay of the eighteenth century—insist that theirs is the survival of Templarism in the modern age is an important piece of information that requires closer inspection—not necessarily to prove or disprove that claim, but to understand the motives behind it.

The Knights Templar were an order of monastic knights whose primary purpose was the protection of pilgrims traveling in the Holy Land. There has been a great deal of controversy over this simple idea, for the reason that the original band of knights consisted of only nine men plus their assistants. They lodged at what was then understood to be the stables of King Solomon's Temple, and it is

believed they got their name—Knghts Templar, or the Templars—
from that fact.

The nine men were French nobles who had given up much of
their property to take the oaths of poverty, chastity, and obedience.
Their leader was Hughes de Payen, and they left France for Jerusalem
in the year 1118. According to one tradition for which there is very
little documentary evidence they found themselves under the protection of Patriarch Theocletes, believed to be a successor to St. John the
Baptist (or St. John the Apostle), to whom it is said the knights owed
special allegiance.[1] This is an important allegation, for although the
history is a little murky there are elements of the story that could
support the reason for the Church's charges that the Templars were
not Christian.

There were a number of groups in the ancient Middle East that
were known as *Johannite*, which is the term we find in the Masonic
documents pertaining to this legend. There was a group of followers
of St. John Chrysostom in fifth-century Constantinople who were
known by that name; there was also an order of knights who were
known as the Knights of St. John Hospitaller, eventually based on
Malta, who were sometimes referred to as Johannites. The group that
the legend is referencing, however, is something altogether different.

According to this theory the Templars made the acquaintance
of a secret Gnostic sect that worshipped St. John the Baptist rather
than Jesus, and were initiated into its service by Theocletes (sometimes spelled Theoclet). In fact, there was such a sect in existence at
that time called the Mandaeans. They worshipped St. John the Baptist, did not recognize Jesus, had secret signals of recognition (in
order to survive persecution by the Muslims), and were generally
dualists who believed in the ongoing conflict between the powers of
Light and Darkness.

There are documents in existence that suggest that this sect existed
as early as the third century CE in the area around Jerusalem and
Palestine. What is surprising is the fact that they still exist to this day.

The Mandaeans were suppressed by their Muslim neighbors, and
forced out of Palestine during the Muslim invasions of the seventh
century CE. They wound up in what is now southern Iraq, where
they remained until the U.S. invasion of 2003 when they were forced

to flee (to Jordan, Syria, and the rest of the world). A few hundred live in Iran and Iraq, but most—like the Yezidis, a unique Kurdish sect that has been accused of worshipping the Devil—have fled Iraq for safe havens.

There is a possibility, but only a slight one, that the Templars made contact with a Mandaean group in Jerusalem. As mentioned, the Mandaeans were forced to flee Jerusalem centuries before the arrival of the Templars. However, the worship of St. John the Baptist, the rejection of Jesus, and the adoption of secret rituals would all speak to the infamous charges of the ecclesiastical authorities against the Templars. The Templars were accused of denying Christ, and of worshipping an idol called Baphomet. This idol was sometimes believed to be represented by a head without a body. This could be a clear reference to St. John the Baptist, who was famously beheaded at the request of Salome and his head presented to her on a platter. The name Baphomet—which has aroused such interest over the years—is either a bastardized form of Mohammed (or Mahomet to many of the Europeans of the Crusader era) and thus an allusion to Christianity's enemy in the Holy Land, or it is what biblical scholar Hugh Schonfield has suggested: a cleverly encoded form of the Greek word *sophia*, or "wisdom." [2]

While the themes of Mandaeanism are consistent with what we know of the charges against the Templars, we have no reliable sources to prove that the two groups were linked. That the late-eighteenth-century and early-nineteenth-century Masonic commentators would have suggested that the Templars had a relationship with "Johannites" in Jerusalem in 1118 or so does seem rather prescient, however, since so little was actually known about the Mandaeans at the time.

Another tradition claims that the Knights Templar were in possession of a Gospel of St. John that differed considerably from the one found in the New Testament in that it lacked several chapters that affirmed the Resurrection.[3] This St. John, of course, is not St. John the Baptist, who was—and is—the center of the Mandaean denomination but St. John the Apostle and Evangelist, and putative author of the Book of Revelation (Apocalypse). We know that the Freemasons celebrated the feast days of *both* of these St. Johns, and this is, perhaps, a clue to keep in mind.

Another text that was circulating in Europe in the twelfth century that may have influenced some of the conjecture concerning the Templars and the Johannites was a Bogomil scripture known as the *Book of St. John* or *The Secret Supper*. In this text, Jesus and St. John the Apostle are sharing a supper in heaven, and Jesus expounds on a dualist theology that is distinctly Gnostic in flavor, particularly as regards the Devil as creator of this world and Enoch and Moses as his servants.[4] The Bogomils—a purist Christian sect from Bulgaria— influenced the appearance of the Cathars, with whom the Templars are often linked, especially as regards the Grail legends. However, the Cathars repudiated St. John the Baptist and initially refused the baptism of water, as this was believed to have come from the Devil. Thus, the Bogomils—and, later, the Cathars—revered John the Apostle but denied John the Baptist. (A confabulation of the two Johns can cause no end of confusion.) If we are to believe that the Templars were in sympathy with the Mandaeans who celebrated John the Baptist, then we must also believe that they would have had nothing in common with the Cathars except, eventually, a conflict with the Catholic Church.

The first nine knights did not cover themselves with glory in the first years of their residence in Jerusalem. They did survive, and performed some of the protection duty they had vowed to do, but eventually returned to France to find themselves under the aegis of St. Bernard of Clairvaux. While the Templars had formerly been under the rule of St. Augustine, they now adopted the Cistercian rule of St. Bernard and returned to Jerusalem where, in the ensuing decades, their power and authority would grow to enormous proportions.

Many historians have focused on their material wealth and political influence, particularly with regard to the Crusades, the repeated attempts by the Roman Catholic authorities to take and keep Jerusalem and the Holy Land from the Muslims. Histories of the Crusades have often given only short attention to the massacre of Orthodox Christians by the Catholic armies, or the murder of Jewish citizens in the Holy Land. There is even less documentation available on the degree to which the Crusaders interacted—on cultural and religious levels—with the people they encountered in Palestine and en route to the Holy Land. Part of the problem stems from the fact that Europeans at the time knew very little about the Middle East and its populations. (At one point, European writers had even identified Muslims as a Jewish sect.) What was being disseminated were largely polemical tracts designed to depict the non-Christians as barbarians or worse. Yet, we are forced to acknowledge that the Crusades—due to their contact with Islamic culture—served to enrich Europe with scientific, philosophical, and mathematical discoveries that changed the face of Western civilization.

The Knights Templar were at the forefront of this enterprise, and their ongoing presence in Palestine and their often mysterious contacts within the Islamic communities eventually served to condemn them in the eyes of the church.

They were based at the site of Solomon's Temple, and this alone has given rise to much speculation as to what they were doing there and what they may have found there. However, at that time, the Muslims long had been in occupation of the Temple Mount and had built the Al-Aqsa Mosque on its summit. The main thrust of the speculation has the Templars digging beneath the Temple in search of buried treasure, and the assumption that they found the Holy Grail.

The problem with this scenario should be obvious at once. What would the Holy Grail—long believed to have been the vessel that Jesus drank from at the Last Supper, or the one (perhaps the same one) that was used to collect his blood at the crucifixion—be doing at the Temple? Why would the followers of Jesus hide it there, and why would the Jewish leaders permit this in the first place?

Had the Templars found something of value at the Temple site, it is much more likely to have been something intrinsically Jewish, something pertaining to the Temple service itself or to the Temple priesthood. This simply may have been treasure—the gold artifacts used in the Temple, buried when the Romans sacked Jerusalem and destroyed the Temple in 70 CE—or it may have been something far more valuable, as has been suggested by Louis Charpentier and others who have popularized the idea that the Templars found the long lost Ark of the Covenant.

This linking of the Templars with either the Grail or the Ark is central to the entire thesis of mystification that surrounds this order. If they were only a band of military men—albeit ones who had taken monastic vows—there would be very little to talk about. The Knights Hospitallers were their rivals in the Middle East, and there is virtually no romantic mystification about this latter group at all. Of course, the Hospitallers were not suppressed by the Church and the King of France and forced to disband. So from where does the legend come, and is there any truth at all to any of it?

THE LEGEND

Now they may become knights who hitherto existed as robbers.

—Pope Urban II, *Patrologiae cursus completus, series latina*

The single greatest intellectual influence behind the creation of the Knights Templar was a Cistercian abbot, Bernard of Clairvaux (now St. Bernard). The author of numerous sermons on the subject of the biblical Song of Solomon (a favorite with Kabbalists as well as Christian mystics), Bernard's was one of the voices raised in Europe demanding a crusade to take back Jerusalem from the Muslims.

This movement had begun with Pope Urban II in 1095, the year of the First Crusade. Part of the rationale behind the Crusades was to find a channel to direct the ferocity and cupidity of the nobility toward something other than robbing and pillaging each other: all of that energy could better be spent overseas—*outremer*—in the lands now held by the Muslim caliphs. It would also reinforce the Church's authority over the landed gentry, by overseeing the development of the knightly class into something more spiritual, with its behavior more outwardly Catholic.

While Urban II had his agenda, Bernard of Clairvaux had a slightly different one. For Bernard, the knights would be an army of Christ, a monastic order of celibate warriors for whom victory was more important than glory.[5] The Knights Templar became his pet project, and when Hughes de Payen returned from his first tour in Palestine he and his fellow knights were consecrated by Bernard as the shock troops of a new Christian army and sent back to Jerusalem.

The Cistercian order that Bernard represented also gave the world the first Grail romance, and it is possible that this was influential in creating the idea that the Templars and the Holy Grail were linked. According to historian Sidney Painter, the famous author Chrétien de Troyes "was almost certainly a Cistercian monk."[6] It was Chrétien de Troyes who wrote *Percival, or the Story of the Grail*, about 1181 (and left it unfinished at his death). It was this work that became, a generation later, the basis for Wolfram von Eschenbach's *Parzival* (c. 1200–1220), which was a retelling of the Grail legend from a German perspective and with substantial differences. Centuries later, this tale became the basis for two operas by Richard Wagner: *Lohengrin* (1848) and *Parsifal* (1882).

The Grail legend is inextricably bound with the Arthurian romances in which it usually appears. It involves King Arthur and his famous Knights of the Round Table, incorporating many unrelated tales and stories around this central figure. The Grail, in most of these legends, has been lost, and it is up to the Knights to find it and restore health to the kingdom. Only the purest and humblest of the Knights are able to locate it—victory over glory—and restore it to its rightful place in Camelot.

This motif of a band of brothers seeking that which is lost reminds one, of course, of the Masonic initiations and the idea of the "lost Word." It is also reminiscent of the lost method of pronunciation of the Hebrew name of God, which became lost at the destruction of the Temple. The Knights of the Round Table—in order to find the lost Grail—must behave as monks. Poverty, chastity, and obedience are required, as well as intense prayer and resistance to all forms of temptation and lust. This insistence on purity will be found among the Cathars—a heretical Christian sect that flourished in France at the same time that the Grail romances were at their height of popularity—and among succeeding generations of spiritual seekers in Europe and America, as we shall see in chapter 4. It was also a major preoccupation of the dissident Jewish Qumran sect of the Second Temple period.

It is in the same context of chivalry and Crusade that we encounter another famous writer on these themes, the Catalan genius Ramon Lull (c. 1232–1316). Also known as Raymond Lully, Ramon Llull, and by other variations, Ramon Lull was a Catholic missionary to North Africa who attempted several times to convert the Muslims using a wide variety of techniques and approaches. He also wrote an important treatise on knightly behavior and chivalry as well as books on alchemy and astral medicine. One of his epithets was Doctor Illuminatus, due to his tremendous degree of spiritual and philosophical insight and a range of learning that included his fluency in Spanish, Catalan, Arabic, Latin, and other tongues.

Lull lived in Spain in the thirteenth century, and was the beneficiary of the fact that the three major Abrahamic religions—Christianity, Islam, and Judaism—all found expression there. The Muslim Caliphs had control over large parts of Spain, and the *Sepher ha-Zohar*—that iconic text of the Jewish Kabbalah—was being written in Spain during Lull's lifetime. Lull himself is famous for having developed a complicated Kabbalistic system of his own, using Latin letters and correspondences that mirror closely those of the Jewish Kabbalah. It was Lull's idea that the three religions shared many ideas in common, most notable among them the concept of the four elements—earth, air, fire, and water—as well as the divine attributes of God.[7] It was thus Lull's intention to bring about a union of the three faiths based on their similarities while ignoring (or downplaying) their differences.

To accommodate this approach, Lull developed a system of concentric circles or wheels upon which were written letters of the Latin alphabet representing various qualities. By turning the wheels, one created "words" that combined these letters—and, hence, their respective qualities—to form new concepts that could be interpreted according to Lull's thesis of the essential unity of the religions and the assumed supremacy of Christianity. The Lullian method had as its original motivation the conversion of the Muslims, but the novelty and complexity of the system he invented became popular among philosophers, mathematicians, and occultists throughout Europe. In fact, Lull is often credited with having "invented" the scientific method.

Frances Yates identifies the Lull system as an "art of memory," that scholastic discipline that enabled philosophers and mystics to commit enormous amounts of material to instant recall. This was a great advantage in an age when books were in scarce supply and printing presses still a long way off. It was also an advantage in the art of rhetoric and debate, which enabled a speaker to bring to mind the right citation or quotation at the right moment, without recourse to notes. Sadly, owing to advances in technology, a prodigious memory is no longer considered an asset or cultivated in the schools, but in the Middle Ages it was tool and in some cases even a device of occult power.

The art of memory uses various methods to create a mental space in which images, ideas, words, names, and the like can be inserted. In a typical example, one selects a building with which one is very familiar: a home, a church, something large and with enough architectural details to serve as "pigeonholes" in which the information can be retained. The famous Globe Theatre of William Shakespeare is one example of a building that might have been used for just that purpose. The memory artists realized that it was easier to retain an image than a string of words; so they used the image of a familiar building as a mental storage device. To memorize a sentence, for example, one would put the first word in the doorway, the next word in the hallway, the next in a niche in the right-hand wall, the next in a niche in the left-hand wall, and so on. In this way, with each word in a familiar place, recall becomes easier.

Using images instead of words is also something we find in occult societies and orders. There is a dual purpose in their use, of course: while useful as a memory device, occult images were also obscure and impenetrable to outsiders. They served as a kind of code that could only be broken by an initiate to whom the secret had been imparted at the time of the initiation; and in the mainstream Church, images (of the saints, of Jesus, of the sacraments or scenes from the Bible) were an instructional medium for the illiterate.

To the memory artist, however, an ornate church building is an excellent memory theater. Churches had a great deal of architectural detail that easily could be committed to memory since one attended church frequently and the church was the center of much social and cultural life in the Middle Ages. Thus, memorizing where statues, pillars, windows, and the like were located in a church came easily due to constant exposure.

Then one could use that image memory as a template for "inserting" the things one wanted to remember. Each pillar might contain one memory quantum or piece of data; the same with the statues, the windows, the altar, and so on. Each time, new memories could be imposed over the same template; the template itself—the church, house, palace, or other building—would not change, only the data superimposed over it.

This was the art of Ramon Lull, as it was of Robert Fludd and Giordano Bruno, among others. Lull's approach was somewhat different, using his system of articulated wheels rather than buildings, but the goal was the same. Information is power; but memory is the ability to use that power.

The Masonic temple is also a kind of memory theater: every piece of furniture, every officer of the rituals, has a specific space to occupy in the temple as well as a specific function and identity. The Masonic instruments—the square, compasses, trowel, and plumb lines—are each representative of discrete ideas and associations. The Masonic tracing boards are perhaps the best evidence of this, for they arrange many seemingly unrelated images in a single tableau. The very fact that they are stand-alone emblems forces the mind to remember why they are collected on a single board, what the narrative is that unites them as if they were the parts of speech in a single sentence. Add to this the emotional impact of the ceremony, and ideally the various discrete elements take on special relevance.

The context for the Masonic rituals, as for the Templar myths, is rooted in ideas of knighthood, brotherhood, and chivalry. This may not be easy to recognize at once, and indeed many mainstream Masons deny any connection with the Templars; yet it would be the Templars who would constitute one of the most important employers of the operative masons' guilds in the twelfth and thirteenth centuries and specifically in the building of the greatest cathedrals Europe had ever known.

While he was developing his various arts and dabbling as well in alchemy and in an astrologically based form of medicine, Lull was also a troubadour and poet who idolized the practice of chivalry and knighthood. While Bernard of Clairvaux devoted his attention to the Knights Templar, Lull was interested in the general concept of chivalry and wrote extensively on the subject. It is important to understand this link between knighthood and the other disciplines that Lull studied and about which he wrote, such as alchemy and astrology. They were all part of the same symbol system, the system represented by the memory theater and by Lull's unique form of *ars combinatoria*, the art of combination. The various elements of astrology were linked to alchemy, and the idea of the transmutation of metals and the perfectibility of matter is linked to the chivalric ideal. The alchemical quest and the quest for the Grail were both heroic endeavors that required isolation from society, strict discipline, piety, and a spiritual focus. The Knights Templar were, after all, Knights of the Temple of Solomon: Christian soldiers and monks who were originally based at the Temple ruins and whose raison d'être was the protection of pilgrims to the Holy Land. These pilgrims were themselves engaged in the equivalent of a Grail quest: a long and hazardous journey through strange lands and hostile cultures, the goal of which was to set foot on the same soil where Jesus walked. Pilgrim and knight were united in their beliefs and in the deprivations they would suffer in order to attain their goal. As the Crusades wound down by the fifteenth century,[8] this exterior quest would become increasingly internalized until the Temple, the Grail, and the Holy Land were to be found within the human soul.

While some popularizers of the Grail tradition focus on the Templars and the Cathars—about whom more will be discussed—the influence of chivalry and the romantic ideal of knighthood in general is largely ignored. The literature of chivalry extends from Bernard of Clairvaux in the early twelfth century to Chrétien de Troyes in the late twelfth century and eventually to Ramon Lull in the thirteenth century. These are all names to conjure with in the history of occultism, Grail legend, and Templar mystique, and they set the stage for the rumors and scandals that would follow.

The medieval knight was much more than a soldier, according to this tradition. Like the samurai of feudal Japan, the knight was in a class of his own. He was of noble birth, had taken an oath to king (or queen) and Church, and lived a life of adventure mixed with high culture. There were no "satanic" knights who opposed the Church and took up arms against it, although they might oppose individual clergy on various grounds. There were no Jewish or Muslim knights. It was a Christian occupation, designed for well-born Christian men, and replete with arcane symbols and strange ceremonies of initiation.

Their purpose was to defend the faith as well as their liege lords; and those who had not taken vows of celibacy (and some who had) were notorious in their pursuit of women. Hence we have the Arthurian stories of Galahad and Lancelot, as well as the pious Parzival. We are entertained with tales of love triangles mixed with jousts, encounters with strange beings in the forest, and all the rest of the Celtic (and, later, Teutonic) mythology that infuses these narratives.

Yet, in the early years of the fourteenth century, the sanctity of this vision would become seriously challenged in one of the most traumatic episodes of the Middle Ages: the arrest of the Knights Templar and the suppression of their order.

SEVEN HUNDRED YEARS OF CONTROVERSY

We have not spent a lot of time examining the two-hundred-year history of the Knights Templar. Many other books have been written on the subject, and the basic details are well known. There are only one or two salient facts that deserve our concentration here.

In the first place, the Templars did enjoy a high level of contact with their Muslim "hosts." As most know, there are two distinct Islamic sects, the Sunni and the Shi'a. The Sunni are considered to be the more orthodox of the two, but the Shi'a contest this. The debate is over the legitimacy of the successors to the Prophet Muhammad. That is the exoteric difference; on an esoteric level, there are far more differences between the two denominations, with the Shi'a noticeably more mystical in their approach to Islam. That is not to say that the Sunni are not mystical; the Sufi sect is one example of Islamic mysticism that probably had its roots in Sunnism. Yet, the Shi'a hold a belief in the "Hidden Imam," a kind of Messianic figure who will rise and lead Islam to global victory. Among the Shi'a themselves there are several divisions. While too complex to explain in any detail, suffice it to say that these differences are based on the number of recognized imams, among other theological points. The major opponent—and sometime collaborator—of the Templars was the Arab military leader Saladin (c. 1137–93).

Born to a Kurdish family in what is now Tikrit in northern Iraq, Saladin was able to restore Sunni superiority in a region that had been dominated by Shi'a caliphates. A wise strategist, Saladin understood that it was useful to him to have the Christians in control of Jerusalem, for it divided Egypt from Syria and he had designs on both. He left the Christian Kingdom of Jerusalem alone until he was able to consolidate his power base in Egypt and have himself proclaimed sultan in 1174, creating in the process the Ayubbid Dynasty (his full name was Salah ad-Din Yusuf ibn Ayyub) and bringing back Sunni superiority in Egypt.

However, he remained in conflict with another Muslim leader, Nuradin, who wanted desperately to capture Jerusalem from the Crusaders and who attempted it twice, but without Saladin's help. After Nuradin's death in 1174, Saladin took Damascus and eventually—after failing to capture the city of Mosul in northern Iraq and Aleppo in what is now Syria—he turned his attention toward Jerusalem and conflict with the Knights Templar. Before he could, however, he was the object of several attacks by the Assassin cult in 1176; both these attacks ended in failure, but Saladin was now on his guard not only from the Crusaders but also from the Isma'ili Rashid al-din Sinan, the "Old Man of the Mountains."

The full story of the Assassins—the Hashishin—is too long to detail here and has been the subject of much recent scholarship.[9] As Isma'ilis, they were members of the Shi'a branch of Islam with whom Saladin had been in conflict for several years. The Sunni-Shi'a conflict gave both the Assassins and the Templars room to maneuver and intrigue as they played one side against the other. In addition, both the Assassins and the Templars were religious zealots who were members of secret societies with their own initiation rituals and their own unique perspectives on spirituality and warfare.

In 1177, Saladin was defeated by the Templars and a combined force from Jerusalem in the disastrous Battle of Montgisard, and he retreated to Egypt with his army in tatters.

He would try again in 1179 and succeed to the extent that a temporary truce was declared between Saladin and the Templars. (Saladin had better luck at times with the Templars than with the Hospitallers; each of the military orders formed their own allegiances in that fluid political environment and were basically autonomous. They reported directly to the pope and had no secular leadership. This sometimes led to conflicts between the orders, when the Templars, for instance, had a truce with Saladin and the Hospitallers did not.)

In the twelfth century, when the Templars were growing in strength in Palestine, the Sunni and the Shi'a were in a serious political and military struggle for supremacy in the region. The Templars found themselves in the middle of this conflict. In order to play one side against the other, the Templars formed some suspicious alliances. A by-product of these alliances was the fact that some Templars became fluent in Arabic, studied Islamic texts, and even—according to some of the charges leveled against them from time to time—converted secretly to Islam.

While there is probably little or no truth to this latter charge, Muslims did have one thing in common with the Mandaeans and the Johannites: they did not believe in the divinity of Jesus. This charge was the most powerful one leveled against the Templars when they were finally suppressed and their leader, Jacques de Molay, put to death. The trials of the Templars in the early fourteenth century contained reports that the initiates to the order were forced to spit on the Cross, deny Christ, and trample the Cross underfoot. There is actually some evidence that this was so, but not for the reasons that most believed.

According to recent scholarship in the field,[10] it appears as if these bizarre rituals were intended to weed out the spiritually or morally weak from the strong. Because the Templars were subject to capture and imprisonment by the Muslims—including torture and death—they would find themselves in situations where their captors would try to force them to give up Christianity and embrace Islam. Thus, the ritualized enactment of this scenario, with the initiate being forced to deny Christ in front of the other Templars under penalty of death. It was to reinforce the mortal seriousness of their quest that these young men were subjected to this seeming blasphemy.

However, even though there was a rationale for these rituals they were used against the Templars as an excuse to have them arrested for blasphemy and heresy. Indeed, documents suggest that Jacques de Molay himself was unnerved by these practices and sought to have them changed or eliminated altogether . . . but too late to do him or the order any good.

The second important fact consists of the actual arrest, torture, and execution of the Templars and the destruction of their order. Much ink has been spent on this issue, and some of it is speculation and some of it rather too cautious. On the speculative side, many popular histories of the Templars insist that the order never died but that it went underground and eventually resurfaced as the Masonic order. On the cautious side, many academic authors have insisted that the order was effectively destroyed and that no survival had taken place. The truth is probably somewhere in between.

In my previous work *Unholy Alliance: A History of Nazi Involvement with the Occult* I have documented the survival of Nazi ideology and Nazi personalities long after the end of World War II.[11] While the survival of war criminals is a fact, what is not so well understood is the role that they have played in other countries around the world. They had formed networks—under the financial and organizational patronage of such men as former Nazis Otto Skorzeny and Hans Ulrich Rudel—across Latin America and the Middle East, networks that became involved in the military and intelligence organs of their host countries. This is perhaps unique in the history of the twentieth century: that a defeated army and discredited political ideology would continue to exist and even thrive underground for decades. In *Unholy Alliance* I suggest that the reason for this is that the Nazi Party is not a political party in the way that is popularly understood but a cult. And true believers do not give up simply because they have lost a war. As an example, Christianity existed underground for more than three centuries—surviving torture, murder, and suppression—before Constantine finally made its worship legal in the Roman Empire.

Could the same have happened with the Templars?

At dawn on Friday, October 13, 1307, there occurred throughout France a wholesale arrest of Templar leaders and the closing of temples. This included the arrest of Master of the Temple Jacques de Molay. Charged with heresy, many of these men were tortured, imprisoned, and later executed in a series of trials that went on throughout Europe for seven years. The real reasons for this smack more of realpolitik than they do of any serious concern about Templar loyalty to the Church, and was the result of a conspiracy between the French king, Philippe le Bel, and a reluctant pope, Clement V. The aim seems to have been to seize Templar treasure and forgive the debts the French monarchy had owed to the order, and to remove the Templars as a political influence. Over the course of the next few years the Templar organization in France was, for all intents and purposes, totally dismantled, and the pope officially dissolved the order in 1312.

Yet the Templars had a far-flung operation, with temples in Germany, Italy, England, Spain, and Portugal, among other countries. While the Templar operation was closed down in Germany, Italy, and England, it did not seem to suffer so badly in Portugal, where the order was rechristened and its operation left mostly intact. Some of what remained of the Templars was allowed to merge with the Knights Hospitaller (then based on the Isle of Malta), thus effectively surviving, albeit in somewhat altered form. What was lacking was central leadership: Master Jacques de Molay was burned at the stake on March 18, 1314, in Paris, not far from Notre Dame Cathedral. This left many of the Templars in a state similar to *ronin*, the famous samurai warriors of Japan who lacked a leader to follow and who became outlaws on the run as a consequence.

This occurred as the result of a string of events that began in the year 1291 with the fall of Acre to the Saracen armies, signaling the end of two hundred years of Christian dominance in Palestine. The Latin Kingdom of Jerusalem was no more, and the Templars now lacked a purpose. In the meantime, however, they had grown to become the richest and most powerful order in Europe, rivaling even entire countries in the amount of their amassed wealth. Oddly, though, they had no real home. Palestine had been their base, even though France had been the country of their birth and Paris was their headquarters. The king, Philip IV (known as Philippe le Bel) now had to contend with a heavily armed, highly trained, enormously wealthy and idle army within his borders, an army that was blooded in the Middle East and returning now to seek other opportunities in France.

France itself had been no stranger to internal military conflict. On March 16, 1244—almost seventy years to the day before the execution of Jacques de Molay—the Cathar stronghold of Montsegur had fallen in the south of France, in a region known as Languedoc. For more than two hundred years the Cathars had been a political and religious problem in France, at least from the year the first Cathars were burned at the stake in 1002 until the fall of their last stronghold in 1255. Adherents of a strict yet simple Christian faith that attacked the Church for its wealth, ostentation, and corruption, the Cathars had come to France from origins in Asia Minor and the Balkans. Their leaders were known as *perfecti*, or "perfect ones," and the name Cathar itself means "the pure." They were enormously popular, not only among the peasant classes but also among various members of the nobility in the south of France who had tired of what they perceived to be the greed, arrogance, and oppression of the Church.

The Cathar heresy spread quickly throughout the Midi. The danger it posed to the Church was so great that the same pope who had authorized the first Crusade in the Holy Land and the same monk who had written the rule for the Knights Templar found themselves engaged in a crusade on their home territory. Pope Innocent III and Bernard of Clairvaux spearheaded the Church's reaction against the Cathars even as they were calling for a crusade against Jerusalem.

On the face of it there was no ideological common ground between the Templars and the Cathars. There was no reason why they should have made common cause, and there is no evidence to prove that they did. The Cathars represented rebellion against the Church, whereas the Templars became the Church's shock troops in the Middle East. When the Templars finally returned to France after having lost Jerusalem, it was already almost forty years after the last Cathar stronghold had fallen to the Church.

The possibility exists, however, that the doctrine the Cathars brought from Asia Minor into France via Bulgaria was the same or similar to doctrines to which the Templars were exposed while in Palestine: some form of Mandaeanism or Gnosticism, for instance. As Barber points out,[12] the founder of the dualist Manichaean heresy with which Catharism is often linked—the prophet Mani—began his life as a Babylonian Mandaean. The channel through which this particular Gnostic-type theology, which sees the cosmos as a battleground between the forces of light and darkness and rejects the God of the Old Testament as evil—moved from Mani to the Bogomils of Bulgaria in the tenth century and thence to the Cathars in the eleventh century—is a matter of some academic dispute. Manichaeanism is said to have disappeared from the scene in the sixth century, thus creating a gap of some three hundred years before the arrival of Bogomilism. The same might have been said, however, about the Mandaeans themselves, who certainly predated all of these heresies and who were suppressed (most notably by the Muslims) but continue to exist to the present day—as do the Yezidis. Thus, one has to admit the possibility that the Manichaeans also survived. Unfortunately, most of the records we have of these "heresies" were written by their opponents: mostly Catholic churchmen whose accounts are largely the product of polemic and patristics. They are thus unreliable. At the same time, we have no documentary or other evidence that the Manichaeans did indeed survive to the time of the Cathars, so we are left holding a puzzle without a solution.

The Templars and the Cathars did cross paths, however. The region that knew the most Cathar activity in France was in the south, in Languedoc. This area happened to be a rich vein of financial support and a source of recruits for both the Templars and the Hospitallers at the same time that the Cathar heresy was raging. In fact, Languedoc was a hotbed of all sorts of religious activity, from the establishment of numerous Cistercian monasteries, to the Cathars, to the military orders like the Templars and the Hospitallers. To generalize, the nobility supported the military orders and the church, while the peasant class felt greater sympathy for the Cathars; eventually, however, the Cathars enjoyed a certain degree of support among the nobility as well. We do not know to what extent the Cathars and the Templars interacted in Languedoc; again, we can only make an educated guess that there was *some* interaction. *If* the Templars were open to discussions with the Mandaeans and Muslims, it is entirely possible that there were conversations with the Cathars, as well. Ironically, it would have been more difficult to hold these conversations in France, under the watchful eye of the church, than with the Muslims a thousand miles away in Palestine.

In any event, in 1307, with the arrest of Templar leaders throughout France, the order suddenly found itself on the wrong side of the Church and State. The fate that the Templars faced at that time was not quite as serious as that suffered by the Cathars, of whom many tens of thousands were slaughtered in the name of Christ; but the Knights now had to consider that there was no longer any home for them in the church, and hardly any room for them anywhere else in Europe. Their rituals were mocked and denigrated, their integrity cast into doubt, their leadership tortured and killed. The Knights Templar, who had seemed the veritable Army of Christ, had become the foot soldiers of the Antichrist, and all on a single Friday the thirteenth.

The Templars, however, were not without friends. On the Continent they enjoyed a certain degree of protection in Portugal. On the British Isles, there is substantial evidence to show that they were held in high esteem by the Scots. Many other Templars found refuge with the Hospitallers on Malta. While the organization was disbanded, the true believers did not abandon their occupation but sought other ways to keep their network together.

These were men who had taken solemn oaths, who had risked their lives for their church, and who had been exposed to other cultures and religious faiths. Would they have simply given up, taken off their distinctive tunics and become farmers? Or would they have vowed to keep their brotherhood alive in the face of a greedy king and a vacillating pope? There is no brotherhood like men who have served in combat together; the Templars were even more than this, since their lives also were infused with religion, ceremonial initiations, and monastic vows. Their leader, Jacques de Molay, had been martyred, refusing to the end to give credibility to the hideous charges proffered against his order; refusing to ask forgiveness, refusing to submit, refusing to accept the ignominy that had been laid at the door of the Temple. Would the Templars—fierce warriors who at one time were the scourge of the Arab world—have simply "gone quietly into that good night"?

It is the core of the current wave of speculation concerning the Templars, the Cathars, and the Grail that they did not, that they continued to survive in Portugal, Scotland, and elsewhere, keeping alive the flame of the Temple although changing names, changing rituals, and adapting as much as they had to. There was also the legend of the famous Templar treasure.

The Templars had virtually created international banking, by issuing notes on funds kept at Templar treasuries in one country that could be redeemed for the same amount at Templar treasuries elsewhere. They charged fees for this service, and soon became powerful throughout Europe as bankers. When the Templars were rounded up and arrested in 1307, much of these funds were believed to have gone missing and since then the legend of the Templar gold—and what happened to it—has never failed to capture the imagination of treasure seekers. For a more modern example, rumors of hidden Nazi wealth at the end of World War II turned out to be founded on fact: organizers of the Nazi underground such as Skorzeny had access to these funds, and used it to finance the network of former SS officers in Latin America, the Middle East, and elsewhere.[13] That the Templar treasure may have been used for a similar purpose is one possibility among many.

The survival of the Knights Templar in Scotland is central to the theory that the Masons are their latest manifestation. It is, in fact, the theory that has the most—admittedly largely circumstantial—evidence supporting it. It has been devalued by some of the more outlandish claims, including some by Masons themselves, but it nonetheless contains a germ of truth. In order to fully understand the fascination that the public has with Freemasonry in the present age, as well as the possibility that Masons as a group were involved in some eighteenth-century political intrigue, it is necessary to understand the theory of Templar survival in Scotland.

The legend of the Templars in Scotland invariably hangs on a single event: the Battle of Bannockburn, where Robert the Bruce defeated the armies of King Edward II in a field only a few miles from present-day Edinburgh and even closer to Roslin—the site of Rosslyn Chapel. The battle is important because the heavily outnumbered Scots under Robert managed to defeat the English handily. According to historical accounts, the English lost their nerve and fled the field in the face of the rapidly advancing Scots.

The aspect of the battle that has never been satisfactorily explained is how the Scots managed this rout. One of the theories put forward is that a contingent of Knights Templar came to the rescue and once the English saw the Templar banners—the famous white banner with the red cross—they knew they would face one of the fiercest and most battle-hardened of any troops in the Western world.

There is no evidence to prove one way or another that the Templars were present on the field of battle that day, but the assumption that they were leads us into the crux of the matter of this study. If the Templars did indeed come to the rescue of Robert the Bruce at the Battle of Bannockburn, then questions about the survival of the Templars are answered, and the implications for how and where they survived play right into popular histories like Michael Baigent, Richard Leigh, and Henry Lincoln's *The Holy Blood and the Holy Grail.*

The Battle of Bannockburn took place on June 24, 1314, which is St. John's Day, a holiday sacred to the Freemasons. This may be a coincidence, but perhaps it is a meaningful one.

In 1306, the King of Scotland, Robert the Bruce, had been excommunicated by the pope (for reasons that have nothing to do with this examination). This meant that he was under no obligation to obey any orders coming out of the Holy See. Thus, when the Templars were finally ordered arrested and imprisoned the following year, and their property confiscated and turned over to the Hospitallers, there was no legal requirement for Robert to do the same. In fact, only two Templars were ever arrested in Scotland during these trials and there is no record of their having endured any hardships or punishment. Indeed, the Templars in question were two Englishmen.

The order was officially disbanded by order of the pope in 1312, as we have seen, and Jacques de Molay burned at the stake in March 1314. The Battle of Bannockburn took place only three months later. The English had cooperated in the arrest and imprisonment of the Templars and the confiscation of their property; the Scots had not. Thus, it is not so far-fetched to believe that some Templars had fled to Scotland to avoid their fate on the Continent and in England, and sided with Robert the Bruce against the English at that famous battle.

The Templars had, in fact, a long history in Scotland. David I of Scotland had granted some lands to the Templars in the twelfth century, at a town about four miles from present-day Roslin. The earliest known Templar charter is that of the town of St. Andrews, and is dated to 1160. The Templars were not the only military order in Scotland, in fact. The Knights Hospitaller also had property in Scotland, as did the Teutonic Knights. As in France, these holdings provided a source of revenue and recruits for the knightly orders.

In 1312 all Templar property in Scotland was granted to the Hospitallers, as was happening throughout Europe. However, there is no record that the Hospitallers actually took advantage of this in Scotland at the time. Indeed, although the two orders were merged legally, they seemed to have maintained their separate identities for at least a century to come. We know that, in 1488, James IV of Scotland issued a statement in which he upheld the rights of both the Templars and the Hospitallers, referring to them as separate entities.[14] This documentation implies a close relationship between the Scottish monarchy and the Templars. We do not know if this relationship was based upon common goals and agendas, or was more a reflection of the political (and perhaps economic) realities of the times. Nonetheless, there was a demonstrable Templar presence in Scotland that outlasted the papal edicts.

What becomes more interesting—in light of the speculation concerning the Freemasons and their origins—is that Freemasonry was known to have been practiced in Scotland as early as 1590,[15] thus predating the creation of the Grand Lodge of England by more than a hundred years. The oldest Masonic "catechisms" come from Scotland,[16] and thus the oldest mention of the "Mason's Word" and other Masonic ritual and ideology. According to David Stevenson, these were probably the creation of the Scotsman William Schaw, the man to whom Stevenson traces the earliest forms of Masonic initiation and organization dating from the very late sixteenth century.[17] In fact, Stevenson contends that these rituals may be older and that they may have been created by Schaw "out of earlier practices of the craft."[18]

More compelling still is the existence of Masonic traces going back at least to the fourteenth century, to the very era when the Templars were being rounded up, imprisoned, and dispossessed. As we mentioned previously, the *Halliwell Manuscript* may date from about

1390 and the *Cooke Manuscript* from 1450. These manuscripts contain some of the first Masonic allusions and legends. If the dating on the Halliwell document is reliable, then it was written less than eighty years after the Battle of Bannockburn; the Matthew Cooke document was written *before* James IV of Scotland issued his statement upholding the rights of the Templars and Hospitallers. Although proximity—in space and time—is not proof of connection, the fact that some Masonic authors attribute their society's origins to the Knights Templar becomes more plausible when we realize that there is sufficient evidence to suggest that both Masons and Templars did exist at the same time—no later than the fifteenth century—and the same place: Scotland and England.

What would the Freemasons and the Templars have in common, however? How did an order of military monks become identified with stonecutters and builders? What was the connection?

CHAPTER FOUR

Sacred Geometry

Little need be added to the story of Freemasonry during the cathedral–building period; its monuments are its best history, alike of its genius, its faith and its symbols . . . Keeper of an ancient and high tradition, it was a refuge for the oppressed, and a teacher of art and morality to mankind.

—Joseph Fort Newton, *The Builders*

No brother should wear leather gloves, except the chaplain brother. . . . And the mason brothers may wear them sometimes . . . but they should not wear them when they are not working.

—*The Templar Rule*, Section 325

AS WE HAVE SEEN IN CHAPTER 3, the putative relationship between the Knights Templar and the Freemasons is based on circumstantial evidence. This is nowhere near proof of the connection, and indeed most modern Masonic historians do not credit the idea at all. One of the problems with the story is the tale of the *Leviticon*, a document used as evidence of an "underground" Templar order, which is presumed to be a clever forgery. Another problem, which we will discuss in chapter 6, is the role of the Chevalier Ramsay in the creation of a Templar myth concerning the Masons.

However, as with the charges against the Templars of spitting on a Cross and denying Christ, there is some truth to the matter although interpretations of it may differ. The most suggestive data concerning a link between the Freemasons and the Knights Templar is to be found in possibly the most glaring piece of physical evidence imaginable: the very three-dimensional Templar castles and cathedrals.

When the Templars first arrived in the Holy Land they were astonished at the degree to which architecture—and particularly military architecture, such as forts and castles—had progressed in the Middle East under Arab rulers. The earliest stories of the Templars in Palestine has them enlisting the expertise of a local man to design siege engines for them, in order to be able to scale the walls of enemy castles. Thus, very early on, the Templars became aware of the importance not only of the Cross and the sword but of the Trowel as well.

In 1139, Pope Innocent II had given the Templars the right to build their own churches, but during the first hundred years of their presence in the Holy Land the Templars were not involved in ambitious building projects and only had possession of less than a dozen castles in the region. After the disastrous Battle of Hattin in 1187, however, which the Templars lost to Saladin, it became obvious that a new strategy had to be employed. The Battle of Hattin was a tremendous setback for Templar pride and reputation. It also represented a terrible drain on Templar finances and recruits.

Until the election of Pope Innocent III at the end of the twelfth century, the Templars were struggling to maintain their position. They were accused of being overbearing, arrogant, and abusive toward those under them, and without victory in battle there were those who wondered if maintaining the order was worth the candle.

Innocent III changed all that, and during his lifetime issued more than fifty papal bulls in defense of the order. That prestige was what the Templars needed, and soon they had the funds—and the motivation—to begin a more ambitious building project in Palestine. The castles of Safed, 'Atlit, and Beaufort were built in the thirteenth century and they were designed with defense in mind.[1] Much ingenuity (and a great deal of gold) was spent in their construction, such as having the main gate open onto a wall, requiring a sharp turn to actually enter the castle; this made it doubly difficult for an invading army to gain entry. Richard I of England—King Richard the Lionhearted of *Robin Hood* fame—had taken Cyprus on his way to the Holy Land and sold the island to the Templars, where it became another source of revenue for the embattled order.

Within a hundred years the Middle East was dotted with Templar edifices, a very few of which are still visible today, having withstood the vicissitudes of wars, tempests, earthquakes, and city planning.[2] The Templars did not restrict their building campaign to Palestine, however, but extended it to Europe as well.

Most of the Templar properties were known as commanderies, and they numbered as many as nine thousand throughout Europe. The commandery was a small affair, usually comprising a farm, storage facilities, and a chapel, and was used to support the order, and provided a kind of network for the Templars—who were, after all, from both the farming class and the noble class, and even the nobles were not unfamiliar with the operation of farms and husbandry. In addition, there were some churches and, of course, the main Templar buildings in Paris and London.

It has been suggested that most, if not all, Templar churches were round, and based on the design of the Holy Sepulcher in Jerusalem. This is not the case, however. While the main headquarters buildings in Paris and London were certainly round, few other Templar buildings followed this design. Normally, a Templar church was the shape with which we are familiar today: a rectangular building with perhaps a semicircular apse at the far end where the altar is located. Some of the popular histories of the Templars insist that they were responsible for the building of Chartres Cathedral, and Chartres is most definitely not a round church but a Gothic-style cathedral with a cruciform design.

The Templars were certainly practical people. They had a war to win and a kingdom to maintain in Palestine. They had to survive intrigues against them by Church and State; they had to raise money; they invented international banking; and they had to learn how to deal with a mysterious enemy in the Holy Land who spoke an unfamiliar tongue, ate unfamiliar food, worshipped in strange ways, and, above all, wanted to kill the Templars in the name of their God just as the Templars did for theirs. These were not pale mystics with robes redolent of frankincense and musty parchment. These were men of action who valued reliable tools: a healthy horse, a sharp sword, and a steady supply line. Their commanderies were a brilliant creation that had the effect of scattering Templar holdings across a wide swath of territory rather than keeping everything in one place. This system could also serve as an underground railroad or series of safe houses, at least until they were rolled up by the king and the pope in 1307.

One of the reliable tools they valued was architecture. The Templar order was international in scope and reach. The Templars had access to the best information on a wide variety of subjects that could be useful to them in their major goal of seizing and holding the Holy Land. The architectural designs and innovations of the Middle East contributed to Templar abilities in that regard, as they mixed and matched what was best from each country, each system of design, until they came up with methods and materials that worked best for them. (The Templars were, in fact, one of the first multinational corporations and they left behind many examples of what to do—and what *not* to do—for present-day CEOs.)

To claim with complete authority that the Templars were directly responsible for the near miraculous explosion of cathedral building that took place in France in the twelfth and thirteenth centuries would be a mistake. The archives of the Templar order on Cyprus were destroyed by the Turks in the sixteenth century, so we are left without a paper trail to prove or disprove Templar involvement. On the other hand, the Templars—as an essential and iconic emblem of the Crusades—were at least indirectly responsible, because the period of the Gothic cathedral phenomenon parallels almost exactly that of the Templars, as well as of the Grail romances. All of this occurred within the same time frame, from the twelfth to the early fourteenth centuries, and their locus was to be found mainly in the same place—France.

Henry Adams (1838–1918) was an author and the grandson of the sixth American president, John Quincy Adams. He was a professor of medieval history at Harvard University, wrote historical novels and biographies, and traveled the world. A student of history and architecture all his life, he wrote *Mont-Saint-Michel and Chartres* as a study of the Gothic period and came to the conclusion that during the period 1170–1270 CE, the Catholic Church built eighty cathedrals and hundreds of other churches of the same class *in France alone*, at a cost of some one billion in 1905 U.S. dollars.[3] It was also a dramatic flowering of the Gothic style, which contained elements believed to have been adapted from Middle Eastern models and therefore, due to the influence of the Crusades, on the European mind-set. It is entirely possible that some of the funds for this impressive spate of construction also came from the Crusades, in the form of taxation and other booty derived from the landholdings of the Templars and the Hospitallers throughout Palestine. We do not have the financial records that would permit us to make a definitive statement on how these cathedrals were financed, but we can make an educated guess that it was not solely from donations by nobles, royals, and pilgrims since so much money was being raised from them already to finance the Crusades.

The actual builders themselves—the architects, foremen, stone-masons, and carpenters, not to mention goldsmiths and sculptors—were probably not Templars or Hospitallers. They were contract labor, hired by the person or persons in charge of the building pro-gram. If Templar money was paying for the construction, they would have had a say in the hiring of appropriate personnel. More impor-tant, if the architectural innovations came from the Middle East, then it stands to reason that someone had to train the local European craftsmen in these techniques and designs. These would have been men who had served in some capacity in the Crusades, either as masons and carpenters hired by the military orders to build fortifica-tions or as members of the orders themselves.

John James, in his authoritative *Chartres: The Masons Who Built a Legend*, remarks, "The client's supervisory staff were clerics, con-cerned almost exclusively with the arrangement of the plan, the sculpture, and the interior. They were uneducated in building mat-ters, and left those difficulties to the men trained to solve them."[4]

So, we have identified three tiers of personnel involved in cathedral building: the client, the clerics, and the actual builders. The client would have been the noble in charge of the project, the lord on whose property the building would be erected, or a churchman: a bishop or someone with enough authority (and access to funds) to instigate a project of this magnitude. The clerics would be the clergy-men who were credited with the overall design: cruciform or rectan-gular or circular, for instance, as well as the saints to be represented in statues and other details of the interior (which, in a Gothic cathedral such as Chartres, can be as important to an understanding of the builders' ideology as the general blueprint). The actual builders themselves came from the guilds: the mason guilds, carpenter guilds, and the like, which had been established as voluntary organizations on the ancient Roman and Greek models. These groups had their own internal structures, passwords, occupational secrets, and meeting places. The mason guilds were the forerunners of the Masonic organizations of today. Known as "operative Masons," they were the actual stonemasons and people actively involved in the erection of very real structures. Today's Freemasons are known as "speculative Masons" because they do not actually cut or dress stone but use the ideas contained within the stonemason's craft as representative of deeper, more "cosmic," secrets.

That, anyway, is the traditional understanding. However, as James describes in some detail, the "cosmic" secrets believed to be the property of the speculative—or modern-day—Masons might actually have been the inspiration for the operative Masons who built the Gothic cathedrals.

The work of James is important because he is an architect, and spent years studying the Gothic cathedrals of Europe from an architect's perspective. He has identified a number of different builders at Chartres, based on the layers—like a stratigraphic analysis—of the building's stonework, and has isolated the design and building techniques of each. His work may be difficult in places for the nonarchitect or for those without a good basic knowledge of geometry, but the effort is rewarding. Since there are precious few documents to be had on the history of the building of Chartres Cathedral, recourse must be had to the available evidence at hand, which is the stonework itself. Careful measurements taken at every angle, of every protuberance, revealed some interesting data.

One of the most important tools of the master stonemason was his personal cubit. An iron ruler or square on which a unit of measurement was frequently etched, this instrument went with him wherever he would go and was passed down as a legacy to his heirs. The length of the cubit would vary from mason to mason. Today, one can go into virtually any hardware store or stationary shop in the world and pick up a ruler marked either in inches or centimeters and it would be identical in measurement to a similar ruler anywhere else in the world. Centimeters are centimeters and inches are inches; the measures are universal. Such was not the case in the medieval world.

There was the Roman foot, of 295 millimeters. There was the Teuton foot, of 333.33 millimeters (or one third of a meter). Then there were units that were particular to various towns and regions. As James notes, "There were hundreds. Each town had its own, often maintained in a metal replica set up in some public place so that strangers could equate the foot of their own region with the local one."5

Each of the trades had their own foot, as well, which only complicated things even further. Add to this the fact that each region had its own currency, and anyone passing through town had to do a lot of mental arithmetic in order to adjust his own measures and values to those of the locality. Therefore, measurement—which we take for granted today—was a critical issue in the Middle Ages. Although there were literally hundreds of different versions, there were only a few that had pride of place among the builders.

James mentions the case of the *pied-du-roi*, the "king's foot" or royal cubit, which measured exactly 325 millimeters: "It was one of the measures adopted by the Moslems during the Conquest, but even then it was old. It has been found in the Minoan civilization of Crete, and in ancient Egypt, and may have originated on the Persian plateau some five thousand years ago. Its value has not changed by more than a couple of millimeters over the centuries."6

Thus, when a Mason tells you that his order goes back to the days of ancient Egypt, in a very real sense he is telling the truth. The iron square with the cubit engraved upon it was passed down from generation to generation, along with the master's gloves and other tools. Together they represented the craft and had about them an air of importance and the hint of a sacred legacy. It was reliable and hallowed, the measure used by ancestors who themselves had taken on the patina of demigods. It is no wonder that the speculative Masons of the eighteenth century would have found in these tools the echoes of a venerable and ancient society.

As James began to measure distances at Chartres in search of the length of the cubit that was used to build the cathedral, he was struck by how much the structure was influenced by notions of geometry that are far beyond what today's architects would employ. Of course, all architecture is based on geometry: on length and breadth and on depth and height; but the medieval architects and craftsmen often used geometry in a meaningful way, as a play of opposites and to demonstrate sacred truths, often through the interplay of ratio and proportion. To study the deep architecture of Chartres is to be introduced to the concept of sacred geometry.

Sacred geometry is not a New Age invention. Builders of everything from the Egyptian pyramids to the temples of India and China were obsessed with duplicating ideas of cosmology, religion, and spirituality in stone. The mason's art was once considered indispensable to everything from defense (forts and castles) to religion (churches and temples) to government (palaces). With the move from hunter-gatherer societies to more centralized and stationary agrarian ones, the art of erecting buildings that would last through environmental conditions (rain, wind, intense heat or cold) to social stresses such as war and pillage became increasingly specialized and sophisticated. In the present day and largely in the West, architecture is understood in terms of aesthetics: how to make a building both useful and pleasing to the eye; ideas of form and function predominate. In Asian countries, however, there is still an emphasis on a building's layout and orientation according to principles we have either lost or never had in the first place. The famous Chinese science of feng shui is one of those, and is still practiced aggressively in Hong Kong, Taiwan, among the Chinese diaspora around the world, and increasingly in China itself now that the influence of austere and purely functional Soviet architectural concepts has declined and the old practice of feng shui enjoys a comeback. In India, the practice of *vaastu* is a Vedic parallel to feng shui in which orientation and design are equally as important as they are in the Chinese version. While these practices are suitable for any kind of building, from homes and shops to commercial and government buildings, in the design, construction, and orientation of the religious edifice they are indispensable.

What James discovered in the complicated ratios and proportions of Chartres Cathedral, however, was a distinctly Western approach to the same ideas as are found in the Asian versions. Architectural allusions to numerology and magic squares predominate at Chartres—especially *gematria*, of assigning numerical values to letters (the Hebrew alphabet is at once a letter system and a number system) and thereby obtaining numerical values for words.

In this case, reference is made to the western rose window at Chartres, which consists of thirty-seven openings. James relates this to the magic square of the sun—an occult figure that is a kind of chessboard pattern made of a six-by-six pattern of squares (for a total of thirty-six).[7] Each square contains a number, from one to thirty-six. The numbers of each column or rank, when added together, always total 111. According to James, therefore, 111 is the numerical equivalent of the phrase "Jesus Maria." If we multiply the number 111—which is the sum of any rank or column of the six-by-six magic square—by the number six itself, the result is 666: the Number of the Beast. The word *Beast* occurs 37 times in the Book of Revelation.

If we then count the number of glazed circles in the rose window, we find there are 193. From there, James eventually arrives at more Kabbalistic numerology. While some of this may seem outrageous to a scholar, the numbers that appear in these minute calculations are usually consistent with the overall spiritual message of the building. In the case of the western rose window, we are shown there are ninety-six stones forming the window, and ninety-six spells—in gematria, Beata Virgo or Blessed Virgin.[8]

Thus, what began for James as a study of the architecture of Chartres Cathedral eventually became a study of religion and mysticism as represented by stonemasons operating in the thirteenth century in France: home of the Cathars, the Knights Templar, the Grail legends, the Cistercian order, and so much else that pertains to this study. The importance of the cubit was such that it was handed down as a legacy to future generations, permanently inscribed on an iron square. The manipulation of the cubit was such that complex architectural games were played using hard stone, stained glass, and space. Chartres Cathedral began with one stonemason and architect and went through many more before it was completed, and yet the integrity of the building remains obvious to anyone who has seen it. It grew, almost as a plant from the ground, obeying laws of nature that were encoded into its dimensions. This was able to happen because each succeeding master mason understood the theory behind the dimensions employed and could solve the riddle proposed by his predecessor through the use of compasses and square, string and cubit. The stone masons of the thirteenth century *thought* in terms of ratio and proportion, and sacred numerology. This was not a technique written down on paper, to be passed on to anyone who could read, but literally written in stone—in a language only other masons would have understood.

This concept led automatically to the assumption that the layout of Washington, D.C., is somehow an encoded form of Masonic symbolism. Perhaps the most eloquent defender of this idea is David Ovason, whose book on Washington contains a foreword by the head of the Scottish Rite in America, C. Fred Kleinknecht.[9] This theory is denied by many Masons who are quick to point out that Pierre L'Enfant—who designed the basic layout of the city—was not a Mason.[10] Yet it could be argued that, by this time (1791), so much Masonic material had been published that to incorporate Masonic elements if one wished would not have been difficult. However, there is no documentation to suggest that L'Enfant had any possible motivation for doing so unless, of course, it was at the suggestion of Masons themselves (such as George Washington or any of the other Freemasons active in government at the time). In addition, Ovason insists that the presence of so many zodiacs throughout the city and their suggestive placement with respect to each other and to the heavens betrays another level of mystery.

Ovason's erudition where hermeticism is concerned is impressive, and his argument for an encoded Masonic message in the arrangement of the city makes for compelling and fascinating reading. Of course, there are statues to many important Masons in the capital, which is only reasonable once it is realized that many prominent Americans were, indeed, Masons. Do the statues represent their Masonic affiliation, or their contribution to American society as citizens? It depends, of course, on where you stand.

Ovason does not seem to insist that Masons were directly involved in building the city or creating a Masonic code; but he does suggest that Masonic code is built into the city anyway. The only explanation for this seeming contradiction is that the encoding was somehow unconscious or that one layer of Masons did not know or understand what another layer of Masons was up to.

The idea that sacred geometry may have had its origins in ancient Egypt received a boost during the post–World War II period with the publication of the works of R. A. Schwaller de Lubicz, an Alsatian philosopher and hermeticist who spent years in Egypt measuring the temple complex at Luxor. His work is based on a similar approach to that taken by John James in that he began with precise measurements of all available stonework at Luxor and then began to analyze the dimensions. To Schwaller de Lubicz, the dimensions were those of a human being. In other words, the Egyptian temple was itself a representation of a humanoid figure, a man or a god, created in magnificent monuments of stone in order to produce a mystical sort of effect on those who worshipped therein. While the details of the approach differ—there was no *gematria* in ancient Egypt, for instance, but there was the idea that numbers were sacred—the end result that was sought was the same: by using principles of sacred geometry one created a building that was also, in a way, a kind of machine or laboratory of consciousness. The secret of the Secret Temple is the Temple itself.

In a previous work I tried to bring attention to the fact that the science of astronomy usually has been neglected by archaeologists who focus on the digs themselves and the artifacts and writings discovered there from a purely literal point of view.[11] The suggestion by some authors and researchers that much of the Pyramid Texts, for instance, may have been referring to astronomical phenomena has usually been ignored or even misunderstood. The same is true of "sacred" geometry and the application of ratios and measurements considered important in a religious context. This in spite of the fact that—in Egypt, for instance—gods were in charge of measurement and computation, and these gods were often also in charge of magic and alchemy.[12]

This area is one that has been largely neglected by modern scholars. The reason for this may be due to the unsavory reputation such investigations enjoyed among German academics during the Nazi period. (Schwaller de Lubicz himself was not free of the taint of anti-Semitism and fascism.) Any research involving ancient origins, sacred geometry, "ley lines," astrology, and theosophical-type studies risks attracting the same type of opprobrium as eugenics, "race science," and all the bloody experimentation that took place under the aegis of the SS-Ahnenerbe. The study of esoteric material has been devalued due to the extremes to which such studies were taken under the Nazi aegis, and postwar philosophers such as Theodor Adorno have characterized all occultism as essentially fascist in nature. There is an element of truth to this assertion, and that concerns the idea of a spiritual elite in possession of secret knowledge. If this elite is a family—that is, in possession of a sacred bloodline, as in the "divine right of kings" or the ideas perpetrated by Michael Baigent, Richard Leigh, and Henry Lincoln of the bloodline of Jesus—then immediately we are confronted by a host of issues that are uncomfortably close to the "race science" programs of the Third Reich for a sacred bloodline implies that other bloodlines are not sacred, are of less importance or even somehow polluted or degenerate. The imposition of ideas of sacredness onto a bloodline also includes ideas of secret knowledge that can only be shared by members of the same bloodline. It encourages old ideas concerning monarchy—ideas that were at the root of the ideology of the Third Reich, albeit in a different form. The Nazis believed in a sacred bloodline, of course, but that included anyone who was pure "Aryan." They were also the most mystically oriented of all the political regimes of the twentieth century, with the possible exception of Tibet before the Chinese invasions. (It is interesting to note in this context that the Nazis had high regard for Tibet, almost alone of all the other cultures of the world. Yet, the Tibetans believed not in the sanctity of the blood but of the spirit: for instance, the High Lamas do not descend from a single family the way monarchs in Europe do, but are selected from among any members of the Tibetan population and, in some cases, non-Tibetans as well, who are deemed to be reincarnations of the previous Lama. The author is not certain if any studies have been done on the sociological implications of this type of "spirit line" as opposed to bloodline but it could be well worth the effort.)

In the case of the Freemasons, however, we do have an elite class that believes itself to be in possession of sacred secrets that are intimately connected to a symbol system that wholly revolves around architecture and construction: sacred geometry. What removes the stigma of fascism from the idea of Freemasonry is the insistence that anyone can become a member by simply passing through the initiations and taking the requisite oaths. There are other stipulations: that one be a monotheist and believe in a life after death, as well as several other requirements that are equally broad and not specific to any one religion or culture. Freemasons are adamant that their organization is not a religion in any sense of the word; yet, the initiation system represents a high degree of spirituality. It is a difficulty for many individuals that ideas such as religion and spirituality are so intertwined that it is virtually impossible to separate one from the other. Indeed, in the early days of Grand Lodge Masonry, Jews were forbidden membership. One had to be a Christian and a Trinitarian to belong to the Society, even though the initiation system refers to the building of Solomon's Temple, an event that took place about a thousand years before the birth of Christ. Because of this and other evidence, Freemasonry was seen through a religious lens and even considered to be a threat to the Catholic Church.

PART TWO

AMERICA BEYOND

It is in Nature as it is in religion: we are still hammering of old elements but seek not the America that lies beyond them.

— Thomas Vaughan, alchemist and Jacobite,

in *Anthroposophia Theomagia*

CHAPTER FIVE

The First Rosicrucians in America?

MOST AMERICAN HISTORY TEXTS IN SECONDARY schools in the United States mention the Puritans and the Quakers as some of the earliest Christian refugees to find themselves in the New World. Students are taught about William Penn and Roger Williams, the first a Quaker and the second a Puritan. Penn is largely credited for setting up what would later become Pennsylvania as a haven for freedom of religious expression, as Williams did in Rhode Island after a controversial stint as pastor in Salem, Massachusetts.

What most students are not taught, however, is that these two colonies would become an axis for one of the strangest of the early religious groups to settle in America from Europe in the seventeenth century. This group would number no more and no less than forty persons and their leader would be a young Rosicrucian mystic who was born in Transylvania: Johannes Kelpius. It would later contribute to the creation of the Seventh Day Baptist denomination as well as the Moravian Church, and represents a little-known episode of early American history, moreover one steeped in the arcane and the occult.

Kelpius (1673–1708) and his Monks of the Wissahickon are a prime example of how America's climate of religious tolerance enabled not only orthodox religious and their followers to thrive, but allowed the flowering of some of Europe's most mystical ideologies as well. That Kelpius and his band of ascetic disciples would make their monastic home a short distance from Benjamin Franklin's Philadelphia is perhaps no coincidence. At least one historian of the period has claimed that Franklin and one of the last surviving "Monks" were acquainted.[1]

In order to understand how Freemasonry could develop and thrive in a land that was so aggressively Christian—and Puritanical in many areas—it is necessary to examine the role that groups like those of Kelpius and the later Ephrata community had in the creation of a uniquely American form of mystical spirituality, one that embraced not only standard Christian ideas of the Resurrection but also those of the Jewish Kabbalah, alchemy, and what is perhaps the least understood system of all: Rosicrucianism. In Kelpius we may have all of these, and more.

THE ROSICRUCIAN FUROR

The Rosicrucian movement had failed on the continent. Refugees from that failure poured into Puritan England as the refuge from Antichrist. And the Puritan revolution took over some of the aspects of the projected Rosicrucian revolution.

—Frances Yates, *The Occult Philosophy in the Elizabethan Age*

A forerunner to the Masonic phenomenon was that of the Rosicrucians, with whom the Masons are often (sometimes erroneously) linked. According to the standard histories of the subject, the Rosicrucians seem to have been the invention of the Swabian theologian Johann Valentinus Andreae (1586–1654) who claimed he wrote the *Chemical Wedding of Christian Rosenkreutz* (one of the key documents of the Rosicrucian episode). Andreae claims that it was a *ludibrium*, a kind of game or hoax, when he was still a young man at the university. If so, it was remarkably complicated and heavily articulated, as any sort of critical and textual analysis would demonstrate. It is possible that his claim was itself the hoax.

Rosicrucianism is based on a legend and a philosophy. The legend involves one Christian Rosenkreutz, an adept of esoteric and hermetic mysteries who, after travels to the mysterious East, returned to Europe to lead a small group of other adepts in the spiritual and mystical practices he had learned. Among these mysteries is that of the Philosopher's Stone of alchemical legend, a powerful substance able to change lead into gold; and the Elixir Vitae, a medicine able to cure the sick of any illness and to provide immortality.

The Rosicrucian myth is a Christianized form of what would ordinarily be considered pagan ideas of transmutation, projected onto the figure of Jesus Christ as the prototype of spiritual (and chemical, biological) regeneration. The Rose and the Cross united as a single symbol is an icon pregnant with meaning. While the Cross may be interpreted as the device to which the body of Jesus was nailed, the rose symbol seems to indicate a redemptive force. The Rose and Cross combined call to mind the flowering Rod of Aaron or the Staff of St. Joseph: symbols of spiritual purity as well as occult potency. To later, twentieth-century, mystics these were sexual symbols; as we will see, there is evidence that to the seventeenth-century mystics of America they were understood sexually as well.

The first document connected with the Rosicrucian "movement" was the *Fama Fraternitatis*, published in Germany in 1614, followed by the *Confessio* in 1615, and the *Chemical Wedding* in 1616. It should be noted that these documents were all published in Germany at the beginning of the seventeenth century, a time and place of tremendous religious upheaval, and that Andreae—the self-proclaimed author of the *Chemical Wedding*—was himself a Protestant theologian.

The *Fama* introduced the idea of a group of adepts gathered around the figure of Christian Rosenkreutz who was buried in a secret tomb, awaiting resurrection. The *Confessio* expands upon this theme with less historical romance and more polemic and philosophy, including references to "Magick learning" and the secret "Languages of Adam and Enoch." These documents were eventually translated into English by the Welsh alchemist Thomas Vaughan (writing as Eugenius Philalethes) in 1652, thus providing an all-important link between the ideas of the Rosicrucians and those of European alchemy and the Kabbalah.

There is no evidence that the secret society known as the Rosicrucians ever really existed, but they did provide a template for some of the most influential groups of intellectuals and mystics in the centuries since then, including the Royal Society of England; the Pietist, Quietist, and Chiliast movements of the seventeenth century; the Masonic societies of the eighteenth century, and the occult orders of the nineteenth and twentieth centuries. The excitement generated by these Rosicrucian manifestos—that there was a secret society of Christian adepts who desired nothing but the improvement of humanity and its liberation from the stranglehold of church and state—was profound and far-reaching. Many groups since 1616 have claimed to be *the* Rosicrucians, including the Societas Rosicruciana in Anglia (SRIA) formed by Freemasons, or the American Mystical Order Rosae Crucis (AMORC), with their large park and library in California and their aggressive mail-order instruction and initiation system. All of these groups have based their ideas on the primary documents of the movement—the *Fama, Confessio,* and *Chemical Wedding*—as well as interpretations of some of the most mysterious spiritual documents to come out of the Kabbalistic and Hermetic schools, with an emphasis on meditation, spirituality, and social responsibility.

Heretofore, many of the most important hermetic and esoteric texts had been produced by the Florentine Academy. With translations of Kabbalistic and late Egyptian documents commissioned by men like Giovanni Pico della Mirandola and Marsilio Ficino, the Academy had put forward some of the most ambitious interpretations of both Kabbalah and orthodox Christianity to date, using the one to interpret the other. This gave rise to something called Christian Kabbalah, a methodology that uses a Jewish Kabbalistic approach toward interpreting biblical texts from a Christian perspective, thus "verifying" or even "vindicating" Christianity with the tools of this "secret science."

That there could be an esoteric form of Christianity—what the Kabbalah is to Judaism—is an idea that appealed to generations of scholars and scientists, including such men as Isaac Newton. The popularity of the works of Pico della Mirandola among others created a market for translations of the most important Kabbalistic texts, such as the *Sepher ha-Zohar.* The most accessible of these translations was that of a friend of Kelpius during his student days: Christian Knorr von Rosenroth, who published his magnum opus the *Kabbala Denudata* or "Kabbalah Unveiled" in three large volumes during the years 1677–84,[2] the last volume being published only ten years before Kelpius's voyage to Pennsylvania.

THE WOMAN IN THE WILDERNESS

Kelpius had been a member of the Pietist movement, which was then being persecuted in Germany. Pietism, a movement within Lutheranism that had been inspired by the writings of a variety of Christian mystics, from Jacob Boehme (1575–1624) to Andreae, was itself a reaction against the intellectualism of the Protestant movement of the seventeenth century which had become locked within Lutheran and Calvinist dogmatic structures. A broad-based ideological reaction to Lutheran orthodoxy, Pietistic movements could be discerned not only in Germany, Switzerland, and the Scandinavian countries but also in England, where versions of it took root in the Philadelphian movement, and eventually it found a home in the New World with the arrival of religious refugees.

Pietism was personal and mystical. Some Pietist groups, like Kelpius's own, were celibate and devoted themselves entirely to prayer and good works. They were also at times apocalyptic. In the form embraced by Kelpius, the "End Times" were believed to be near. Kelpius thought he would see the end of the world in his lifetime, and his group concentrated on the Book of Revelation (Apocalypse), and particularly upon chapter 12, which speaks of a "woman in the wilderness" who was to give birth to a male child that would rule the earth with an iron scepter. From their focus on this message, the group became informally known as the The Society of the Woman in the Wilderness, as well as the Monks of the Wissahickon or even the Mystics of the Wissahickon.

Yet, there was an even greater emphasis on the Western esoteric tradition among the members of Kelpius's group, an emphasis that has caused them to be labeled Rosicrucians and occultists. The evidence is in their activities in Pennsylvania leading up to the death of their leader from consumption in 1708.

Kelpius, as a man of only twenty-one years, found himself in charge of the group known as the Chapter of Perfection, which was leaving Germany for the New World when his mentor and the leader of the pilgrims—Johann Jacob Zimmerman—died in Rotterdam on the eve of their departure. The tale of their voyage to America is fraught with incidents of tempests, battles, and attacks by pirates. It took four months for their ship—the *Sarah Maria*—to make it to the shores of Pennsylvania in 1694, but all members of the group arrived safely and made their way to the Germantown area of what is now Philadelphia. Prior to their leaving Europe, however, Kelpius was able to meet with Jane Leade (a cofounder of the group known as the Philadelphians) in England. Named after the Church of Philadelphia in the Book of Revelation—and once again demonstrating the Pietist obsession with millennialism—the Philadelphians were heavily influenced by the writings of Jacob Boehme. In fact, Leade believed herself to be a prophet and a medium for the "Virgin Sophia." Sophia in this case was analogous to the idea of the Shekinah in Jewish mysticism: the uniting of the Shekinah (the Bride) with the Bridegroom (God) would signal the end of the world and what Christian Evangelicals term the Rapture. The term is to be found in Jacob Boehme's theosophical writings and in alchemical literature, and most especially in Rosicrucian texts such as a complicated illustration in *The Secret Symbols of the Rosicrucians* that was published in 1785 but incorporating much older material.[3] In addition, this concept of a divine virgin forms the centerpiece of David Ovason's work on the presumed Masonic influences in the design of Washington, D.C.[4]

The group arrived in Pennsylvania on June 23, 1694, and that evening—on the eve of St. John's Day—performed a ceremony in the forest that involved lighting a bonfire. This commemoration of St. John's Day has been described by Julius F. Sachse, one of the few Kelpius biographers, as a common German tradition that was kept alive by the Chapter of Perfection in Pennsylvania.[5] However, Masons will recognize at once the significance of the date as being one of the two St. John's Day's held sacred in the Masonic calendar, the other being December 27. It should be noted that the hotbeds of Masonic activity in Europe were England and Scotland; Germany was not particularly Masonic at the end of the seventeenth century, and Kelpius's short interval among the Philadelphians in London would not be evidence that he had somehow become initiated into the Craft at that time.

His background, however, was steeped in the hermetic arts of the time. His mentor, Zimmerman, had been an astronomer and astrologer and had studied Rosicrucian and Kabbalistic texts as well as biblical exegesis. These studies were revived at the Wissahickon, Pennsylvania, compound, complete with a set of astronomical equipment—including a telescope and a horologium—that was erected on the roof of their main building to enable the mystics to search the heavens for a sign that the End Times were near. Zimmerman had predicted the end of 1694 as the date when the Second Coming would take place. When that did not happen, the mystics continued to scan the heavens and create complex astrological charts. In addition to astrology, the group also created herbal medicines, for which they were well-known in the region, as well as amulets and talismans to protect against various diseases, evil spirits, and the like. These services, including astrology and dowsing for metals and water, were offered free of charge to the neighboring communities. Yet, besides preaching and healing, the group did not interact much with local society, another indication of their Rosicrucian sentiments, for—as the core documents of the Rosicrucian furor tell us—Rosicrucians are not to interfere in the affairs of humanity except to heal the sick.

Kelpius and his followers settled on the banks of the Wissahickon River. The number of the group's members was strictly limited to forty, as that was considered a sacred number to the Christian mystics of the time. References to the number forty abound in biblical literature, from the forty years' wandering in the desert of the newly liberated Jews to the forty days and forty nights that Jesus spent in the wilderness.

Kelpius would die a young man in 1708, and it is claimed that many of his books and instruments eventually found their way into various local museums and private collectors after his death and the gradual dissolution of his community. Copies of his letters to various correspondents demonstrate his interest in astrology, alchemy, and the hermetic arts, and his belief that these arts were part and parcel of the chiliastic Christian message. In one letter, to a Steven Momfort of Rhode Island (probably Stephen Mumford, the founder of the Seventh Day Baptist denomination, then living in Newport, Rhode Island), dated December 11, 1699, Kelpius writes,

> No wonder then, if your continual Gazing upon this Supercaeles-
> tial Orb and Sphier from whence with her Children causeth you to

observe every new Phoenomena, Meteors, Stars, and various
Colours of the Skei, if peradventure you may behold at last an Har-
binger as an Evidence of that great Jubelee or Restitation of all
things and glorious Sabbathismos or the continual days of Rest
without intervening or succeeding Nights, whereof God hath spoken by the mouth of all His Prophets since the world began (Acts
3,21) and whereof both the Testaments prophesie in evey Title and
Iota. . . . I do not question, but it will be your as well as my desire,
who would rejoyce not only to give you full satisfaction as to this,
but to see with you, yet in our days, that happy day, which when its
new Earth swallows all that forementioned Floud and where its
glorious Sun causeth all other Stars and Phoenomena to disappear,
no Night succeeds it, but that the Night is swallowed up in ye Day,
Darkness into Light, Death into Life, Judgment into Victory, Justice into Mercy, all imperfect Metals into Gold, and Gold itself is
refined seven times. . . .[6]

The letter goes on to include the inevitable references to the
Woman in the Wilderness as well as "baptisms" by pillars: the first a
"Pillar of Cloud" and the second a "Pillar of Fire" (per Exodus, but
eerily reminiscent of the first- and second-degree Masonic initiations).

The indefatigable Sachse—who, as it develops, was not the most reliable of historians but a Freemason himself who might have had his
own agenda[7]—has included a photograph of his collection of early
Pietist books and objects in his study of Kelpius, and there we can see
an open volume of Kabbalistic diagrams (such as those found in *The
Secret Symbols of the Rosicrucians* or the *Kabbalah Denudata*) among
the other interesting items on display. The sober piety of the group is
possibly what protected it from charges of witchcraft or sorcery.
Another possibility is the general acceptance of Kabbalistic, Rosicrucian, and Hermetic ideas, texts, and practices among some of the
most influential early American leaders.

As historians of Mormonism such as John L. Brooke and D. Michael
Quinn have shown,[8] early America was awash in occult ideas. While
alchemy is generally assumed to have been a European phenomenon,
casual observers may be surprised to learn that the study and practice

of alchemy was alive and well in the American colonies long before the American Revolution and that, indeed, elements of this and other occult practices—such as astrology, ceremonial magic, and Rosicrucianism—influenced the ideas of Freemason and founder of Mormonism Joseph Smith Jr.

For instance, John Winthrop Jr., governor of Connecticut (1659–76), was an alchemist who owned more than 275 books on the occult, including manuscripts of the legendary Elizabethan magician John Dee, and corresponded with other occultists and Rosicrucians. Prior to his stint as governor he had been corresponding with a New London, Connecticut, merchant John (or Jonathan) Brewster on methods for developing the "red elixir"—one of the goals of the alchemist's art.[9] Even such a notable Puritan cleric and author as Cotton Mather—who was an observer at the Salem, Massachusetts, Witchcraft Trials—was interested in alchemy and esoterica and was actually a member of the Royal Society in the period when many alchemists and persons of Rosicrucian sentiments were members.

Until the year 1717—oddly corresponding to the year when Freemasonry became officially organized in London—students at Harvard University were expected to attend lectures in the medical applications of astrology.[10]

Thus, from these very few examples alone, we can discern the outlines of an occult underground in America in the late seventeenth century. When Kelpius and his Chapter of Perfection arrived in Pennsylvania in 1694, then, it was in an atmosphere of tolerance not only for religious differences but for the study and practice of the occult arts, as well.

News of the Kelpius group spread not only in Pennsylvania among the German immigrant community but also to Europe, where it attracted much attention from like-minded Christian preachers and mystics from Germany and Scandinavia. A number of Pietist ministers and theologians were attracted to the idea of a haven in the New World and followed Kelpius in the years that followed. The most notable of these was the man who would eventually found the famous Ephrata Community, Conrad Beissel.

Johann Conrad Beissel (1690–1768) was born in Germany and became a devoted student of Jacob Boehme after encountering a group of Philadelphians in Strasbourg in 1711. Prior to his emigration he was a baker and member of a baker's guild; in that capacity, he went through three "degrees" very similar to those of Freemasonry: apprentice baker, journeyman baker, and master baker. In his journeyman status, he went from village to village for a year to practice his craft before returning to the place he started, eligible for the master baker status. In this he mirrored in his own life the speculative journey of the Freemason. In addition, and according again to Sachse, Biessel received an initiation into a Rosicrucian society in Heidelberg through "a learned mystic and theosophist named Haller."[11] Unfortunately we don't have any more details at our disposal about this intriguing episode, only that it took place in Heidelberg and that his association with the Rosicrucians was cause for him to be arrested and fined. Sachse states that it was a Pietist "conventicle" which provided the cover for the Rosicrucian order that Beissel joined, thus implying the close association between the mystical fraternity and the religious movement.

Frances Yates has written extensively on the relationship between Protestant movements in seventeenth century Europe and the appearance of the Rosicrucians.[12] She places special emphasis on the court of Frederick V, Elector Palatine, at Heidelberg as a nexus of Rosicrucian and other mystical Christian sects. A full account of the relationship between Frederick V and James I of England—and thus the relationship between the Rosicrucian movement and the Jacobins—would require much more space than is available here. What is important to remember is the role of Frederick and the start of the Thirty Years War, the conflicts between different Protestant entities at the time, and the overall conflict with the Catholic Church, which was firmly opposed not only to Protestantism, of course, but also to the mystical Christianity that was represented by Rosicrucianism and the Christian Kabbalah. Although Yates is able to trace the Rosicrucian influence as far back as Edmund Spenser's *The Faerie Queene* and its Knight of the Red Cross character, this is a strain of Hermetic tradition that has long been overlooked by scholars.

The first volumes of Spenser's poem were published in 1590, and thus more than a decade before the publication of the *Fama Fraternitatis*. At the time, Spenser had been in communication with the circle around the Elizabethan magician John Dee and it is clear from an examination of both Spenser's correspondence and his famous poem that he had been greatly influenced by Rosicrucian and Kabbalistic ideas, and that these were represented in *The Faerie Queene*, ideas that were later picked up by John Milton in his most famous work, *Paradise Lost*. When we consider that both Rosicrucianism and Freemasonry were anti-Catholic but piously pro-Christian at the outset of each, we can better understand how these mystical, crypto-Kabbalistic ideas were carried into the New World and gained such prominence among the English, German, and Scandinavian settlers who had embraced some form of Protestantism. While Catholics may have been attracted to these doctrines and practices, this was taking place at a time when religious affiliation was representative of political affiliation. Church and state were not separate entities in seventeenth-century Europe. Religious persecution as well as religious tolerance were at the discretion of the monarchs. Secret occult societies were as dangerous as secret political societies and, in fact, might even be considered identical. Secrets were secrets; groups of men meeting in the dead of night, sharing these secrets, were something no monarch could tolerate.

Beissel emigrated to America in 1720, settling first in Boston and then making his way to Germantown, Pennsylvania, in an attempt to join the Kelpius community. To his dismay, he discovered that Kelpius had died in 1708, long before Beissel had made the Atlantic crossing. Instead, he studied for awhile with Kelpius's successor, Conrad Matthai, before eventually moving out to start his own community in Lancaster County.

Matthai (1678–1748) was the community's last leader. By 1720, the Society of the Woman in the Wilderness was down to two or three old men, living as hermits in the woods. All around them, Philadelphia had grown and expanded from a few dozen buildings to hundreds, with thousands of inhabitants. Matthai cut a singular figure in those days, in his broad-rimmed hat and simple homespun outfits and sandals. A venerable figure to some, he was a source of unease to others. He had retained the knowledge and inclination to practice the occult arts, and was renowned as an astrologer, diviner, and healer, and as someone who communicated with the Other

World. He was also believed to practice astral traveling, the ability of the soul to leave the body and journey to other places.[13]

When Beissel arrived from Europe to join the community, it was Matthai who took him under his wing and eventually convinced him to move out and make his own way. This Beissel did, eventually forming the famous Ephrata Community in Ephrata, Pennsylvania.

The full story of Ephrata is beyond the scope of this study, but it is worthwhile mentioning a number of relevant data. Among these is the fact that Beissel and Benjamin Franklin were acquainted, and that Franklin printed many of Beissel's works on religion and music. Even more important, Ephrata was the scene of mystical rites, a quasi-Masonic secret society, and supernatural occurrences.

Within Beissel's community of celibate men and women leading a simple life in the Pennsylvania countryside there was a growing tension between two forms of occult practice: the Rosicrucianism practiced by Beissel and a kind of Freemasonry urged by one of his lieutenants, Gabriel Eckerling.

Eckerling was promoting something called the Zionitic Brotherhood, a fraternity whose aim was "physical and moral regeneration"—that is, alchemical transformation.[14] Gabriel Eckerling was the "Perfect Master" of this order, and he was assisted in his duties by his brothers Israel, Samuel, and Emanuel.

It should not come as a surprise that there would be Masonic activity—legitimate or not—in Lancaster County at the time. Benjamin Franklin himself had published his famous *Constitutions of the Free Masons* in 1734, a book containing the "History, Charges, Regulations, &c of that most Ancient and Right Worshipful Fraternity, For the Use of the Lodges. . . . "[15] It was the first Masonic book printed in America, and was printed by order of the Pennsylvania Grand Lodge, of which Franklin had recently become an initiate in Philadelphia.

At Ephrata, however, the Zionitic Brotherhood was something of a special case, an anomaly in Masonic studies since there seems to be no reliable documentation as to the source of the order's teaching and rituals. Be that as it may, their rituals do deserve a closer inspection.

By the end of 1738, the Zionitic Brotherhood had managed to erect a building for their own use, a secret temple to which only initiates were allowed access. It was three stories tall, perhaps in imitation of King Solomon's Temple. (A three-story temple is also central to the initiation system of the Freemasons.) The first story was a general-purpose area that contained the kitchen and refectory. The second story was designed as a circular chamber for the use of the Brothers as a sleeping area. The arrangement of this room is curious, for it consisted of thirteen beds, small cots arranged in a circle "like the radiating spokes of a wheel."[16] In the center was a single lamp that was kept lit constantly during a forty-day ceremony, a description of which follows. The room had no windows or any other source of light.

There are a number of issues with this. In the first place, the room was circular and the beds arranged in a circle. There were thirteen of them, which suggests the lunar year of thirteen months, Jesus and his twelve apostles, or King Arthur and his Knights of the Round Table. Then, the name of this room was Ararat, signifying the mountaintop on which Noah's Ark rested. Why this should be so is a matter of some interest, since some of the earliest Master Mason initiation texts in existence refer not to the murder of Hiram Abiff at Solomon's Temple but to the sons of Noah who "raised his body from the grave in search of a valuable secret."[17] The legend of Noah is important to Masonic mythology, since there is a tradition that Noah hid the secrets of the universe inside two pillars so they would survive the Flood. There are, of course, two pillars at the entrance to King Solomon's Temple and pillars are an integral part of the first- and second-degree initiation ceremonies.

The arrangement of the thirteen beds in a circle, however, recalls the discovery of an ancient burial site in Kiefer, Ohio. This site—said to be an Adena Indian burial mound—contained twelve bodies in a circle, arranged around a thirteenth in the center, "like spokes in a wheel"[18] (oddly, the same analogy used by Sachse for the Ephrata group). The same method was used by another Native American group, found at a site in Greene County, Alabama, in 1875. In this case there were twenty-five bodies in a circle, with heads in and feet out.[19]

That there were no windows and only beds and a single lamp implies a kind of burial or entombment scenario for the ritual. This room, as mentioned, was circular; but the third story was a square room with oval windows, one window in each wall facing the four cardinal directions. It was in this room that the main ritual took place.

For forty days the initiates would remain in this square room, absorbed in prayer and meditation. What rituals were performed has not come down to us, but some details have managed to make their way into the available documentation.

The thirteen "elect" were locked into the temple for the duration of the ceremony so they would not be disturbed. Every hour of their day was accounted for, from six hours for silent reflection, three hours in prayer "in which each votary offered his body and soul as a living sacrifice," nine hours to the "study and practice of the esoteric problems of the ritual" and finally six hours in which the elect discussed "the regaining of the lost or ineffable word."[20] This latter is most interesting, since the "lost or ineffable word" is central to the idea of the Masonic "lost word." This lost word has its roots in the operative Masonic practice of a password or shibboleth that allowed the members of the various degrees to identify themselves to each other and to the paymaster in order to receive their just wages. It was the struggle over this word that allegedly led to the murder of Hiram Abiff when lower-ranked masons working at Solomon's Temple wanted to know the word so that they could cheat their way into higher wages.

The "lost word," however, has a deeper connotation than that. According to Jewish tradition, the correct pronunciation of the sacred name of God has been lost since the destruction of Solomon's Temple and the scattering of the priesthood. This name—usually spelled YHVH in Hebrew letters and pronounced "Jehova"—was known as the Tetragrammaton ("word of four letters") to the medieval magicians who held it in high esteem as a word of power. It was believed that anyone who knew the correct pronunciation would be able to summon divine energy itself. Since Hebrew was written without vowels, there is no way of knowing precisely how the four-lettered name should be pronounced.

Thus, the search of the thirteen elect in the upper chamber of their secret temple for the lost word of God has resonance not only with the practices of ancient Judaism but also with Freemasonry. The Freemasons as a group, however, did not—and do not—occupy themselves with such rituals or attempts to discover the lost word; it is merely part of their rituals and their mythology. It is the systematic search for sacred secrets that marks the Brotherhood of Zion as well as the Rosicrucians and groups stemming from them as constitutionally different from modern, mainstream Grand Lodge Freemasonry. In the case of the Zionitic Brotherhood, this intense forty-day ritual resulted in what can only be described as supernatural occurrences. Starting at the end of the thirty-third day, according to the record of the Ephrata community, seven archangels made their appearance to the gathered elect and remained in communion with them until the end of the forty-day period. They were Anael, Michael, Raphael, Gabriel, Uriel, Zobiachiel, and Anachiel, who gave the adepts a parchment on which appeared the "seal, or the sacred pentagon, containing the ineffable name."[21] This signified the success of their endeavors, the attainment of "moral regeneration" and spiritual rebirth.

This ritual has much in common with practices from other times and places. In every case, though, these other practices were considered occult, magical, and not normative for any of the religions under discussion here: Catholicism, Protestantism, or Judaism. It is similar in nature to the rites of the Qumran group as evidenced by the *Songs of the Sabbath Sacrifice* in which a group of the elect would gather together in what appears to have been an ecstatic state of prayer in order to find themselves in the company of the angels. Even the numerology is significant, for the number seven and the number forty were as important to the Qumranites as to the Zionitic Brotherhood. The latter could not have known of the Qumranite practice because the Dead Sea Scrolls, which record the activities of the Dead Sea Scrolls sect, were not discovered until 1947.

What is equally compelling is the preparatory ritual undertaken by the prospective adept before he was admitted to this arcane rite. The neophyte had to spend forty days in a "hut or cave in the forest" accompanied by an attendant. This period of quarantine had to begin in May, on the night of the full moon. The candidate was to drink only rainwater that had fallen in the month of May, and his food was to consist of broths made from herbs, with the occasional crust of bread. The usual mortifications of the flesh were required and the aspiring adept had to spend his days and nights in prayer.

On the seventeenth day, however, a curious development took place. Several ounces of blood were taken from the candidate, who was then given twelve drops of a white elixir—six in the morning, six in the evening—to drink. This elixir is nowhere identified or explained. The formula seems never to have been written down.

On the thirty-second day, at dawn, more blood was drawn from the adept. On the thirty-third day, also at dawn, the adept was administered a grain of "materia prima." Again, this substance is not described or identified, except through the hyperbole of Sachse, who writes, "This *materia prima* is the same substance which God created to confer immortality upon man when he was first made in paradise, but which, by reason of man's wickedness, was lost to the race, and at the present time was only to be obtained through or by the favor of such adepts as were within the highest circle of the Rosicrucian Brotherhood."[22]

The physical effect of this substance, however, is described and the results are somewhat alarming. The candidate for adepthood "lost his speech and power of recollection" and three hours later went into convulsions and "heavy transudation."[23] "Transudation" may have been intended here as a genteel way of saying "perspiration" since the word today means the excretion of liquids through a membrane or through the pores of the skin. That this may be so is revealed by the next sentence, in which Sachse notes that the candidate's bed was changed. He was then given beef broth with more herbs.

On the next day, more of the mysterious materia prima was administered and in addition to all of the above symptoms the candidate now became delirious with fever, "which ended with a complete loss or shedding of the skin, hair and teeth."[24] On the thirty-fifth day, the candidate had a bath "of a certain described temperature" and the following day the third and final dose of the materia prima was given in wine, after which he fell asleep. During this sleep, new skin, hair and teeth appeared.

He was then placed in another herbal bath. On the thirty-eighth day, another bath was taken, this time with plain water and saltpeter. On the penultimate day of this ordeal, he was given ten drops of the "elixir of life" which Sachse says was known as the "grand-master's elixir"; this was taken in red wine.

Thus was this strange fast ended, on the fortieth day. At this time, the newly born adept was "restored to the state of innocence of which mankind had been deprived by reason of original sin" and now had the ability to lengthen his life to 5,557 years.[25] In order to remain effective, this strange ritual had to be repeated every forty years, commencing always in the month of May.[26]

Anyone familiar with the work of Mircea Eliade will recognize at once many of the symptoms of the shamanistic trance, voluntarily undergone by those who wish to attain spiritual perfection by first mortifying the flesh.[27] Eliade writes of several cases in which the candidate for the role of shaman must repair to the forest and undergo serious deprivations, to the point of hallucinating that his internal organs had been removed, washed, and then reinserted; or other examples of physical torture, death, putrefaction, and resurrection. What is different in this scenario is the addition of elixirs, the formulas for which are so far unknown. Were they hallucinogens? It is possible that, with the combination of austerity, near starvation and thirst, constant prayer, and the addition of a drug (imported peyote, mushrooms, even cannabis or some other plant native to the region) one could attain the same state of trance as that assumed by the Siberian shamans of which Eliade writes.

The elixirs, however, take us also into the realm of alchemy. Alchemy is also a subject on which Eliade has written,[28] as the idea of the transmutation of metals is mirrored in the transmutation of human flesh and spirit. The consumption of miraculous elixirs that cause one to putrefy and then become reborn is familiar to alchemists from the Yangtze River in China to the Rhine in Germany.

What is a little disconcerting in Sachse's account, however, is the list of the seven angels. Many of them are, of course, familiar: Michael, Gabriel, Raphael, and Uriel are all well known from many ancient sources, starting with biblical accounts and working through the centuries to Kabbalistic literature and the grimoires of ceremonial magic. Anael, while perhaps less familiar, is also a common figure in these texts. Anachiel and Zobiachiel, however, are a little more curious.

Anachiel does appear in the *Greater Key of Solomon*, a magician's workbook that dates to the fourteenth or fifteenth centuries at the earliest. In this text, Anachiel is attributed to Saturn and appears in a magical seal of that planet. Zobiachiel, however, is elusive.

The only place I have been able to locate a similar mention of this angel (as *Zobiachel*, not *Zobiachiel*) is in a poem by Henry Wadsworth Longfellow, "The Golden Legend" (1851). The great commentator on European history Thomas Carlyle (1795–1882), mentions *Zobiachel* as one of the seven planetary angels invoked by the magician Count Alessandro di Cagliostro and, in fact, numbers *all* of the seven angels as given by Sachse. The problem is that Carlyle's book on *The French Revolution* does not appear until a century after the events at Ephrata. In fact, Cagliostro himself introduced these angels—if Carlyle can be believed—in 1777. As Zobiachel/Zobiachiel does not appear in any other occult or esoteric text I have been able to locate, I am forced to conclude that Sachse has either added these details himself based on his reading of Carlyle, or—more improbably—that the Brotherhood of Zion had access to this particular lineup of angels in advance of Cagliostro and his "Egyptian Freemasonry." Thus does the appearance of an angel throw the entire episode into doubt.

Julian Friedrich Sachse was himself a Mason and the Librarian of the Grand Lodge Library in Philadelphia,[29] which may explain his romantic fantasy in describing the events at the secret temple. Yet he did not make up the entire episode, for we discover that other would-be adepts had tried to penetrate the brotherhood's mysteries and failed. The one mentioned by Sachse is verified by the original source, a manuscript by Johann Frantz Regnier published in Frankfurt, Germany, in 1747 from which Sachse's account is taken. In this document, the hapless Johann tries as he will to perform the necessary forty-day ritual of purification, but begins to go insane.[30] In an interesting aside, Regnier mentions that the leaders of the brotherhood had tried the ritual but he implies that they did not complete it. If that is so, then we can safely assume that the entire story related by Sachse never took place. The problem with making that assumption is that Regnier himself never completed the ritual, and may have accused the leadership of the brotherhood of similarly failing so that he himself would not appear quite so pathetic by comparison.

Further, the building, with its strange details, did exist as described, as did the Brotherhood of Zion who built it. For what purpose was it then intended, Sachse's description notwithstanding? We are forced into an uncomfortable realization that the best source we have available on this bizarre episode in early American religious history has, until very recently, been that of a Freemason.

THE CHOIR OF FAUSTUS

He had . . . sat in English, French, and Italian opera houses; that had been music for the ear, but Beissel's rang deep down into the soul and was nothing more nor less than a foretaste of heaven.

—Thomas Mann, *Doctor Faustus*

Other than the mystical rites and strange brotherhood, Ephrata also was known for its music—Beissel was an amateur musician, and Kelpius had written numerous hymns using a notation system he himself had developed. The most famous Christian Kabbalist of the time—Christian Knorr von Rosenroth—was actually better known as a composer of hymns (some of which are still in use today), and this is one of the ways in which Knorr von Rosenroth influenced the young Kelpius (the other being, of course, Kabbalah). This musical tradition found its most emotional and esoteric expression in the choral arrangements of the Ephrata community.

Beissel was himself the composer of some one thousand of these hymns, which were arranged in a way that deeply impressed the visitor to Ephrata. The same spiritual rigors that were imposed on the candidates for the Elect were also imposed—greatly modified—on the singers at Ephrata. They were expected to fast, to conduct themselves ethically and morally in every case, to remain celibate, and to pray continually. The result was a choir of exceptional intensity.

These were not the rousing hymns of the Lutheran Church, but ethereal compositions sung by weak, pale, spiritually distracted souls according to a simple yet effective arrangement by Beissel. As if in a trance, these devoted votaries held notes that seemed to float above the heads of the listeners in what Jan Stryz has called "The Alchemy of the Voice."[31]

Stryz's thesis is that the division of the sexes at Ephrata contributed to a kind of alchemical tension. He notes that "tradition calls for the male alchemist to enlist the help of a female in some instances, in order to provide the complementary energy necessary to the alchemical process. . . . under the direction of their founder and 'Father,' Conrad Beissel, the choral group at Ephrata cloister did engage in work that can be defined as alchemical."[32]

As the Brotherhood of Zion grew in importance at Ephrata, Beissel was determined that its corresponding sisterhood not be neglected. The Order of Spiritual Virgins that he had created as the female branch of Ephrata now became the Spiritual Order of the Roses of Sharon, and Beissel became the only male member of the community allowed to eat with the sisterhood—and to attend their secret rituals. His relationship with women had always been problematic for a spiritual leader. Rumors of possible dalliances with women both single and married had dogged him since his time in Europe, and he was involved in one or two romantic scandals in Pennsylvania as well.

The sexual tension that Beissel represented in this sexually divided and celibate community could charitably be construed from an alchemical standpoint. The men and women of the Ephrata cloister—the Brotherhood of Zion and the Spiritual Order of the Roses of Sharon—could be conceived as the male and female "energies" necessary for the completion of the alchemical Great Work. Celibacy's purpose was to increase the sexual tension while directing it toward spiritual—rather than material—gratification. In this case, it was no different from the overall goals of sexually oriented European and American secret societies of the later nineteenth and early twentieth centuries.

The impossibility of maintaining that high degree of control, however, gradually had its effect. The Ephrata community began to dissipate after the death of Beissel in 1768, and was absorbed into the Seventh Day Baptist denomination with whom they—and Johannes Kelpius before them—had maintained a lengthy correspondence and cordial relationship. Some of the individual members found themselves marrying and creating households of their own, the mysteries and rituals of the secret temple fading into memory and submitting at last to the oaths of secrecy of their respective orders.

If the United States is a Christian country, as many Evangelicals and conservative citizens insist, then the underground currents of alchemy, astrology, the Kabbalah, and Rosicrucianism are the black sheep of the American family. They do not comprise some recent, New Age phenomenon redolent of marijuana fumes, incense smoke, and the unwashed California Hippies of the 1960s but are a legacy of our earliest religious refugees. The occult has been with us since long before the Salem Witchcraft Trials. It was brought over, a silent passenger, with the first Puritans and the first people we call the Pennsylvania Dutch. Governors and university professors were alchemists in those days; preachers were Rosicrucians. This was the environment in which Freemasonry began to take root and blossom in the years leading up to the American Revolution.

CHAPTER SIX

New Rites, Ancient Memories

[A] limited code is unfolded to the E[ntered] A[pprentice], and in practice that code is enlarged as he advances from degree to degree, and even the code of the third degree is not meant to be exhaustive, but simply a bare minimum, and implies that until a man has lived up to this bare minimum he is not fit for deeper spiritual teaching.

—J. S. M. Ward, *An Interpretation of Our Masonic Symbols*

THE THREE DEGREES OF BASIC FREEMASONRY—the so-called Blue Lodge degrees—were not enough. Although established by the practices of the Grand Lodge in 1717, there were enough different Masonic groups already functioning (many with their own versions of the rituals) that dissatisfactions were bound to arise. Some of these problems were purely those of any organization: internecine squabbling, office politics, and power plays. The initial aura of fellowship and brotherhood began to dissipate under the pressure of nationalistic, class, religious, and occupational tensions. To make matters worse, the political situation in Europe was having its effect on the stability of governments, and international intrigues were having their effect on every level of society.

Secret societies like Freemasonry occupied a strange twilight world between the two major institutions of church and state. Masonic lodges were meeting places for men, a space where likeminded individuals—motivated by a desire to improve their lives and the lives of society in general by digging more deeply into matters more properly the province of religion and government—could find validation and reinforcement away from the prying eyes of king and pope.

On the Continent, Freemasonry was not as popular as it was in England and the American colonies. Perceived as a kind of club for the working class and a venue for amateur theatricals, the French in particular had no use for it. That was until the political situation in England became volatile and a power struggle ensued between those who were supporters of the Protestants and Parliamentary forces under Oliver Cromwell, and the Royalists who supported the Stuart line. A conflict that began in the late sixteenth century as a civil war in England would culminate in some of the most bizarre worldwide conspiracy theories concerning Freemasons in the twentieth and twenty-first centuries.

THE JACOBITES

Without burdening this story of Freemasonry with too much historical detail, it is still necessary to provide a little context for what will follow. We will choose as an arbitrary starting point the succession struggles among the Stuarts, the Puritans, and the Hanoverians in the seventeenth century.

King Charles I of England (1600–49) was the son of King James VI of Scotland. When Queen Elizabeth I died in 1603, James VI became King James I of England. Charles was born in Scotland and spent the first few years of his life there before moving to England to be with his family. His older brother, Henry, died at an early age, thus leaving Charles as the heir apparent to the throne. His sister married Frederick V, Elector Palatine, in 1613.

Although he was a Protestant, Charles was suspected of having Catholic sympathies after his marriage to a Roman Catholic, the Princess Henrietta Maria of Spain, in 1625 when he assumed the throne. His suspected Catholic loyalties and his belief in the divine right of kings—that kings should be answerable only to God—combined with an autocratic relationship with Parliament, made him an unpopular monarch. He was officially crowned on February 2, 1626.

Due to a series of conflicts and struggles—both with his Parliament and in a fruitless war with Spain—Charles I was gradually losing control of his kingdom. Calvinism was the popular faith, and Charles wanted to bring the country back to the Church of England

and a more ritualistic observance. This was perceived to be the influence of his Catholic wife, and her impeachment was being discussed among the members of Parliament. A rebellion was in progress, and Cromwell and his colleagues fled London and began to form the New Model Army to wrest control of the country from Charles.

The English Civil War broke out in 1642. Although Charles had the support of the Scots, his forces were finally defeated in 1648. Charles was captured, tried, and beheaded on January 30, 1649.[1] This made his eldest son (1630–85) King Charles II of England, but Parliament refused to recognize him as such and instead put Cromwell in charge of the country while not actually crowning him as a king. Charles II was crowned in Scotland but eventually fled to the Continent. He was allowed to return and ascend the throne in 1661, inaugurating what is known as the Restoration, and he ruled until his death in 1685 amid more assassination plots and political maneuvering involving Catholics, Calvinists, Anglicans, and others. He converted to Catholicism on his deathbed, some say as part of an agreement with his friend and supporter, King Louis XIV of France. His brother, James II of England (1633–1701) also known as James VII of Scotland, would become king after him. James II had, however, become a Catholic while in exile in Europe in 1668, a secret he kept until 1676. He married a Catholic and then faced a series of internal struggles as various factions plotted to assassinate him and replace him with a Puritan government.

Eventually, James II was forced into exile in France where he died virtually destitute. His son (known as James III of England and James VIII of Scotland) was recognized as the rightful king by Louis XIV of France, but in England George I ascended the throne, thus inaugurating the Hanoverian succession. James III (1688–1766) attempted to gain his throne in an invasion of Scotland in 1715, but was defeated. He spent the rest of his life in Europe, mainly in Rome. His son, the famous Bonnie Prince Charlie (1720–88), attempted another takeover in 1745 but failed as well.

The family and supporters of James II and his son James III were known as the Jacobites[2], Jacobus being the Latin form of the English name James. Their exile in France and Italy served to romanticize their movement, especially as their claims to the throne had been recognized by the French and Spanish monarchs. Bonnie Prince Charlie was the last of the Jacobites to claim kingship.

All during this time, Masonic lodges had functioned as underground meeting places for Jacobite supporters. While the lodges had struggled to maintain neutrality during the English Civil Wars of the seventeenth century—Elias Ashmole, the famous alchemist and founding member of the Royal Society was initiated a Freemason in a lodge composed of both Royalists and Parliamentarians in 1646—the bonds of brotherhood became more difficult to maintain. Into this romantic atmosphere of espionage, intrigue, and "pretenders to the throne" stepped one of the major personalities of modern Freemasonry: Chevalier Michael Ramsay.

Ramsay (1681–1743) was a Scot who had attended Edinburgh University and the University of Leiden, and received a doctorate in civil law from Oxford University in 1730. For a while he moved in the same Pietist circles as Johannes Kelpius but, later converting to Catholicism and throwing in his lot with the Jacobites, he wound up in France and then in Rome (in 1724) as the tutor of the young Bonnie Prince Charlie. He was also a Mason, and Grand Chancellor of the Paris Grand Lodge. His most lasting contribution to Freemasonry was a speech he made in 1737 in Paris, before a meeting of a Masonic lodge there. What he had to say caused reverberations down through the centuries, and Freemasonry is still struggling to come to terms with the ideas he presented there for the first time.

In this speech he connected the practice of Freemasonry not with the stonemasons' guilds of medieval Europe but with the nobles who conducted the Crusades in the Holy Land. Ramsay claimed—without actually mentioning the Knights Templar by name—that the chivalric orders that had operated in Palestine were the direct ancestors of the Freemasons; that their oath was not "execrable" as had been claimed (and thus immediately connecting these orders with the accusations against the Templars); that they had only the highest ideals; that they recognized each other by passwords and signs in order to differentiate each other from the Saracens; and that later they had merged with the Order of St. John of Jerusalem (which is precisely what the Templars had done, as we saw in chapter 3). According to Ramsay, this is why their lodges were called Lodges of St. John.

Ramsay was very specific in his speech about which Scottish nobles had been involved in protecting and supporting these Masonic forebears, and used 1286 as the date when the Kilwinning Lodge of Scotland was in operation as the only surviving lodge of the Crusader period.

In other words, Ramsay claimed that Scotland—and only Scotland—had indisputable Masonic credentials, and he went further to claim that France would become the center of the restored Masonic order.

The effect of his words was electric. He had single-handedly caused a sensation throughout France that elevated the reputation of Freemasonry and made it as noble as, if not nobler than, existing chivalric orders. Suddenly Freemasonry was no longer about stoneworkers in a quarry but about educated men, nobles, princes, and Crusaders. In his later work, he deliberately linked Freemasonry with the Templars: a connection that has yet to be broken, no matter how hard many have tried. (In the process, the Mason-Templar connection became the raw material of the Holy Grail legend as interpreted by Michael Baigent, Richard Leigh, and Henry Lincoln in their nonfiction work *The Holy Blood and the Holy Grail,* which later would become the theme of Dan Brown's famous novel *The DaVinci Code.*)

Thus was the Scottish Rite born.

Although Ramsay did not create the thirty-three degree system that is the structure of Scottish Rite Masonry today, his insistence that Freemasonry descended from Crusader knights via Scotland and then to France was the impetus for a major Masonic revival in France and other parts of Europe. It was called the Scottish Rite so as not to confuse it with the practices of the English lodges, which was just fine as far as the French were concerned. The Scots were the strange and exotic element in France, pretenders to the English throne yet not really English themselves. What Ramsay said had a ring of truth about it, and his speech was copied and reprinted and distributed throughout the country. The Freemasons suddenly had an ancient European pedigree but with the problematic associations of heresy and "execrable oaths" connected with the Knights Templar. Jacobitism and Freemasonry became conjoined.

While this new paradigm seemed to attract a number of French Catholics, the Catholic Church itself was not amused. Pope Clement XII issued a bull in 1738 making it very clear that membership in Freemasonry was forbidden to Catholics, and had Ramsay's speech burned in public in Rome. At the same time, King Louis XV of France became concerned that Masonic lodges were hotbeds of anti-monarchical sentiments and plotting, and in 1737 ordered an investigation. When it was revealed that many nobles and members of his own court were Freemasons, and that no seditious talk was permitted in the lodges, the king relaxed and did not continue to prosecute a case against them. It was, however, an uncomfortable replay of what had transpired in France four hundred years earlier with the arrest and execution of the Templars by the king and pope. As for Chevalier Ramsay himself, he melted into the background and became a private rather than public figure and died in Paris in 1743, the city that had been his home since 1730, where he is buried in the St. Germain Cemetery. The damage, though, had been done. Political intrigue and the hermetic society had formed a partnership from which it has never been able to recover.

THE INVISIBLE COLLEGE

Michael Ramsay was one of the earliest members of the Royal Society. As mentioned above, Elias Ashmole (1617–92), after whom the famed Ashmolean Museum is named, was a Freemason, alchemist, Royalist, and also one of the founders of the Royal Society. Another member was Isaac Newton, the scientist, alchemist, and biblical scholar. Like a genuine Rosicrucian Society, these adepts pooled their researches in every aspect of Nature in an attempt to unlock her secrets.

The Royal Society was formed in 1660, only eleven years after the beheading of King Charles I and during a time when it appeared that the tremendous political and religious turmoil that had been taking place in England was about to end with the Restoration and the coronation of Charles's son. In 1661 Ashmole was elected a Fellow of the Royal Society, and the newly crowned King Charles II became its patron.

Ashmole was not only an alchemist and a scientist but also an astrologer. Like his hero, the Elizabethan magician John Dee, he found himself in the unusual position of giving astrological advice to the king's court on political issues and even, it was suggested, to Charles II himself.[3]

This was the environment of the Royal Society during the period of the Restoration, when life in England began to relax a little under a tolerant monarch who valued diplomacy and accommodation with his internal enemies. Astrology and alchemy shared the stage with astronomy and chemistry; there was no discernible difference between the two. In Ashmole's view, the sciences revealed—rather than concealed—the hand of God, the Great Geometer, in his creation. This was a point of view shared by many, and not only Freemasons. However, Ashmole had designed a coat of arms for the new society along purely Masonic lines. It shows a divine hand from above holding a plumb line that disappears into the darkness below.[4]

In the 1650s Ashmole began a serious study of the Kabbalah and even began learning Hebrew from a Rabbi Solomon Frank in London. He had already accumulated a large library of alchemical texts and was immersed in their study as well, writing his own comprehensive overview of alchemy, the *Theatrum Chemicum Britannicum*, in 1652.

Ashmole was a walking encyclopedia of knowledge, the consummate polymath and Renaissance man. His museum was the first in the world to be operated as a public museum. He had a vast collection of antiquarian artifacts and was, in fact, a noted historian and antiquarian. More than any other of his contemporaries, he represented the highest ideal of the man for whom education is a jewel and not a chain: an end in itself and not simply a means toward accumulating wealth or prestige. Yet he remains one of the most neglected—and misunderstood—of the original founders of the Royal Society.

Today the website of the society admits that it began with an "invisible college" of philosophers who met to debate issues concerning Francis Bacon and his works. The society states that its "official foundation date" is November 28, 1660, when the group decided to formally organize themselves after a lecture by Christopher Wren.

Oddly, though the society's brief history mentions Wren, the scientist Robert Boyle, and others, it omits the name of Elias Ashmole, who was present at that same meeting and was one of its most important members.[5] This omission may reflect more on present-day attitudes of the society than anything more accidental.

In a survey of Royal Society members that was the subject of many newspaper articles in 2008,[6] it was revealed that only 3.3 percent of respondents to the survey believed in God. In such an atmosphere, someone like Ashmole could only be an embarrassment. Newton, despite his well-documented alchemical, biblical, and Kabbalistic researches, can be acknowledged because of his tremendous contribution to science; his other interests would be considered the quaint pastimes of an eccentric genius.

In the seventeenth and eighteenth centuries, however, spiritual forces were still very much a part of the operation of creation. Men like Ashmole, Newton, and Ramsay would see in the scientific method an instrument for understanding the mind of God. It was a tool they used for measurement, like the square and the compass, knowing full well that creation, but not the Creator, could be measured that way. They cherished a belief in a deity and recognized that Catholics and Protestants could work together to find a solution to society's problems regardless of their doctrinal differences. With the Kabbalah they had the beginnings of a mathematical approach to the mysteries; the endless combining of numbers and letters to coax meaning out of enigmatic phrases was the inspiration for the scientific method, for it introduced the idea that religion should not be taken at face value but its scriptures "deconstructed" to find hidden meanings based on number and proportion, and that recourse must be had to the original languages of the Bible in order to accurately understand its meaning. Once this idea had taken root—that the Bible could be subject to investigative scrutiny by men who were not priests, theologians, or ministers—it provided an emotional impetus for a wholesale examination of nature and the dissection of each of its mysteries, that the hand of the Great Geometer and Architect of the Universe could be found hidden in plain sight. The tools of the Kabbalah were available to anyone who took the time to study them; it provided a democratization of the theological process, putting a rare form of biblical exegesis in the hands of Everyman and taking it out of the grasp of the self-interested priesthoods that had, until the time of Luther, managed to keep the Bible away from the eyes of the masses and who had later set themselves up as its guardians and interpreters.

Ashmole and Newton, for example, were not only alchemists and Kabbalists of a kind; they were also scientists. A scientific approach to biblical texts was probably the last thing any of the organized churches wanted to see. Copernicus and Galileo had felt the wrath of the church, as had Giordano Bruno as late as 1600 when the Italian priest, magician, and philosopher was burned at the stake. The relationship between church and science was tense, and all the temporal power was in the hands of the church and not scientists. It helped, ironically, that the Protestant Reformation divided the Christian base and splintered itself into various factions and sects, thus providing some breathing room for the great thinkers and philosophers of the age. The disorganization of Christianity allowed the growth of contending points of view since there was no single power in Europe that could control the dissemination of new ideas through the use of the Inquisition, torture, and the stake. New ideas were still dangerous, of course, and hysteria over witches and sorcerers had not disappeared with the Restoration. Traffic with the devil was traffic with the devil, regardless if you were Catholic or Protestant; if you were Jewish, you were always living in a limbo of tension with the threat of expulsion—or worse—hanging over you and your community.

Men like Ashmole were great believers in tolerance, however, and they had found a champion in Charles II. Because of their own dangerous beliefs and practices, they had learned sympathy for those who were oppressed due to religious beliefs. Ashmole was aware of the example of his hero, John Dee, the Elizabethan mathematician, magician, and polymath who had suffered from angry mobs and suspicious monarchs. As a Mason, Ashmole was also sensitive to the requirement that one should treat everyone fairly and equally, and that the goal of the brotherhood was to create a society based on the bonds of friendship and mutual respect. That there were inner secrets to Freemasonry—secrets of geometry, arithmetic, music, and the other liberal arts—made it seem all the more credible because they were secrets of science as they were of God.

Eventually, though, the Royal Society would come to represent what is known as "hard science" only, reflective of the times and the change of attitudes toward such superstitious ideas as alchemy and magic. The society had outgrown all that; either that, or it had realized early on that commingling science with religious and mystical concepts was one way to court disaster. Someone eventually would object to a religious or mystical interpretation or doctrine being introduced into the proceedings, and the witch hunts would begin again and with them the loss of royal protection and subsidy. The "pure science" or "hard science" approach guaranteed neutrality. It was mathematics without the Kabbalah, the laboratory without the devotions of the alchemist. The church was still standing, but it had become a conference hall. The element that was missing was initiation.

Without initiation—either in Masonic terms or even in priestly terms—there was no psychological or emotional preparation for the study of the sciences. Ideas of personal responsibility or accountability—issues considered moral or spiritual and therefore unrelated to science—were no longer relevant. Concepts of social justice had no place in the laboratory or classroom. For better or worse, the scientific method had become the royal cubit of the modern age. From this approach came modern medicine, the marvels of telecommunication, and a host of inventions and developments that have lengthened and eased the lives of billions of people, even as billions more are impoverished by the strain on natural resources these innovations require as well as the development of powerful new military weapons. But the cubit had other uses, as well, and instead of using it to build cathedrals the scientists used it to build bomb shelters.

The great shortcoming of the Age of Reason—subsumed into the overall rubric of the Age of Enlightenment—was the near impossibility of adequately defining either reason or unreason. The only way it could be successful in its laudable program of eliminating the source of the horrors of the religious wars and the oppression of human populations by greedy or incompetent monarchs or popes was to elevate reason and science above everything else and to deny the importance or relevance of faith, superstition, and religion; in essence, it was necessary to create unreason as a demonic or chaotic elemental force. This was an easy image to materialize, since the Church had already thrown down the gauntlet where science was concerned in the great trials against Galileo and Bruno, among others. The line in the sand had been drawn. What Thomas Kuhn called the "Scientific Revolution" began to take form in the meeting rooms of the "Invisible College" that gave birth to the Royal Society,[7] which was itself an imitation of that other Invisible College, that of the Rosicrucians. What began as a defense of science and alchemy and Kabbalah (the Church had proscribed all three) resulted in the elevation of one over the other two. The ancient ideal of the magus—the Renaissance magician and worker of miracles through understanding the actions of nature and the angels, the magus of Newton and of Ashmole—had become reduced to that of the popular conception of the scientist: a magus without the charm.

But it was early days and Freemasonry (and the Enlightenment) had other arrows in its quiver. One of them was revolution.

THE LODGE OF NINE SISTERS

While England had the Royal Society, France had the Masonic Lodge of Nine Sisters (Lodge de Neuf Soeurs), which was developed for the same reason: to create a community of scientists and researches whose discoveries and innovations would benefit society. Unlike the Royal Society, the Lodge of Nine Sisters required Masonic initiation. Although the trends had been there among French Freemasonry for some time, the Lodge of Nine Sisters was only officially created in Paris on July 5, 1776—that is, one day after America signed its Declaration of Independence from Britain. And a prime mover behind the creation of that lodge was none other than an American icon: Benjamin Franklin.

Franklin had been initiated into Freemasonry in 1731 in Pennsylvania, and it was on his presses that the first Masonic book in America was printed. An inventor, diplomat, author, publisher, and scientist, Franklin could have been an American Ashmole, but Franklin—more than Ashmole—represented the new age that was dawning. Ashmole was the last of the Renaissance magi; Franklin was the first of a new incarnation of the magus. Based more on reason and science, and less on alchemy and the Kabbalah, this magus was the magician who created new social orders, new forms of government, new ways of looking at political problems. Franklin grounded the lofty ideals of spiritual enlightenment until they became the more worldly accomplishments of the Age of Enlightenment. As he did with his famous kite and key, Franklin tapped the forces of nature in a thunderstorm and brought down fire from the gods.

It seems obvious that Franklin saw Freemasonry as a new kind of guild for the intellectual and the rationalist. He seemed dismissive in his writings where Freemasonry was concerned, once famously writing, "Their grand secret is that they have no secret at all."[8] Whether this was the coy statement of a Mason concealing the secret doctrine by claiming it did not exist or the bewildered complaint of a man who never quite understood what was happening is up to readers and historians to decide. Nevertheless, Franklin continued to be active in Freemasonry and especially during the period when the Continental Congress sent him to France to negotiate a military arrangement with the king.

Official Freemasonry in France had been established by the London Grand Lodge in 1732, which authorized the establishment of a French Grand Lodge at Paris. The first grandmaster of the lodge was an Englishman, but he appointed some French nobles as officers. The innovation of Freemasonry in France was similar to that experienced in England: it introduced concepts of community organization and equality in an environment that was primarily monarchical. It was a laboratory for the experience of liberty, equality, and fraternity, ideals that would become the slogan of the French Revolution.

It should be mentioned that Freemasonry did not advocate the overthrow of governments but instead tried to inculcate ideas of social responsibility and respect for the existing government. However, in the atmosphere of prerevolutionary France it was indeed difficult to maintain a cordial attitude toward the monarchy while at the same time promoting ideas of liberty, tolerance, education, and reason. To a certain extent, Freemasonry could be considered a kind of *secular religion*, to borrow the term from Emile Durkheim, father of modern sociology.[9] Indeed, the idea of secular or civil religion can be traced to the ideas that inspired the French Revolution itself.[10]

Masonic symbols, motifs, and ideas were so prevalent at this time
that it is no wonder that many contemporary chroniclers suspected
direct Masonic involvement in the Revolution. The movement had
attracted such notables as Baron Montesquieu and Voltaire, the later
initiated into the Lodge of Nine Sisters shortly before his death.
Although French Masonry had managed to avoid a disaster during
the regime of Louis XV, and English Masonry was under a degree of
protection during the Stuart Restoration, that situation would not necessarily last forever. The Church had made its position clear concerning Freemasonry: it was an enemy. Therefore, Freemasonry lived under
a constant threat of suppression in nominally Catholic countries.
Regardless of the ideals of good citizenship that Masons formally
adopted, to maintain Masonic status under these circumstances was to
court censure, imprisonment, and in some cases even death.[11] Added
to this was the fact that some French Masonic lodges were sympathetic
to the Jacobites, which meant that these lodges were, ipso facto, political. Masonic lodges were composed of human beings, and as they
failed to live up to the neutrality requirements of their fraternity they
became increasingly polarized. The more strategically minded among
them realized that the Masonic lodge structure and network—complete with its protective firewall of passwords and grips—could provide a valuable asset in terms of espionage and safe houses. Although
espionage was not the proper occupation of a gentleman in those days,
the Jacobites had made international conspiracy romantic.

Ramsay's contribution gave Freemasonry and Jacobitism a high
moral context by linking them with the Crusades, the Templars, and
the Scottish nobility. Decades later, another Mason would expand
Masonry's profile in France by associating it with higher learning,
culture, and sophistication; but it would never be completely rid of
the faint aroma of political intrigue and covert action.

A French Freemason, Jerome Lalande, determined that a society
of learned gentlemen with Enlightenment ideas should form a separate lodge to promote the study of art and science. For Lalande, this
new society would support a wide variety of disciplines and subjects,
from painting and sculpture to music and science, all topics consistent with Masonic teaching in the degree rituals, with their emphasis
on the liberal arts and sciences.

Lalande obtained approval from the Grand Orient to create his Masonic society, and on July 5, 1776, the Lodge of the Nine Sisters was formally created. Less than twenty-four hours earlier, the American colonies had proclaimed their independence from England and its mad Hanoverian King, George III. The connective tissue, of course, was Franklin himself.

As he was one of the philosophical and political architects of the new American republic, Franklin's presence in France was necessary to ensure that the French remained sympathetic (especially financially and militarily) to the American cause of freedom from England. In fact, as every American schoolchild knows, France sent General Marquis de Lafayette to help Washington in his war with the British forces. What is perhaps not so well known is that Lafayette was also a Freemason and a friend of Franklin.

The symbol of the Lodge of Nine Sisters was a pyramid, and inscribed within it were the square and the compasses, along with the vaguely unsettling motto, "Truth, Union, and Force."[12] The pyramid, along with the All-Seeing Eye in the triangle, also would appear on the reverse of the Great Seal of the United States.

The initiation of Voltaire on April 7, 1778—the frail philosopher and author being led into the lodge on the arm of Franklin—was a major development in the history of the lodge and gave it considerable credibility. It was also a statement, aligning the lodge and by extension all of Masonry with the Enlightenment principles of which Voltaire was the best and most visible representative.

The following year—on May 21, 1779—Benjamin Franklin himself became lodge master, and the political activities of the Nine Sisters Lodge increased dramatically. As thirty-second-degree Mason William Weisberger writes, "The cultural operations of this assembly and those of the May 1, 1780 session revealed that the Nine Sisters would function as a center for Masonic supporters of the American Revolution. These activities flagrantly violated Masonic regulations, but for unknown reasons were never questioned by Grand Orient authorities. The cultural operations encouraged by Franklin conversely permitted the lodge and French Masonry to become identified with this American political and cultural movement."[13]

The "cultural operations" referenced by Weisberger pertain to books, speeches, and articles presented before the lodge on the subject of America and American independence. These French Freemasons were impressed by American attempts to rid themselves of what they perceived to be English tyranny, and were effusive in their praise of Franklin. The official journal of the lodge even published the Declaration of Independence, as well as some of the state constitutions (this was before the U.S. Constitution had been composed, and each state was busy creating its individual constitution). Aside from the propagandistic value of the meetings, the speeches, and the official publications, there is little available documentation on the degree to which (or if) the Nine Sisters actively supported the revolution in more material ways. In fact, many of the internal operations of the lodge were never committed to writing at all.[14]

By the time of the French Revolution, however, the Nine Sisters found that they had outlived their welcome. Meetings were cut short, or not held at all. Gradually the lodge ceased to function, as the revolution—and then the Terror—took precedence in everyone's lives. Ironically the Jacobin revolutionaries feared that the Masonic societies would be uncontrollable and a threat to their administration even as Freemasonry and its Enlightenment principles had provided the intellectual context for the Revolution.

No matter. The Lodge of Nine Sisters never made it to the nineteenth century, but it had served its purpose well. At the same time as the Nine Sisters Lodge was being formed in France, however, another secret society was being formed in Bavaria. With a reputation far in excess of its actual accomplishments, the Bavarian Illuminati of Adam Weishaupt became the ultimate conspiracy theorist's nightmare.

DOCTOR FRANKENSTEIN'S COLLEAGUE

I was nourished with high thoughts of honour and devotion. But now crime has degraded me beneath the meanest animal. No guilt, no mischief, no malignity, no misery, can be found comparable to mine. When I run over the frightful catalogue of my sins, I cannot believe that I am the same creature whose thoughts were once filled with sublime and transcendent visions of the beauty and the majesty of goodness. But it is even so; the fallen angel becomes a malignant devil.

—Mary Wollstonecraft Shelley, *Frankenstein, or the Modern Prometheus*

One hesitates to even mention the Illuminati in the context of Freemasonry, as there has been so much written about them from so many different perspectives that it is a virtual certainty that anyone reading these words has already formed very concrete ideas about them. They are also an annoyance to modern Freemasons, who must suffer the usual questions and accusations, some of which have been generated by popular culture.[15] The problem we face is that, as with the Freemasons themselves, the historical records are not complete and the actual or verifiable influence of the Illuminati on historical events is difficult to prove—or to disprove. Yet, a confluence of events calls them to our attention for their legend lives down to the worst expectations of monarchists and priests alike.

The Illuminaten Orden was created out of whole cloth by Adam Weishaupt (1748–1830), a professor of canon law at the University of Ingolstadt in Bavaria. Schooled by the Jesuits, who were eventually banned by Pope Clement XIV, Weishaupt was acknowledged as having a mastery of languages, including German, Czech, Latin, Greek, Italian, and Hebrew. At the age of twenty he had received his doctorate and was teaching law at Ingolstadt, coming under criticism from the university officials for his rationalist and secular approach.

He had, during these times, dreamed of creating an order that would mimic that of the Jesuits but be organized around an Enlightenment ideal. This he accomplished, on May 1, 1776, creating what he at first had called the Order of Perfectibilists: an awkward nomenclature derived from the *perfecti* of the Cathar movement. This was later changed to the Illuminaten Orden, or Order of the Illuminati, the "Enlightened Ones."

Thus, in 1776, we had the creation of three separate entities espousing Enlightenment principles: the Illuminati, American independence, and the Lodge of Nine Sisters, in three different countries and all within the space of about five weeks. The following year, Weishaupt was initiated into a Masonic lodge in Bavaria with the intention of trying to take over the Masonic order for his own purposes. For a while he seemed to have been successful, as his scholarship and academic credentials made his claims of ancient lines of succession and the "real Freemasonry" seem credible. Many Masons were attracted to this new development—as the French had been drawn to the Nine Sisters—but eventually Weishaupt's thirst for unbending control and his increasing paranoia made him difficult to endure. When word of his antimonarchist ideas reached the Elector of Bavaria, an investigation was ordered. Incriminating documents were found, and Weishaupt was forced to flee to Gotha where he remained until his death in 1830. During his time in Gotha he wrote several books explaining the Illuminaten Orden and defending it against various slanders. His desire was to have created a thing of beauty and goodness, but the angel had fallen and become—in the eyes of many—a malignant devil.

One of the main sources of complaint against the Illuminati—accusing the order of complicity in the events leading up to the French Revolution—was the book about Jacobinism and secret societies by the Abbe Barruel. Filled with inaccuracies and speculation, it was nevertheless the standard reference work on the subject for years, as was John Robison's *Proofs of a Conspiracy*. However, Thomas Jefferson himself defended the Illuminati and Weishaupt in particular,[16] and attacked the work of Barruel as the "ravings of a Bedlamite," even as George Washington expressed his concerns about the Illuminati and the Jacobins and denied they had any involvement at all in the American Revolution even though he suspected they had agents in America.[17] Later, a statesman of no less prestige than Winston Churchill would declaim against the Illuminati, mentioning Weishaupt by name and even using Weishaupt's name in the order: Spartacus.

> From the days of Spartacus-Weishaupt to those of Karl Marx, down to Trotsky (Russia), Bela Kun (Hungary), Rosa Luxemburg (Germany) and Emma Goldman (USA), this world-wide conspiracy for the overthrow of civilization . . . has been steadily growing. It played . . . a definitely recognizable part in the tragedy of the French Revolution. It has been the mainspring of every subversive

movement, during the Nineteenth Century; and now, at last, this band of extraordinary personalities from the underworld of the great cities of Europe and America have gripped the Russian people by the hair of their heads and have become practically the undisputed masters of that enormous empire.[18]

This is an extraordinary document, which cites conspiracy theorist Nora Webster as a source and takes for granted the existence of a "world-wide conspiracy for the overthrow of civilization," laying the blame squarely at the door of the Illuminati. Written in 1920, it was an article by Churchill preaching to the Jews about the need to embrace Zionism and reject Bolshevism. In so doing he becomes invested in every stereotype about "international Jews" that were embraced by Henry Ford in America at about the same time. To Churchill—whose above list of evildoers is composed almost entirely of Jews—Weishaupt was the originator of the conspiracy. Oddly, though, Weishaupt, a Jesuit, was certainly not a Jew.

The problem we face in confronting the story of the Bavarian Illuminati is obvious. Hyperbole and hysteria have overcome sober scholarship where the dreaded Illuminati are concerned. Even Thomas Jefferson and George Washington disagreed about the essential nature of the society, and Churchill saw it as the source of modern evil. Weishaupt was concerned with the creation of a new man, a "perfect" man, and in this he shared the Enlightenment laboratory with another intellectual intent on the same goal: Doctor Victor von Frankenstein.

The central character in the famous horror story by the then nineteen-year-old Mary Wollestonecraft Shelley (1797–1851), Victor Frankenstein is also a student at the University of Ingolstadt in the late eighteenth century. Frankenstein's celebrated monster is the result of is desire to create, literally, a new man. As someone who was fascinated by the works of Cornelius Agrippa, Paracelsus, and Albertus Magnus, his interest in occultism mirrors that of Weishaupt, who studied the ancient Egyptian mysteries and whose Masonic initiations would have introduced him to still more esoterica.

Frankenstein's monster becomes a murderer in search of love and acceptance. It grows out of the control of its creator and becomes more infamous, out of all proportion to the actual evil it creates. One wonders if the teenaged Mary Shelley had Weishaupt in mind when she wrote *Frankenstein*, so close does it parallel some of the same themes of Weishaupt's notorious order. As a daughter of the feminist Mary Wollestonecraft and the anarchist William Godwin (who wrote a book called *Lives of the Necromancers*), Mary Shelley was certainly in a position to have picked up a lot of Enlightenment gossip and occult ideas.

I myself entertain a fantasy of Adam Weishaupt and Victor Frankenstein as colleagues in that cold laboratory workshop in Ingolstadt, perhaps being admonished by a visiting Benjamin Franklin whose research, after all, provided the necessary electricity.

THE ASIATIC BRETHREN

In addition to the normative Masonry of the Lodge of Nine Sisters, and the unrecognized Illuminaten Orden, there were many other Masonic and quasi-Masonic lodges on the Continent at the time of the American and French Revolutions. It would be a strain on the reader to try to cover them all; even worse, to describe their beliefs and practices, as well as their Masonic bona fides or lack thereof. Yet, some of the personalities involved in these creations are such that some of them are still with us today, as characters in novels and popular histories.

In the following pages we will touch on only a few. No study of Freemasonry, no matter how abbreviated, can afford to neglect mention of Count Alessandro di Cagliostro and Count Saint-Germain. And no proper approach to the subject of revolutionary Masonic movements can avoid discussing the Asiatic Brethren or its relationship to a fascinating movement of Jewish mystics from Ukraine, including one who became a Jacobin during the French Revolution and who died—along with Danton—under the guillotine.

No one is certain when the Order of the Knights of St. John the Evangelist for Asia in Europe—more commonly referred to as the Asiatic Brethren—was founded, but its existence was known for certain in 1783, and possibly as early as 1780.[19] The fact that it was named for one of the St. Johns of Freemasonry is not necessarily proof that it was a recognized Masonic order. In fact, it probably wasn't; but one of the founders of that order would find himself in France during the French Revolution as a Jacobin.

Moses Dobruschka was a relative and close associate of a Jewish heretic and Sabbataean, Jacob Frank. I discuss this story in more detail in another work,[20] but a brief summary will be given here.

The Sabbataean movement was the subject of a massive volume by the respected Kabbalah scholar Gershom Scholem.[21] Sabbatai Zvi (alternately *Zevi* or *Sevi*) (1626–1676) was a Jewish mystic whom many believed was the Messiah; so much so, that many pious Jews began selling their homes and moving to the Holy Land in the expectation that the Third Temple would be built and a New Age would dawn. During his wanderings Zvi had been captured by the Turks and forced to convert to Islam, thus alienating most of his followers, who saw in this apostasy the ultimate betrayal. Others, however, believed Zvi when he insisted that he had to convert to Islam in order to "gather the sparks together"—that is, to perform *tikkun*, a repairing or perfecting of the world. This is a complicated topic pertaining to Kabbalistic teaching, but basically it means that Zvi saw the Muslims as sparks of the original creation, and it was his intention to bring all humanity together to receive the new Messiah. Those who continued to follow Zvi despite his conversion became known as the Doenmeh, and they lived mostly in Turkey, where some of them are to be found to this day.

One of the Sabbataeans was Jacob Frank (1726–91), who formed his own version of Zvi's sect by converting first to Islam and then later to Catholicism. His followers were known as Frankists, and he expounded an almost incoherent doctrine of Kabbalistic teaching that encouraged various forms of vice as well as piety.

His cousin, Moses Dobruschka (1753–94), had been considered as Frank's successor, but Dobruschka demurred and found his way into Western Europe. The Frankist amalgam of Jewish, Muslim, and Catholic spiritual teachings gave him a broad range of references and contexts to employ, as well as a confused religious heritage. Upon converting to Catholicism in 1773 in Austria, he was raised to the Austrian nobility in 1778, taking the name Franz Josef von Schoenfeld. With another Frankist—Ephraim Joseph Hirschfeld—he formed the Lodge of Asiatic Brethren as a Masonic organization that would admit Jews. Another cofounder of this lodge was the Baron von Ecker und Eckhoffen, a member of the Hapsburg nobility who had belonged to a Rosicrucian lodge known as the Guelden und Rosenkreuzer. There is some confusion among historians as to which lodges would be properly called Rosicrucian and which Masonic. In many cases, the members themselves would have been hard put to classify them.

It is more or less certain, however, that the Asiatic Brethren were not Masons in any traditional sense, since their degree system differed so remarkably. If we are to believe the work of Heckethorn,[22] the degrees were five in number, and the costumes worn by the officers rather more outlandish than anything the Masons themselves employed. Dobruschka, however, changed his name yet again. This time he was Junius Frey, he was in France, and a Jacobin.

By the time he arrived in France in 1792, the revolution had already begun but the Terror was a year away. After less than two years in France, the newly minted Junius Frey was suspected of being a spy—probably for Austria, which was then at war with France. He was arrested, tried, and executed at the guillotine on the same day in 1794 as Georges Danton, the famous moderate Jacobin, during a purge of the Jacobin Party. The influence of the Asiatic Brethren on other lodges—Masonic and Rosicrucian—was probably more intellectual than anything else, but it did pave the way for a Kabbalistic current in the more modern Masonic and quasi-Masonic groups that came out of the Enlightenment period. One of these was the Rite of Strict Observance.

Promoted by the Jacobite Karl Gotthelf Baron von Hund und Alten-Grotkau (1722–76), the Rite of Strict Observance was intended to be a restoration of Templar Masonry. Like Chevalier Ramsay, Baron von Hund believed that the Templars were the real ancestors of modern Freemasonry, and he also believed he had received that information plus additional instruction from Unknown Superiors of the Order. Hund was appointed Provincial Grand Master of the Order in about 1765. The Order may have developed originally from the Masonic Kadosh Degree, which memorializes the Templars and had been created by French Masons at Lyons in 1743.

Hund, however, was by all accounts sincere in his belief that he had been contacted by the Unknown Superiors of the Order and waited patiently for their return, which did not take place. Regardless of its actual origins, the Rite of Strict Observance had spread to a half dozen countries in Europe in a very short time before disappearing soon before the end of the nineteenth century when a Masonic convention declared officially that there was no connection between Freemasonry and the Templars. Hund's Rite of Strict Observance, however, was to have lasting consequences.

One of these was the founding of yet another Masonic lodge—the Society of the Shining Light of the Dawn—in 1807 by Prince Karl of Hessen-Kassel. Created in Frankfurt as a branch of The Rectified Rite of Strict Observance, it was a Jewish lodge and may have been the parent of the famous nineteenth-century occult society the Hermetic Order of the Golden Dawn. Gershom Scholem even references this lodge in his own autobiography, passing by its temple in Frankfurt when he was a young man.[23] This order would become extremely influential in the creation of modern British and American New Age practices and concepts in the twentieth century.

Another Masonic society that has had tremendous influence over the formation of a number of Masonic organizations in Europe and the United States derives from the creative genius of Count Alessandro di Cagliostro (1743–95). So much is controversial about this figure that I must qualify much of the information given herein.

Cagliostro—whose real name was possibly Giuseppe Balsamo, a native of Palermo, Sicily—claimed he had been initiated into the Egyptian mysteries. Becoming a Freemason in London in 1776 or 1777 (possibly in a lodge of the Rite of Strict Observance known as the Esperance Lodge), he became for a while thereafter the toast of European society. Insisting that the true mysteries were to be found in Egypt, he proclaimed his desire to create an order of Egyptian Masonry to which only previously initiated Masons would be permitted to join. However, since Cagliostro's Masonic connection was with Hund's Rite of Strict Observance, his order admitted both men and women (as did Hund's). The Rite of Strict Observance was very popular in Europe at this time, and Cagliostro was welcomed in lodges throughout the Continent. This Egyptian Rite consisted of three degrees, and initiates were given the names of Jewish prophets.[24] Cagliostro himself adopted the name of Enoch (in the Jewish manifestation) and the Grand Copt or Cophta (in the Egyptian fashion). His wife, the Countess Cagliostro, held the title of Queen of Sheba. They conducted initiations into the new Masonic sect, and gained the support and enthusiasm of the nobility as well as the mercantile classes.

Cagliostro, however, was accused of various crimes throughout his career and was deemed a man of mysterious origins. Was he really Giuseppe Balsamo, or did he, as he claimed, have a childhood on the Isle of Malta and thereafter travel extensively throughout the world? The official biographers were usually so hostile to Cagliostro that it is impossible to trust their records. His life culminated in an equally mysterious end. Arrested by the Inquisition on charges of being a Freemason (which was proscribed by the Catholic Church and an endless series of papal bulls), he was sent to prison for life and died (somehow, somewhere) in 1795. Although sent to a remote hilltop castle known as San Leo in Tuscany, which could only be approached by being lifted up in a basket, the official prison cell of Cagliostro is in Rome, where other authorities said he had died. Like the enigmatic Count de Saint-Germain with whom he is often linked, Cagliostro's birth and death were as ultimately unknowable as his life.

Cagliostro's idea of an Egyptian form of Freemasonry, however, outlived him by more than a century. Like the Chevalier Ramsay's idea of a Templar Masonry, Egyptian Masonry took on a life of its own. This received additional impetus from Napoleon's invasion of Egypt (1798–1801), an episode that contributed to Egypt mania back in France. The discovery or rediscovery of the magnificent architecture, temples, pyramids, and statues of ancient Egypt convinced the casual observer and the Freemason alike that there were sacred mysteries buried in the sands. It seemed as if Cagliostro's boast that the pyramids were really initiatory edifices could be true, and that Cagliostro's insistence on the importance of Egypt to spiritual regeneration had been either a farsighted prediction or the result of Cagliostro actually having been initiated there, as he claimed.

The result of this Egypt fever was the creation in 1805 of a Masonic entity known as the Rite of Mizraim in Milan, *Mizraim* being a Hebrew form of the word for Egypt. The creators of the group were said to be men who had been refused initiation into regular Masonry. The group moved its headquarters to Paris in 1812, where it ran afoul of regular Freemasonry and was shut down.

Another group, the Rite of Memphis, was formed in 1839 in Marseilles and then in Paris, and was based on the same Egyptian Masonry as the Rite of Mizraim and, in fact, was believed to be a revival of the dormant Mizraim group. Neither the Rite of Mizraim nor the Rite of Memphis are or were "regular" Masonic societies—that is, they were unrecognized at best and irregular at worst. The same can be said for a host of other groups calling themselves Masonic, including the popular European system of Co-Masonry. It is at this point that one must take a longer view before making any kind of value judgment on the value or lack of value of any of these orders.

Initiation in the Western tradition is a curious phenomenon. Among the preliterate peoples of Siberia, for instance, shamanic initiation could be self-selecting. In other words, one woke up one day and felt the calling to become a shaman; or one had some peculiar mental or physical disability that indicated a proclivity to shamanism. There was no paper trail, no line of apostolic succession, no committee or "Grand Orient" to determine what was, and was not, a valid initiation.

In the Western tradition, however, initiation is as much a bureaucratic phenomenon as it is a spiritual one. Taking its cue from the Catholic Church—which was, after all, the dominant religious and spiritual force in Europe for many centuries—secret societies began to focus more on the legal establishment of lodges and the legitimate lines of initiatory succession than they did on the rituals and their correct performance and the transmission of spiritual or esoteric teaching. Secret societies were power centers, and unscrupulous persons would see in them the potential for worldly gain and authority over large numbers of individuals who had voluntarily joined in the expectation of receiving secret wisdom. Later, as the Age of Enlightenment dawned, groups that did not have the bona fides bestowed by an authority figure or authority organization were considered irregular or even fraudulent. This led (in the nineteenth century) to a tremendous rush to accumulate as many diplomas and certifications as possible, with the emphasis on degrees and titles above all else. Since the leaders of these societies could not prove they had any *inherent* spiritual power or authority, they had to rely on the borrowed authority and implication of spiritual enlightenment bestowed by a paper diploma.

Meanwhile, back in Siberia . . . the newly initiated shaman, who had undergone a rigorous and dangerous period of novitiate alone in the forests, returned to his or her village with the ability to heal the sick, see visions, and communicate with spirits. If the shaman did not have the *inherent* ability to perform these functions, the shaman was not a shaman. The village suffered. No amount of paperwork would remedy the situation.

Thus, initiation—true initiation—is not subject to scientific measurement or bureaucratic approvals. This means that a scholarly history of secret societies may have to diverge significantly from the available documents and look instead at the fruits of their labors. An irregular lodge may, indeed, operate more successfully than a regular one and be more "powerful"—in an esoteric sense—than their more regular counterparts.

In the case of the Rites of Memphis and Mizraim—which became joined together at the end of the nineteenth century—their "fruits" were strange, indeed. Although beyond the scope of this work, their influence on the formation of a series of Western occult lodges and secret societies was considerable.[25]

Another phenomenon was that of Co-Masonry, which saw its beginning in an 1882 schism among various French Grand Lodges of the Scottish Rite. One of the schismatic groups—the Lodge of the Free Thinkers—decided to initiate a woman. As that was against the basic rule of Freemasonry, this caused the group to be declared the Masonic version of anathema. Emboldened nonetheless, the group decided to initiate even more women so that, in 1893, the lodge known as Le Droit Humaine came into being as a lodge of the Scottish Rite. A number of thirty-third-degree Masons of French Scottish Rite Masonry helped in its formation, and thus was Co-Masonry born. It is considered irregular, from the point of view of regular Scottish Rite Masonry, due to the initiation of women; but it has very active lodges throughout the world and a devoted following among both male and female initiates. The presence of female initiates possibly contributes another degree of depth to the rituals and other lodge procedures that would not be found in normative Freemasonry; certainly, the stigma of Freemasonry being a "boys' club" or a strictly male fantasy of spirituality is lessened considerably and new solutions may be sought to the old esoteric problems of alchemy, Rosicrucianism, and Kabbalah that might not have been discovered in a purely male-gendered organization.

CHAPTER SEVEN

A Conspiracy of Intriguing Men

It is meet and right that you should meet here in Philadelphia—the City of Brotherly Love—the mother City of Freemasonry in the western world. We may well say, Masonically speaking, that this is holy ground.

—Julius F. Sachse, "Beginnings of American Freemasonry"

A CULTURAL CONTEXT

Popular culture in the United States since the 1980s has seen a lot of discussion on the subject of secret societies—most especially the Freemasons—and their alleged role in the American Revolution. Films such as *National Treasure* (2004) and its sequel *National Treasure: Book of Secrets* (2007) have introduced the idea that there was a cabal of initiates behind the instigation of the Revolution and the crafting of the Declaration of Independence. This comes in an atmosphere of fascination with ancient secrets that began with the first Indiana Jones film, *Raiders of the Lost Ark* (1981), which was concerned with the discovery of the Ark of the Covenant and the race to keep it out of the hands of the Nazis. The third film in the series, *Indiana Jones and The Last Crusade* (1989), was centered on the Holy Grail and once again the efforts of the Nazis to capture it. The second, *Indiana Jones and the Temple of Doom* (1984), was about a Siva lingam in India and as such was the only one of the three not centered on Western, Abrahamic religious icons and efforts by both Allied and Nazi archaeologists to secure these "objects of power."

Then, in 2003, Dan Brown's novel *The Da Vinci Code* was published, adding an element of historical prestige to the dialogue. Brown insists that the data in his novel is based on facts, a statement that has been ridiculed by many academics and scholars who say that

Brown's data was based on speculative histories—such as Michael Baigent, Richard Leigh, and Henry Lincoln's international bestseller *The Holy Blood and the Holy Grail*—and the misinterpretation of available evidence. While *The Holy Blood and the Holy Grail* has been dismissed by many academics as pseudohistory, with the implication being that Dan Brown's novel is thus a fictionalized form of a pseudohistory, these volumes mark the first time that many people found themselves exposed to medieval European monarchical dynasties, biblical history, and a conspiracist's perspective of modern history. The downside of the phenomenon is that many readers accepted the theories set forth in these books as factual since they did not possess the background—culturally or academically—to critically examine the ideas they encountered.

The same charges were leveled against the Oliver Stone film *JFK* (1991). Historians of the 1963 Kennedy assassination were upset at the way Stone presented theories as facts, even though the film was not advertised as a documentary. However, like *The Da Vinci Code*, which would follow twelve years later, various elements of the most prevalent conspiracy theories were presented for the first time to the American public. They were made aware of personalities such as Clay Shaw (who was later revealed to have worked, at least in a temporary contract capacity, for the CIA), David Ferrie, Jack Martin, Guy Banister, and the entire New Orleans demimonde in which John F. Kennedy's assassin—Lee Harvey Oswald—moved in the year leading up to the president's murder in Dallas, Texas. The film was also at least partially responsible for the declassification of thousands of assassination-related documents by the U.S. government during the administration of President Bill Clinton, due to the public outcry for more information and clarification on various aspects of the alleged conspiracy, aspects raised in a spectacular and compelling form in Stone's work.

While historians may complain about the cavalier way in which speculation is presented as fact in these literary and cinematic productions, the positive aspect of all of this publicity has been the attraction of larger and wider audiences to the investigation of many of Western culture's most enduring mysteries, and to question the "official story" and the "party line," which is the beginning of critical thinking. Indeed, Americans had already been prepared for this during the Watergate scandal of the 1970s, when it was revealed that sitting president Richard M. Nixon had violated the U.S. Constitution and then covered it up. The televised spectacle of high-ranking officials in the government lying under oath and then being caught at it did much to increase the level of cynicism and paranoia among the American public at a time when it was just recovering from the traumatic experience of the Vietnam War—a war and its escalation that was critical to the thesis put forward in the film *JFK*.

In the attempt to assign meaning and value to the experiences of the last century, speculative historians have usually been the only resource many people have. Science cannot provide meaning, yet it is meaning that many crave. In an age of increasingly specialized knowledge and miniaturized focus, combined with the explosion of new technological advancements, it has become all but impossible to understand the world—to understand reality and the experience of reality—without standing back from the massive amount of information available to everyone and trying to find meaningful patterns or, failing that, imposing patterns where none previously existed. This obsession with seeing patterns in history—either in the form of secret cabals of initiates; manipulating financial and political forces toward some unspoken goal; or cosmic trends exposed in the arcs and angles of the stars, Aztec or Mayan calendars, or mundane horoscopes—is reflected in the popularity of familiar cultural icons and television characters, such as the obsessive-compulsive detective Adrian Monk (*Monk*) or the police lieutenant Robert Goren (*Law and Order: Criminal Intent*), both fictional characters who detect crime and criminals by seeing patterns in behavior and physical evidence that the rest of us cannot see or usually ignore. These characters are but the latest iteration of the Sherlock Holmes mythologem: flawed, antisocial personalities who because of their isolation from society see things the rest of us do not. The same was true of the character Fox Mulder on the enormously popular television series *The X-Files*, as well as the equally popular Dr. Gregory House on *House, M.D.*, both based specifically on the Holmes character. The popularity of these fictional individuals may be due in large part to their ability to solve problems using only their minds: a critique of the pervasive culture of high technology and its "labor-saving" mystique. This mythologem insists that power resides in the individual, even as the individuals themselves reside outside the mainstream of American society. It is an acknowledgment, perhaps, that true humanity is to be found where the Net and the Web—both spider metaphors even as they are network images—cannot reach. It's an acknowledgment that the best of us are the ones we have neglected or ridiculed, that "the stone the builders rejected has become the cornerstone" (Psalms 118:22).

This idea that one has to leave society in order to see clearly the patterns of influence and power—and thus to act upon them—is a critical aspect of secret societies everywhere. In order for the initiate to "see," he or she must be removed temporarily from the normal field of action and forced to look at society from a different angle, a different perspective. This dislocation is typical of initiation, and it is to be found in cultures as ethnically and geographically diverse as the Trobriand Islanders of Bronislaw Malinowski; the Sudanese Zande of E. E. Evans-Pritchard; or the cult of Mithra in the days of the Roman Empire. What rescues these societies and their initiations from social stigma has been the fact that they were integral parts of the societies they represented. Although the societies were secret, they served a valuable function in preparing young men (and sometimes women) for their roles in the social order. It is only when we come to modern times that the function of secret societies becomes suspect in general.

This may have to do with a Western division of "religion" and "magic," or "true faith" and "heresy": elements that were unknown to the ancient Egyptians, for instance, who did not admit the existence of "magic" or "witchcraft" as we understand these terms today but who understood spiritual power or force—what they called *heka*—to be a universal quantum, a kind of occult vitality that underlies all of creation. It is only when the European powers—most notably the Romans in the first century BCE—became involved in Egypt that this division of religion and magic began to take place as the Europeans attempted to gain power and control over the spiritual practices of the colonized population, a strategy that involved denigrating the religion and its priesthood and sacred texts.

We in the twenty-first century are not the first to recognize this dilemma. As early as the seventeenth century, Giordano Bruno made an eloquent plea to revive the ancient Egyptian worldview, based on his own readings of the *Corpus Hermeticum*, that compendium of late Egyptian texts that exerted such a fascination over the Florentine Academy of the fifteenth and sixteenth centuries. This idealization of ancient Egypt found a new voice in the person of Count Alessandro di Cagliostro in the eighteenth century, who created a version of Freemasonry known as the Egyptian Rite. There was thus a prevailing concept that ancient Egypt was the real cradle of civilization, that in its religion could be found the eternal truths that the Church could not provide, due to the Church's hostility toward the study of nature and its secrets. The paranoia of the conspiracy theorist may have had its origin in the suspicion harbored by the Renaissance men where the overarching authority of the Catholic Church was concerned. The Church actively suppressed the search for knowledge by independent thinkers, such as Giovanni Pico della Mirandola, Giordano Bruno, Galileo, Copernicus, Tycho Brahe—not to mention the alchemists and magicians Cornelius Agrippa, the Abbot Trithemius, and so many others. There was religion—the true faith—and everything else.

Thus the concept "What I do is religion, what you do is magic or witchcraft or sorcery" is a relatively new idea. When we discuss Masonry in the modern world, we are forced to make a lot of intellectual assumptions that may or may not have any real validity. Is Masonry a religion? Is it magic or witchcraft? Is it the survival of an ancient mystery religion or cult? These may not be the right questions to ask; however, they were the questions that defined the subject for centuries.

When we approach the influence of the Masonic brotherhood on the creation of the United States of America, then, we should keep uppermost in our minds a deep suspicion of any easy answers or characterizations. What drew men like George Washington and Paul Revere—among so many others—to the practice of Freemasonry was an indefinable element that was part brotherhood, part esoteric knowledge, part idealism and vision. It was the desire to take the reins of government away from the iron grip of monarchs and hereditary bloodlines and to create a nation of individuals who saw meaningful patterns—the design of the Great Architect—where others saw only chaos and confusion.

THE POLITICAL CONTEXT

But what do we mean by the American Revolution? Do we mean the American war? The Revolution was effected before the war commenced. The Revolution was in the minds and the hearts of the people; a change in their religious sentiments. . . .

—John Adams to Hezekiah Niles, quoted in Bernard Bailyn, *The Ideological Origins of the American Revolution*.

It would be naive to think that the American Revolution took place in a vacuum. The events and the ideologies that led up to that historic spectacle took place on both sides of the Atlantic: a head of steam that developed over more than ten years as each side grew in suspicion of the other. The paranoia was not restricted to the stamp tax, the tax on tea, or the other ancillary issues that one reads about in grade school textbooks. The paranoia ran deep on both sides, and the colonies themselves were divided into factions that supported the English king and the rule of the monarchy and those that opposed English dominion. Those opposing the king were also divided into factions, neither completely trusting the other's judgment or agenda. Some were in favor of violent revolution from the start; others were more cautious and wanted to negotiate. Most of these individuals were of English descent (a fact it would do well to remember in the pages that follow). In other words, they shared a common language and cultural context. The separation caused by the Atlantic Ocean meant that the colonists would be viewed as less sophisticated and refined as their compatriots in the motherland—as poor cousins, in fact. When set against the revolt that would take place shortly thereafter in Haiti—of African slaves against their French masters—the difference could not be more obvious. The slaves shared nothing in common with their owners; they were brought from Africa in chains and made to work in the cane fields and as household help for white, French-speaking Europeans.

The American colonists, however, were by and large English themselves. They had not been brought to America as slaves, and their

ancestors had fled to the shores of the New World in search of freedom, not servitude. Their revolt against George III, therefore, could be
seen as all the more bizarre for that reason. Its source was not the slave-
master's whip but the somewhat less tangible ideas of the European
Enlightenment: ideas of the rights of humanity, the "inalienable rights"
that would make it into the Declaration of Independence.

These ideas, however, were seen as representing something darker,
something more sinister. Rather than engage these ideas and take them
at face value, it was far more tempting to dismiss the ideals of the
Enlightenment as diversions from the "reality" that was taking place: a
cabal of conspirators, planning the ultimate overthrow of the kingdom.

Power always has at least two forms. One is that of the idea, an
intangible but nevertheless unrelenting force for change with the
ability to alter consciousness in the individual and, by extension, the
masses. The other form is that which we call realpolitik: the prag-
matic application of mechanisms and strategies designed to keep a
group in power regardless of ideas, morals, or even ultimate purpose.
An idea may have been behind the creation of the machinery of
power, but once that machine is in operation it has a life of its own. It
needs another idea, just as strong if not stronger than the first, to
counteract it. However, the existing power apparatus will do all it can
to deflate that new idea: through denigration, ridicule, or fear mon-
gering. It will count on the masses to be more conscious of their own
immediate needs than of anything grander or larger outside themselves. It will rely on the masses to endure the devil they know rather
than the devil they don't know.

And so it was in the late eighteenth century in the English-speaking world. As historian Bernard Bailyn observes,

> The opponents of the Revolution—the administration itself—
> were as convinced as were the leaders of the Revolutionary move-
> ment that they were themselves the victims of conspiratorial
> designs. Officials in the colonies, and their superiors in England
> were persuaded as the crisis deepened that they were confronted by
> an active conspiracy of intriguing men whose professions masked
> their true intentions. As early as 1760, Governor Bernard of Massa-
> chusetts had concluded that a "faction" had organized a conspiracy

... and by the end of the decade he and others in similar positions ... had little doubt that at the root of all the trouble in the colonies was the maneuvering of a secret, power-hungry cabal that professed loyalty to England while assiduously working to destroy the bonds of authority. . . . [1]

So we see that the political and cultural environment of the late eighteenth century in England and the American colonies was as obsessed with ideas of conspiracy as any present-day tabloid or work of thriller fiction. This was a secret conspiracy of "intriguing men" who were believed to be orchestrating the revolution that would come. There was no mention in Bailyn's Pulitzer Prize–winning book of the influence of the Freemasons, even though the Masonic Society at the time was tailor-made for his characterization of a cabal of "intriguing men." That Masons were working on both sides of the conflict is well known: there were leading Masons among both the British elite and the troops sent to put down the rebellion, as there were among the leaders of the American Revolution. A conspiracy theorist would say that they were in some kind of arcane collusion. The Masons themselves insist that discussion of politics was—and is—forbidden in the lodge; that Masons are expected to support the government of whatever country they find themselves—that is, *not* to engage in subversive actions against legitimate powers that be. However, some Masonic lodges in the American colonies were obviously in violation of that rule.

THE BOSTON TEA PARTY

One of the "smoking guns" in the theory that Freemasons were somehow "behind" the American Revolution is the canceled meeting of St. Andrew's Lodge in Boston on the night of the famous Tea Party.

The Boston Tea Party was organized to protest an arrangement the British government had made with the East India Company. Tea was a staple in the American colonies, and it was smuggled into American ports with regularity due to the high tax imposed on the tea by the British. However, a deal with the East India Company by the British meant that the company had a monopoly on all tea imported into America and could charge any price it wished, even up to only half what the smugglers were charging. This was seen as British government interference in local trade, and a protest was staged by the Sons of Liberty on the night of December 16, 1773. The leader of this action was Samuel Adams, considered by many to be a Freemason, though there are no lodge records anywhere to support this. The protest itself did, however, involve so many members of the local Masonic lodges that they were either closed that day or had meetings with only a handful of members. The canceled meeting of the St. Andrew's Lodge is representative of this fact.

A look at the available records of that fateful night show that protests against the East India Company and its tea involved as many as eight thousand people at Boston's Old South Meeting House alone. It would seem mathematically probable that many of the Boston Freemasons would have been among these eight thousand. To claim that the Masons were behind the Tea Party, however, is overstating the case. It would be just as credible to say that Christians were behind it, since most of the men involved were Christians. In order to prove Masonic involvement it is necessary to show that the lodges were themselves organizing or instigating the protests and the eventual revolt against England.

It is far simpler to demonstrate that the same Enlightenment ideas that informed the Freemasons' beliefs also motivated the revolutionaries. Unfortunately, one did not need the Freemasons to become influenced by Enlightenment concepts. These were freely available in the writings of John Locke, Voltaire, Jean-Jacques Rousseau, and many others, as Bailyn points out.[2] Even noted American Freemasons such as Benjamin Franklin and George Washington did not boast about their Masonic credentials or even give them much attention in their writings, which were often voluminous, instead downplaying Masonry's importance in their own lives.

That said, however, there is that same nagging problem that was mentioned at the very start of this study: the fact that Masons took severe oaths of secrecy concerning their initiations and other lodge business. If a person of such generally recognized moral character as George Washington was a Mason—and we know for certain that he was—then is it not reasonable to assume that he would abstain from any detailed description of his Masonic career? This may be particularly true at a time when quasi-Masonic groups such as the Bavarian Illuminati were coming under direct attack by European governments on charges of sedition and rebellion. To be a Mason in the late eighteenth century may have had a greater cachet and would be undertaken with greater solemnity than it would, for instance, in the late twentieth century: the oaths observed, the rituals performed with something like reverence.

Thus, if we agree for a moment that men like Washington and Franklin—and Paul Revere, and John Hancock, and so many other leading lights of the revolution who were also Masons—took their Freemasonry seriously, we must acknowledge that any organized Masonic revolutionary activity would fall under the protection of the oaths of secrecy and would have never been revealed. Absence of evidence is not evidence of absence; but extraordinary claims require extraordinary proofs.

What is more likely is that Freemasonry offered a forum for men of like minds to meet and discuss issues important to them from an Enlightenment perspective. It reinforced ideas that were already held but perhaps imperfectly articulated. It offered a safe place where these ideals could receive important validation from one's peers, in an atmosphere of solemnity and near sanctity. Where neither church nor state was the appropriate venue for expressing "the rights of man"—since these rights were a critique of religious authority as well as the divine right of kings—the Masonic lodge filled that need. The temple of the lodge became a kind of temple of Democracy, at least in those early years of the colonies.

As noted in the epigraph from John Adams above, the American Revolution began in the minds of Americans before the first shot was fired. It included a change "in their religious sentiments"—a serious assertion that can be most easily understood in the context of defiance of the divine right of kings and the insistence on the divine right of every human being. This required a major shift in religious understanding tantamount to that instigated by the Copernican revolution. The king, like the earth he represented and with which he was identified, was no longer the center of the universe. Suddenly, all men became equal in the sight of God, the Great Architect of the Universe.[3]

In a Masonic lodge, there were no class restrictions; a prince could be initiated by a commoner. In this way, Freemasonry represented some of the most cherished ideals of the Enlightenment in a symbolic and representational form. Further, by refusing to allow religious or political discussions in the lodge it actually placed itself outside of—and even above—both.

The truth about the Tea Party, then, is more complex than has been taught in the schools. It was not a protest against the tax on tea, but against the government-approved monopoly of the tea trade by the East India Company. There is no evidence that it was staged by a Masonic conspiracy per se, although Masons almost certainly took part[4]. It was the general environment of the times that contributed most to the growing independence movement in the American colonies among men who had been exposed to Enlightenment ideas either through books and newspapers, or even from fraternal brothers in the Masonic lodges: lodges which were living examples of Enlightenment philosophy. While it is virtually certain that most if not all members of St. Andrew's Lodge were involved in the famous Tea Party, that does not provide evidence that the Masons were organizing or instigating the event. If we wish to find traces of direct Masonic involvement in the revolution, however, we are forced to look elsewhere.

INTRIGUING MEN

Prominent Americans who were Masons and who were involved in the revolution are not difficult to identify. The most prominent of all, of course, was General George Washington (1732–99) himself. The man who would become the first president of the United States had been initiated at a lodge in Fredericksburg, Virginia, in 1752.[5] Although there is no documentation to suggest that Washington was an active member throughout his life, he never repudiated his Masonic affiliation, either. He has left behind several letters in which he discusses Freemasonry as well as the Illuminati and it is clear from his writings that he held Freemasonry in the highest regard while characterizing the Illuminati as something outside the Masonic mainstream.

The papers of George Washington are preserved at the Library of Congress, and the originals may be viewed online.[6] Among these are letters he sent to various lodges around America, usually in the form of thank you notes for books or honors received from them. In one such case, a letter to the Ancient York Masons of Pennsylvania dated January 3, 1792, Washington writes,

> I request you will be assured of my best wishes and earnest prayers for your happiness while you remain in this terrestrial mansion and that we may hereafter meet as brethren in the eternal Temple of the Supreme Architect.

In another letter, this time to the Massachusetts Masons Grand Lodge, dated December 27, 1792, he writes,

> To enlarge the sphere of social happiness is worthy the benevolent design of the Masonic Institution; and it is most fervently to be wished, that the conduct of every member of the fraternity, as well as those publications which discover the principles which actuate them may tend to convince Mankind that the grand object of Masonry is to promote the happiness of the human race. . . . I sincerely pray that the Great Architect of the Universe may bless you and receive you hereafter into his immortal Temple.

Again, in a letter to the same Lodge on April 24, 1797, he writes,

> In that retirement which declining years induced me to seek, and which repose to a mind long employed in public concerns, rendered necessary, my wishes that bounteous Providence will continue to bless and preserve our country in Peace & in the prosperity it has enjoyed, will be warm and sincere, and my attachment to the Society of which we are members will dispose me always to contribute my best endeavours to promote the honor and interest of the Craft.

In another letter to Massachusetts Lodge Number 22, dated April 1, 1797, Washington mentions his gratitude to the lodge for the fact that they are of the opinion that he "acted upon the square" in his "public capacity." Thus, we can see from this selection of letters that Washington held his Masonic affiliation in sufficiently high esteem.

However, in response to an inquiry concerning the Illuminati, Washington was quite forthcoming as to his opinions about secret societies and their alleged intervention in the internal affairs of the United States. His letter, dated October 24, 1798, is to one Reverend George Washington Snyder:

> It was not my intention to doubt that the doctrines of the Illuminati and principles of Jacobinism had not spread in the United States. On the contrary, no one is more truly satisfied of this fact than I am.
>
> The idea that I meant to convey was, that I did not believe that the *Lodges* of Free Masons in *this* Country had, as Societies, endeavoured to propagate the diabolical tenets of the first, or pernicious principles of the latter (if they are susceptible of separation). That Individuals of them may have done it, or that the founder or instrument employed to found the democratic Societies in the United States, may have had these objects—and actually had a separation of the People from their Government in view, is too evident to be questioned.

This is a somewhat problematic statement, to be sure. Washington here defends the Freemasons "as Societies" from charges that they were involved with the Illuminati or the Jacobins, but admits that certain individuals may have had those designs. In fact, he claims that he is satisfied as to the facts of the matter and that, indeed, "Doctrines" of the Illuminati and "principles" of Jacobinism had spread in the United States. His only intention in this letter is to separate the Freemasons as an organization from these charges, while allowing that individual Freemasons may have been involved. Yet it is not the Illuminati or the Jacobins themselves that had penetrated the United States—according to this letter—but only their doctrines and principles. Washington is careful to say that some Freemasons may have "endeavoured to propagate" these ideas without specifically saying that they were members of Illuminati lodges or Jacobin circles of intrigue.

Washington's most public appearance as a Mason, however, was at the cornerstone laying of the U.S. Capitol on September 18,

1793, which was a Masonic ceremony and in which Washington appeared dressed in Masonic regalia. Other than that, there is very little documentation to show that Washington attended lodge meetings or was active in any way in Masonic affairs. He was raised to the Master Mason degree in 1753, and after that there is almost nothing to show his interest in Masonry until the time of the revolution. This is not necessarily unusual; if the force of the initiation—particularly of the third degree, which involves a death-and-rebirth scenario—was sufficiently powerful in young Washington's mind he may have felt no further need to attend meetings after that. He was surrounded by Freemasons, and could have received additional knowledge or clarification (if desired) from them on a casual basis. Looking at Washington's career, one can come away with the assumption that *his* lodge was the army. It was a fraternity, a "band of brothers" united for a common cause and surrounded itself by emblems of death, of sacrifice, of nobility of purpose. Washington had attained an impossible goal in his professional life: he had defeated the greatest standing army the Western world had known at the time, and given birth to a free nation in the process. It is entirely possible that Washington viewed his own life as putting those Masonic ideals he learned as a young man of twenty into practice in the real world—and with a vengeance. The laying of the Capitol cornerstone in 1793 was the capstone to his own career, the laying of a foundation for centuries of American government to come, and it was done with Masonic ceremony. Whatever historians may think about Washington's Masonic fervor or lack thereof, the symbolism of this act—and its implications—cannot be ignored.

The next Freemason deserving of inclusion is Benjamin Franklin (1706–90). Franklin was initiated in 1731, one year before George Washington was born. Records show that he was much more active in Freemasonry than Washington, serving as Provincial Grand Master of the Grand Lodge of Pennsylvania in 1734, the year he published the first Masonic book in America, *The Constitution of the Freemason*. He seems to have remained active in Freemasonry for the next twenty-five years or so, but from about 1760 until the revolution there is little data on his Masonic activities.

Then, in 1776, we find Franklin in Paris as the delegate of the American colonies to France. It was while there that, in 1777, he joined the Masonic Lodge of Nine Sisters (Lodge de Neuf Soeurs), eventually becoming its Honorary Master in 1779. He was partly responsible for bringing Voltaire himself into that lodge, where the famous French author and philosopher was initiated in Franklin's presence in 1778. (Voltaire died soon thereafter and was buried with Masonic honors.)

Franklin was believed to have been involved in numerous other secret societies and underground clubs, mostly in Europe. He traveled to England frequently in the years before the revolution, and persistent rumors have him frequenting Sir Francis Dashwood's Medmenham Franciscans in 1773–74. This was a cabal of libertines, according to the popular histories, and meetings of the "Knights of St. Francis" or "the Medmenham Friars," among other epithets— sometimes casually referred to as the Hellfire Club—were believed to involve sexual orgies and Black Masses, among other outrages. The motto of Dashwood's cabal was *Fay ce que voudras* (the Rabelaisian "Do what thou wilt"), to become the slogan of another Englishman's cult in the twentieth century, that of Aleister Crowley. A painting of Dashwood shows him in the robes of a Franciscan monk, on his knees in adoration before the Venus de Medici (a famous classical sculpture of the goddess of love).[7] The members of Dashwood's circle included some of the most influential English nobles and political movers and shakers of the time, and Dashwood himself was named Chancellor of the Exchequer, so it is no wonder that Franklin is believed to have attended some of their meetings.

Franklin's influence on the ideals of the American Revolution as a kind of eminence grise cannot be denied, but it is his overall genius that is perhaps best remembered today. As an inventor, author, journalist, politician, and statesman he is one of America's most enduring icons; he was also one of the most active Masons among the list of Revolutionary War–era Americans and a man who raised the young nation's profile and credibility among the courts of Europe at a time when the United States desperately needed them both. The Grand Lodge at York, England, even goes so far as to claim him as an "English Freemason," stating on its weblog that "Benjamin Franklin is too important a figure in Freemasonry to leave exclusively to the realms of American history, ideology, and sentiment"![8]

Another active Freemason among the revolutionaries was Paul Revere (1735–1818), whose "midnight ride" was made famous in the poem by Henry Wadsworth Longfellow. Revere was a Freemason who became increasingly involved with the Sons of Liberty and with such notable figures as General Joseph Warren (a Freemason Grand Master who was killed at the Battle of Bunker Hill), John Hancock (another Freemason), and Samuel Adams (yet another Freemason). If we simply list some of the most famous figures of the American Revolution—Washington, Franklin, Revere, Hancock, Samuel Adams, and the foreign military advisors the Marquis de Lafayette and Baron Friedrich Wilhelm von Steuben—we find that they were all Masons. John Adams, however, was not a Mason and his son John Quincy Adams belonged to the Anti-Masonic Party. Thomas Jefferson was not a Mason. So it is hyperbole to suggest that *all* or even *most* of the founding fathers of the American republic were Masons.

Yet the number of those who were is out of proportion to the rest of the population. Of the fifty-six signers of the Declaration of Independence, nine were known and confirmed Freemasons. Thirteen of the thirty-nine signers of the U.S. Constitution were Freemasons—that is, one-third. Of the seventy-four commissioned generals of the Continental Army during the revolution, thirty-three—almost half—were Freemasons. Even Robert Newman, the man who hung the lantern in Old North Church—"one if by land, two if by sea"— was a Mason.

Yet, a look at some membership rolls for Boston and Philadelphia in the immediate prewar period would be instructive. The total number of Masons in Philadelphia in the year 1756, for example, is given as 2,397. The population of Philadelphia at the time was about 30,000—of whom only the men would be eligible to be Masons. Assuming a total male population of 15,000, then, about 15 percent of that number were Masons.[9] If this is in any way reflective of the total number of Masons versus the total number of inhabitants in revolutionary-era America, then it would seem that they commanded a disproportionate share of the decision making of the revolution. Almost 50 percent of all the generals of the Continental Army were Masons, and as mentioned thirty-three percent of all the signers of the Constitution were Masons. One reason for this statistic is the emphasis on wealth and position of the early Masonic lodges in America. The initiations were expensive, and the lodges protected themselves against members whose social status they did not like or of which they otherwise disapproved by using a blackball vote. Thus, the early American lodges were populated by the wealthy, the urban merchant class, and very few farmers.[10]

While the majority were not Masons, the brotherhood still shows up in hugely disproportionate numbers in any examination of the men who founded the nation: the philosophers and idealists, the conspirators, and the generals who fought and died on the battlefields. These men came from the educated and wealthy classes, classes that comprised the majority membership of the Masonic lodges in those days. These were the "intriguing gentlemen" who conceived the revolution and then carried it out, forming the first democratic republic in modern times.

But there was another group of Freemasons—though not fully recognized by the main bodies—that made a significant contribution to the revolution and to American life, politics, and culture for centuries to come. Their names are not as well-known as those of Washington and Franklin, but they held the same ideals and made the same sacrifices. These were the Masons of what has come to be known as Prince Hall Freemasonry.

One of the requirements of Masonic membership is that one be free born—that is, not a slave. Several justifications for this requirement have been made by other authors, most notably the idea that only a free man could make an oath. That does not explain why someone who had been born a slave and was now free could not become a Freemason, however.

If we look again at the previous paragraphs, we will be reminded that the first Masonic lodges in America—known as the "Moderns"—were composed largely of wealthy and socially connected white men. Another Masonic element later crept into American Freemasonry, and that was the group known as the "Ancients." This group more easily attracted the less-wealthy, less-powerful citizens. While the Ancients were not as class-conscious as the Moderns, neither of these two groups admitted either women or African Americans. (While Europe was still struggling over the question of whether or not Jews could be admitted as Freemasons, we find Jews as well as Native Americans among the earliest American Masons.[11])

However, a freed slave named Prince Hall challenged the idea that, even though Freemasonry preached universal brotherhood, this universality did not include African Americans. Born into slavery about the year 1735, he was manumitted by William Hall in 1770 and opened a leather-working shop in Boston. In 1775, Prince Hall and thirteen other black men were initiated into Freemasonry by a British soldier. This initiation was considered irregular, and became the basis for some controversy, but Hall and his brothers persisted and opened African Lodge No. 1 in Boston. They were eventually granted a charter from the Grand Lodge of England after the end of the Revolutionary War, and became African Lodge No. 459; Prince Hall was himself named Grand Master. This initial lodge became the forerunner of the more than forty Prince Hall Grand Lodges that exist today in America. Among the more famous Prince Hall Masons we find Count Basie, Mayor Thomas Bradley of Los Angeles, Nat King Cole, W. E. B. Dubois, Duke Ellington, Alex Haley, Justice Thurgood Marshall, Congressman Charles Rangel of New York, Sugar Ray Robinson, Booker T. Washington, Andrew Young, and countless others.

What Prince Hall accomplished, however, extends far beyond even this prodigious achievement. A tireless organizer and advocate of racial equality, Hall not only fought at the earliest, most iconic battles of the revolution—Lexington, Concord, Bunker Hill—and suffered with Washington at Valley Forge, but he also managed to convince General Washington to accept black troops as full members of the Continental Army.

With the successful end of the revolution, Hall returned to Boston and opened a school for the children of the former African slaves. He continued to campaign for equal rights under the law until his death in 1807.

Those who insist that Freemasonry is a sinister cabal of men who desire to control the world need only study the Prince Hall branch of Freemasonry to realize that such characterizations are weak. The conflict between "regular" Freemasonry and Prince Hall Freemasonry is evidence that the same biases and prejudices that existed and continue to exist in American society also affect Freemasonry itself, which is not the grand, united organization that it is made out to be but subject to the same social stressors as the rest of us. In spite of the insistence of Masons that Freemasonry is a society devoted to universal brotherhood and moral improvement, the organization as a whole has demonstrated a level of class consciousness and race consciousness (not to mention gender bias) that argues against the uplifting message of its publications and official announcements. At the same time, what we call Freemasonry is not a monolithic structure of old white men intent on monopolizing trade and government but a very loosely organized bundle of different societies with sometimes opposing positions on critical issues.

Freemasonry during the American Revolution was not even unified on a position for or against democracy. There were Masonic lodges that were pro-England and lodges that were prorevolution. One of America's most famous traitors—Benedict Arnold—was a Freemason. The British Army itself contained many Masonic lodges within its regiments whose loyalties were normally to the king. That meant that Masons were fighting Masons in virtually every battle of the revolution.

Masonic organization in the colonies was really colonial organization. Some Masonic lodges may have served as safe houses and some Masons as spies. The lodges served as a network of communication and supply. There can be no doubt that Freemasonry played an important role in the events of the revolution, but it is important to remember that the role it played was on both sides of the conflict. This is a far cry from the idea that Freemasonry had somehow instigated or organized the American Revolution. The ideas that were (and are) enshrined in the rituals, initiations, and lectures of Freemasonry were Enlightenment ideas. Freemasonry's importance to the revolution is that it provided a place where these ideas could be experienced directly; the Masonic temple was a laboratory of democratic ideals, equality, and human rights.

CHAPTER EIGHT

Magic and Mormonism

*The details of the case will probably be never known now, though we are
informed upon good authority that the crime was the result of an old-standing
and romantic feud, in which love and Mormonism bore a part. It seems that both
the victims belonged, in their younger days, to the Latter Day Saints. . . .*

—Sir Arthur Conan Doyle, "A Study in Scarlet"

We have the true Masonry.

—Heber C. Kimball, one of the first Mormon leaders,
quoted in John L. Brooke, *The Refiner's Fire: The Making
of Mormon Cosmology, 1644–1844*

TO THE ANCIENT EGYPTIANS, the earth was created when a
mound rose from the sea. The pyramids themselves were stylized
mounds or mountains. In ancient Babylon, the ziggurats were the
equivalent of mountains that had to be climbed. Moses received the
Ten Commandments at the top of Mount Sinai. Noah's Ark landed
atop Mount Ararat. And, finally, King Solomon's Temple was built at
the summit of Mount Moriah in Jerusalem.

In America, the first settlers and pioneers found the countryside dotted with mounds. In some cases, these were burial mounds;
in others, the mounds served no discernible purpose. Eventually,
archaeology would demonstrate that these mounds were representative of an ancient Native American culture and that in many cases
these mounds were as astronomically oriented as Stonehenge:
aligned to the rising and setting of the sun, moon, and certain stars
at certain times of the year. This has its analogue in the *tumulus*
culture of ancient Europe, which saw the building of mounds for
the same purposes.

Thus, for many ancient peoples mounds had sacred significance. They represented an approach to the heavens, the moment of creation, the burial of kings and priests, and the site of temples.

So perhaps it is no wonder that the first religion to be created in the newly independent United States of America would have found its own origins at the site of a mound: Hill Cumorah, in upstate New York.

In the aftermath of the American Revolution, there was a religious revival taking place in the country and especially in the northeastern states. This occurred not long after the War of 1812, which saw the British invasion of the United States, the famous Battle of New Orleans, and the burning of the White House. Millennial panic and chiliasm brought with it anxiety about not only the future but redemption itself. New religious movements were born, new denominations formed, and feelings were running high. At the same time, there was a curious criminal enterprise abroad in the land that had its roots in alchemy and the hermetic sciences: counterfeiting.

Popular notions of alchemy invariably focused on the ability of alchemists to make gold rather than the more spiritual or mystical aspects of the spagyric arts. Thus, it was inevitable that fraudulent alchemists would appear, promising, for example, to convert worthless metal into gold or selling fake gold rings and coins. Alongside the counterfeiters were the diviners.

Diviners claimed to have the ability to locate gold and treasure that was buried beneath the earth. They also claimed the ability to locate copper and other metals for mining. Their instrument was usually a branched stick, or two sticks—one held in each hand—that were held parallel to the earth as the diviner walked along. If the sticks pulled toward the earth, the substance being sought was found. Success depended upon the individual capability of the diviner, of course.

Both the diviners and the counterfeiters fed off of the economic hardships being experienced throughout New England and New York State in the early decades of the nineteenth century. They had found an environment that already had experience with hermeticism, alchemy, Rosicrucianism and Freemasonry, thus making it even easier for the unscrupulous to take advantage of a desperate population. When even the president of Yale University was an avowed alchemist, how could the rest of the population resist the allure of secret societies engaged in the production of untold wealth?

The family of Joseph Smith Jr. (1805–44) had fallen on hard times. They had moved from Vermont to the Burned-Over District of upstate New York in search of a living. It was the time of the Second Great Awakening, and religious revivalism was everywhere, as were occult practitioners, alchemists, astrologers, and diviners. Joseph Smith Sr. had himself been a diviner, and previously had been involved with the Universalist movement back in Vermont, and possibly had been initiated into Freemasonry there.[1] Now they were in Palmyra, New York, and surrounded on all sides by Masonic lodges and occultists with pedigrees going back to the Pietist movement that had given birth to Johannes Kelpius and the Woman of the Wilderness sect as well as the Ephrata, Pennsylvania, commune. Groups such as the New Israelites were fleetingly influential: a sect that claimed to represent the lost tribes of Israel and which believed the Millennium would take place in 1802.

The first "Great Awakening" had taken place over a period of several decades in prerevolutionary America and produced such important and prominent theologians as Jonathan Edwards. The second version would produce the *Book of Mormon*. In both cases, the underground streams of hermeticism, Rosicrucianism, and occultism were flowing strong. The Great Awakenings were also periods of occult renaissance in America, and Freemasonry was perhaps its most obvious vehicle. It provided a space where men could frame their religious and occult ideas within an organized structure that purported to transmit sacred knowledge within the emotional impact of initiation.

The Awakenings were primarily Protestant and independent of the Catholic Church. In fact, Catholicism was looked upon with deep suspicion by many—if not most—early Christians in America. Thus the conflict between Freemasonry and the Church was not the issue in America that it was in Europe. Many American Christians saw no problem in being both fervent in their faith and proud members of the brotherhood.

This is a field that has only recently become a focus of serious academic attention. Works such as John L. Brooke's *The Refiner's Fire* (which investigates Mormon cosmology in terms of alchemical and Rosicrucian influences), Richard Godbeer's *The Devil's Dominion,* and Jon Butler's *Awash in a Sea of Faith* have unpacked the history of early American occultism and its influence over the growth of religions and religious revivalism in the seventeenth, eighteenth, and nineteenth centuries. D. Michael Quinn's magnum opus, *Early Mormonism and the Magic World View,* concentrates specifically on the influence of occult ideas on Joseph Smith Jr. and the *Book of Mormon.* What is presented in these texts is a fundamentally different history of the American religious experience, and a suggestive template for examining the occult revival of the 1970s and '80s in America as a counterpoint to the growth of Evangelicalism and Charismatic theology in the same period. Indeed, the Salem Witchcraft Trials of the late seventeenth century would probably not have taken place had not occult ideas and apprehensions permeated the religious environment in New England for decades prior to that event.

However, as provocative as a study of early American occultism might be, our focus here must be on Masonic connections with the creation, development, and growth of the Church of Jesus Christ of Latter-Day Saints—more commonly known as the LDS Church or simply as Mormonism. The works cited above will provide readers with a good, in-depth account of the state of occult and hermetic thought in the American colonies and the early United States, and in previous chapters we have covered some of this ground already. Now, however, our attention is drawn to Joseph Smith Jr. and his ritual magic operations in New York.

Smith came from a family that had a contentious relationship with organized religion. Neither of his parents had developed close connections with any congregation in Vermont—where Smith was born—or in New York until Mrs. Lucy Mack Smith started going to a Presbyterian church. It was in the diaries of Mrs. Smith that we find the first references to the occult practices in which she and the rest of her family engaged during their hard times in Palmyra. Indeed, she refutes the claims of others that the family had neglected their farm chores to focus instead on ceremonial magic, thus revealing a somewhat intimate knowledge of the subject.[2] Other research reveals that Joseph Smith Sr. had been an experienced diviner and conjurer, searching for buried treasure and gold using magic circles and obscure incantations.[3]

It was his son, however, who had the talent for divining and who had developed a reputation for it in the area around Palmyra. Among his instruments was a seer stone, a rock that was used as a kind of crystal ball. Smith would stare into the stone and see visions.

This practice has a venerable pedigree. Staring into a stone, a glass, a mirror, or even a pool of ink or water is a technique that is almost as old as religion itself. In the seventeenth century, the Elizabethan astrologer and magician John Dee was the proud owner of a piece of polished Aztec obsidian that he called his "shew stone" and with which he communed with the angels. Some of the medieval grimoires—magician's workbooks or manuals—contain detailed instructions for making a "magic mirror" that serves the same purpose.

Both of Smith's parents claimed to have visionary dreams, as did Smith himself. The family had struggled with thieves and scam artists their whole lives, as well as with sanctimonious preachers. Like many desperate but intelligent or simply independent-minded people, they shunned organized groups in favor of individual solutions. Joining a church meant accepting or agreeing to too much that was disagreeable or offensive. The occult arts offered individual paths to both spiritual enlightenment and, perhaps, easy money. So, just as the itinerant Methodist preachers claimed visions and prophetic dreams, so could the individual mystic—without a congregation, without a church building, and independent of ecclesiastical approval.

Smith grew up in that environment, coming of age in Palmyra in a town that boasted Masonic lodges and bookstores selling occult tomes. A barefoot farm boy, living with a family in desperate straits financially, his emotional stresses would find their greatest expression in Smith's picking up the diviner's rod and the diviner's seer stones—as well as grimoires of magic and sorcery—and trekking out into the forest to conjure an angel and find the golden plates.

Brooke has examined the possibility that Masonic lore—picked up from his uncle, Hyrum, or by other family members—might have influenced the Mormon legend of the discovery of the golden plates.[4] As we have seen, there were two competing legends in Masonic rituals and literature concerning the search for esoteric secrets. That of the slaying of Hiram at the Temple of Solomon is well known, even outside Masonic circles. That of Noah hiding the secrets of the universe inside a pillar or pillars is not so well known, but equally suggestive.

In the degree rituals of the Scottish Rite's thirteenth degree, that of the Arch of Solomon or the Ninth Arch, however, we find references to a hidden treasure buried underground by the prophet Enoch before the Flood, as well as references to plates of gold bearing Mosaic inscriptions.[5] In fact, the Ninth Arch degree lecture could be seen as the model for Smith's story of finding the golden plates upon which were written the *Book of Mormon*. This is not a canonical biblical story, regardless of the presence of the prophets in the legend. The only place where Smith might have learned of this tradition would have been from a Scottish Rite Freemason or possibly from a book on Freemasonry, such as the one published in Salem, Massachusetts, in 1818 and titled *The Freemason's Monitor*. Considering that the first vision of the golden plates by Joseph Smith Jr. was not until 1823, there is every possibility that the knowledge lecture of the Ninth Arch had come to him by any number of sources.

Regardless of the ultimate source of the legend, in 1823 Smith performed an occult ceremony at the stroke of midnight on September 22 (the autumnal equinox) and discovered his own golden plates buried underground.

The story is familiar to every Mormon, and is the basis for the scripture known as the *Book of Mormon*, which Smith translated from the hieroglyphic texts inscribed on the golden plates. What is perhaps not so well known are the details of how Smith happened to be there and the methods he used for finding the treasure.

Smith's technique was an amalgam of various occult methodologies, from divination to conjuration. His "seer stone" was a piece of rock, about four inches long, that he placed in a hat. He would stare at the stone in the darkness of the hat and see visions. But the choice of the autumnal equinox for his first vision of the Angel Moroni is evidence of another strain of European magic.

Astrology long has been an essential element of Western European occultism as well as Middle Eastern religious and magical practices. The names of the planets gave us the names of the days of the week. The sun, moon, and planets—as well as many of the fixed stars—became part of the magician's cosmology and arsenal of tools. Each of the planets was believed to represent special powers and abilities—for instance, Mars for war and the shedding of blood since it is a red planet; the sun for life and generation; the moon for anything cyclical and changeable, and so on. As this cosmology grew more sophisticated, the attributes of the planets themselves and in combination with other planets became ever more complex. One's birth horoscope was believed to be a kind of formula by which one could discern the abilities and proclivities of the native by assessing the priorities to be assigned to the powers and weaknesses of the planetary positions relative to the native and relative to each other.

Even before these calculations became that advanced, however, there was the simpler cosmological map of the seasons. These seasons are marked by the voyage of the sun "through" imaginary points in space during the course of a solar year. Thus, the first day of spring falls in March when the rising sun passes over the earth's equator. This is known as the vernal equinox: when both day and night are of equal length, and the sun "passes through" the first degree of Aries. The first day of summer is known as the summer solstice: this is in June, when the sun "passes through" the first degree of Cancer. The autumnal equinox, September 22, is when the sun is now returning on its annual voyage and "passes through" the first degree of Libra. Joseph Smith himself was born on December 23, close enough to the winter solstice to be worth mentioning. That is when the first degree of Capricorn is visited by the sun.

These four days are known as the "quarter days" because they divide the year more or less equally into the four seasons. They were considered to be especially potent times to conduct occult ritual. The four astrological signs mentioned above—Aries, Cancer, Libra, and Capricorn—are known as cardinal signs: the strongest and most representative signs of the four platonic elements fire, water, air, and earth, respectively. Also, for anyone wishing to conduct alchemical experiments involving the transmutation of elements, these days were auspicious.

Joseph Smith Jr. was born under Capricorn, a cardinal earth sign. His visit to the mountain on the first day of the cardinal air sign was certainly a deliberate choice. He was seeking to find treasure buried in the earth, to bring the treasure into the "open air," so to speak.

He was eighteen years old. A spirit who had appeared to him in a vision in his seer stone informed him that golden plates were buried in a cave in the Hill Cumorah. He told others of his vision, but went to the hill at night on his own.

The hill he approached was not called Cumorah at the time; it very probably had no name at all, the name Cumorah having come from the *Book of Mormon*. It was a drumlin, a kind of ripple in the ground created by the movement of a glacier. There are many such drumlins in western New York and, geologically, they have no natural caves as they are only piles of gravel and earth. There is some controversy among the Mormons as to whether the hill known today as Cumorah is really the hill visited by Smith that night and on every September 22 for the next four years, or if he had visited another cave, perhaps in a vision. In any event, this first visit to the cave proved rather startling.

He found the cave, near the top of the hill, and in it a stone box that contained the golden plates. However, as he attempted to seize the plates, an amphibious creature—"like a toad"—jumped out, turned into a man, and struck him in the head. The plates disappeared, and he returned home empty-handed. Smith attributed this loss to the fact that his intention was to obtain gold and riches and not spiritual gifts.

He wound up returning to the same spot, year after year, on the same day until he was finally able to convince the treasure's guardian angel—Moroni—of his blamelessness and purity of purpose. That was in 1827. At this point, he was granted access to the golden plates, on which were inscribed the text of what would become the *Book of Mormon*.

It is not my intention to make a judgment as to the veracity of this story. There have been many published criticisms of Mormonism's origins, almost from its inception. Indeed, as the quotation at the beginning of this chapter indicates, even Arthur Conan Doyle—creator of Sherlock Holmes—was not immune to thoughts of Mormonism as some kind of strange, murderous cult and used the LDS Church as the theme of his very first Sherlock Holmes mystery. Instead, our purpose is to examine the influence of Freemasonry and Masonic ideas on this, the first made-in-America religion. This is a contentious theme, and Mormon apologists have had a difficult time in responding to accusations that Masonry had an undue influence over both the writing of the *Book of Mormon* as well as upon the life of its founder. What are not in doubt are the following facts:

Members of Joseph Smith Jr.'s immediate family were Freemasons.

Joseph Smith Jr. himself was a Freemason.

Many details of Mormon ceremonies are identical to Masonic designs and practices.

In addition, Smith was married to the widow of William Morgan, the famous victim of a putative Masonic murder conspiracy.

THE MORGAN AFFAIR

The kidnapping that led to the alleged murder of Morgan took place on the night of September 11, 1826, in a town only a few miles away from Palmyra, New York and the Hill Cumorah. In another eleven days, Smith would once again attempt to wrest the golden plates from the Angel Moroni, but on this night William Morgan was kidnapped and taken to Canandaigua, New York, and then—so one legend goes—he made it over the border to Canada and lifelong exile. The other version of the story is far more brutal, and has Morgan being beaten, his throat cut, and his body dumped into Lake Ontario. In any event, Morgan was never seen again.

A Freemason of uncertain degree, he had promised to publish the secrets of Masonic ritual in a book that was then being set into type. The print shop was burned to the ground, by agents unknown. Morgan was arrested by the police on what appears to have been a trumped-up charge over a two-dollar debt, and then taken from the prison at night by a group of Masons. After this he disappeared from sight.

That is the standard version of the tale, and one that is repeated in heavily amended form in the work of Christopher Hodapp, a Masonic apologist.[6] However, there are some problems with the story. In the first place, Morgan's work would not have been the first-ever book revealing the initiatory rituals of Freemasonry. As early as 1797, the work of Thomas C. Webb—an important Masonic lecturer—had been published, which described the rituals and legends of Blue Lodge Masonry and the appendant Scottish Rite and York Rite, although omitting some secret material. Other Masonic texts were already in print in England, and editions of them were available in the United States. According to Masonic historian S. Brent Morris (himself a thirty-third-degree Mason), "A total of 626 volumes dealing with Freemasonry were published in America through 1800. Ten of these deal with precursors of the Scottish Rite."[7] The first book on Freemasonry published in America was printed, as was mentioned in chapter 6, on Benjamin Franklin's presses as early as 1734. For nearly a hundred years before the mysterious evaporation of William Morgan, one could obtain copies of the degree rituals quite easily. The French historian of secret societies, Augustin de Barruel, had published his four-volume magnum opus *Memoirs: Illustrating the History of Jacobinism* in 1799, which contained details of the Scottish Rite mysteries in volume 2. Thus, why the special treatment meted out to Morgan?

Brooke has provided some additional evidence that goes a long way to suggesting a more mundane motive in the Morgan affair. This concerns New York State politics more than it does Masonic oaths and ritual retribution, and is worth considering. According to Brooke, "From 1807 to 1827 the elite Rite of Perfection, in which hermetic beliefs were most fully articulated, was divided into competing councils led by Governors De Witt Clinton and Daniel D. Tompkins."[8]

The Rite of Perfection refers to Scottish Rite Masonry, which was developed in France in about 1758 and brought to America by Etienne Morin, who established Scottish Rite lodges in Jamaica and on the island of Hispaniola about 1761. Later, Scottish Rite lodges appeared in New Orleans; Charleston, South Carolina; Philadelphia; and also in Albany in upstate New York as early as

1767. References in popular literature to thirty-third-degree Masons are references to Scottish Rite Freemasonry and its highest degree, the thirty-third. This form of Freemasonry is not intended to replace the first three degrees of traditional Masonry, nor to replace the United Grand Lodge. It offers additional rituals and instructions that are meant to amplify and clarify the original three degrees, and are intended for Master Masons only. However, according to historian Steven C. Bullock, the branch of Masonry that was involved in the Morgan affair was not the Scottish Rite but the York Rite version,[9] a claim that is supported by another Masonic historian, Mark A. Tabbert,[10] who cites Bullock's work as the source. Some of the confusion might have arisen due to the fact that the Ninth Arch of the Scottish Rite is sometimes also called the Royal Arch, which is the formal name of the York Rite (i.e., Royal Arch Masonry). Regardless of which version was involved—and in early-nineteenth-century America there was tremendous confusion over the rites, the lodges, and the chapters of Freemasonry and their respective jurisdictions—ideas about the Rosicrucians, the Knights Templar, and alchemy were explored in these additional rites, as well as legends concerning the building of Zerubbabel's Temple (the temple that replaced the ruined Solomon's Temple after the Jews returned to Jerusalem from Babylon). It was the Scottish Rite, for instance, that gave us the legend of the Ninth Arch and buried treasure that may have influenced the content of Joseph Smith's visions.

The conflict between the two New York governors involved a power struggle between the City Grand Lodge and the Country Grand Lodge, as well as some financial irregularities. One of the people implicated in one of several embezzling schemes was Joseph Enos, who for awhile was Grand Master of the Country Grand Lodge. To make matters more complicated, he was a member of the Canandaigua lodge, which was the one implicated in the kidnapping of William Morgan. As Brooke points out, "Concerns that Morgan was going to expose corruption among the Country Grand Lodge leadership may well explain his death."[11]

While not proven, this is an interesting area for future Masonic scholars to explore, as much for the history of internecine struggles among various Masonic lodges and their connection to New York state politics and the governor's office as for the possibility that Morgan's disappearance was the result of purely political motives.

Whatever the reason might have been for the Morgan affair, his wife evidently felt she was allowed to marry again, and this she did to another Mason, one George Harris. A few years after the Morgan affair, in 1834, George Harris was received into the LDS Church by the famous Mormon preacher Orson Pratt. George and Lucinda moved to Far West, Missouri, with other Mormons and in 1838 they met Joseph Smith. By this time, George Harris was one of the Mormon leaders in Far West, and by all accounts the relationship between Harris and Smith was a cordial one. What is not known for certain is whether Harris knew that Smith had taken George's wife, Lucinda, in a plural marriage ceremony.

One of the facts about Mormonism that always arouses attention is the practice of plural marriage. Smith was known to have as many as thirty or more "wives" obtained in this way: although married in the LDS Church, and although the marriage would be consummated, the plural wife—if she had a husband—would remain with her legal spouse. This is what occurred with Lucinda Morgan Harris. (After Smith's assassination in 1844, Lucinda left Mormonism and became a Sister of Charity in the Catholic Church.)

The long-term effect of the Morgan affair, however, was impressive in its range and in its contribution to the American political landscape. Anti-Masonic hysteria erupted in the United States, and Masonic lodges either closed or kept a very low profile for decades. The Anti-Masonic Party was created in 1828 out of the scandal of the Morgan affair, and ran a candidate for president of the United States, William Wirt, in 1832. When the Masonic hysteria had died down and the single-issue Anti-Masonic Party lost its luster, many of its members left in 1838 to join the Whig Party.

It is odd, then, that in this atmosphere of paranoia and suspicion where Freemasonry was concerned Joseph Smith—who had, after all, produced a new scripture and a new religion almost single-handedly—would accept initiation into a Masonic lodge.

THE MASONIC MORMON

On the evening of March 15, 1842, Joseph Smith Jr. was initiated into the Entered Apprentice degree of the Craft at the Nauvoo, Illinois, lodge. The following evening he was evidently both passed to the Fellow Craft degree and then raised to the Master Mason degree. This was done with unseemly speed, but such was the influence of Smith and the Mormons in Nauvoo at the time that the initiations took place at Smith's own business office.

Smith then went on an aggressive campaign on behalf of Masonry by having hundreds of Mormons in Nauvoo initiated into the brotherhood. By the time he was finished, there were more Masons at the Nauvoo lodge than there were in all the lodges in the rest of the state of Illinois combined. This led to some unrest among the other lodges, who complained that initiations were being carried out wholesale—that, in fact, the Nauvoo lodge was a kind of Masonic diploma mill. They demanded that the Grand Lodge take notice and conduct an investigation.

Eventually, the open wound between the Masons and the Mormons began to fester and would not heal. According to the Mormons, the reason was due to polygamy and the Masonic reluctance to accept as brothers those who practiced it. According to the Masons, it was the hijacking of the Craft and Craft rituals by the cavalier actions of Smith and his associates that ruptured the relationship.

Regardless of the status of the official relationship, however, Masonic ideas, symbols, and rituals had made their way into Mormonism as early as the writing of the *Book of Mormon* and lasted well beyond that point. Smith had—unconsciously or deliberately—incorporated standard Masonic concepts into his scripture and, eventually, into the rituals of Mormonism. Mormon apologists have tried to explain away these similarities on the basis that Masonic symbolism is universal and that there was no deliberate borrowing from Freemasonry. However, upon closer examination, it is easy to see that the similarities are such as to argue strongly against such reasoning.

In the *Book of Mormon* we find the following suggestive verse:

> And it came to pass that they did have their signs, yea, their secret signs, and their secret words; and this that they might distinguish a

brother who had entered into the covenant, that whatsoever wickedness his brother should do he should not be injured by his brother, nor by those who did belong to his band, who had taken this covenant. (Helaman 6:22)

This is as good a description as any of the practice of the passwords and other recognition signals used by the Masons. What is more to the point is that it refers to a band of brothers who had "taken the covenant," with the adjuration that one brother should not injure another regardless of what crime that brother may have committed. This was precisely the objection that the anti-Masons had concerning the order. At the time the *Book of Mormon* was being written, about 1827–28, the Morgan affair had reached a fever pitch, with the Anti-Masonic Party being formed in 1828. It is perhaps no wonder then that the text would contain—conscious or unconscious—allusions to this event, particularly as the Morgan affair began in the towns of Batavia and Canandaigua, New York, only a few miles from the Smith farm in Palmyra, and was making national news.

However, the citation from the *Book of Mormon* above casts the practice of secret signs and words between a band of brothers in a bad light. The text later refers to the "Gadianton robbers" who are guided by Lucifer and take over the Nephite government:

Now behold, those secret oaths and covenants did not come forth unto Gadianton from the records which were delivered unto Helaman; but behold, they were put into the heart of Gadianton by that same being who did entice our first parents to partake of the forbidden fruit—Yea, that same being who did plot with Cain . . . Yea, it is that same being who put it into the heart of Gadianton to still carry on the work of darkness, and of secret murder. (Helaman 6:26–29)

The reference to secret murder is compelling, and may be a direct reference to William Morgan who was—it was widely assumed—secretly murdered.

Well-known critics of Mormonism Jerald and Sandra Tanner of Salt Lake City, Utah, who run the Utah Lighthouse Ministry and Bookstore there, have pointed out that the origin of the problematic name Mormon actually may be a direct reference to the Morgan affair.[12] The name *Mormon* has perplexed scholars who can find no Hebrew equivalent that makes any sense, which is interesting since Mormon was believed to have been a member of one of the Lost Tribes who wrote the history of the Nephites contained in the *Book of Mormon*. Smith himself claimed that *mon* was an Egyptian root meaning "good." (This was disproved once Egyptian hieroglyphics were deciphered upon the discovery of the Rosetta Stone.) The *Book of Mormon* is, in fact, filled with fanciful names that seem to have no equivalent in the ancient Middle Eastern languages from which it was presumably derived, nor from Native American languages that were believed by Smith to represent the remnants of the Lost Tribes.

Recourse to newspaper articles that were popular at the time of the Morgan affair, however, reveals a possible source for the name Mormon. According to the Tanners, this appeared in the *Wayne Sentinel* of November 2, 1827, in an article discussing the discovery of a body that had washed up on shore from Lake Ontario, the same lake where it was believed the body of William Morgan had been dumped.

According to the article, the body was discovered not to be that of Morgan but of one Timothy Monroe (spelled "Monro" in the *Sentinel*). Due to the typeset of the article, the name MORGAN (capitalization in the original) had been broken into two syllables, MOR and GAN. Directly below the MOR syllable in the same paragraph and sentence was the name of MONRO (capitalization in the original). Thus, we have the very suggestive placement of MORMONRO. The Tanners feel it quite possible that the word Mormon derives from the two names, MORgan and MONroe—two names associated with the Masonic murder mystery.

Considered in isolation from other evidence, this may appear to be a slim possibility. However, careful examination of other clues does point to a Masonic origin for many Mormon ideas and practices.

One of the practices that has been discussed in many places is a special Mormon garment that bears a close resemblance to the Masonic apron (made famous in the painting of George Washington laying the cornerstone of the U.S. Capitol). This garment must be worn by a Mormon desiring to enter the temple.

This is a secret temple in every sense of the term. No one except a Mormon in good standing is allowed to enter the temple, and even then is not allowed to do so unless in possession of a Temple Recommend, a document signed by several authorities in the Church, including the local bishop and branch president, after the applicant has been personally interviewed. Thus, it is impossible for outsiders, non-Mormons, and Mormons in bad standing to enter the temple.

There are, at present, 126 Mormon temples around the world, including the famous temple in Salt Lake City, Utah, representing a tremendous growth in Temple building in the last fifty years or so. There are, of course, many thousands more Mormon church buildings that are used for everyday services. The Temples belong to a different category of religious experience and are the result of a vision Smith had that his movement was a "restoration" of the King Solomon's Temple service. In other words, the Mormon temple is a modern incarnation of King Solomon's Temple, and this is a concept with a great degree of similarity to Masonic custom.

Further, examination of the history of the temple "endowment" ceremonies reveals many parallels with Masonic ritual and specifically with Royal Arch degree work. (It will be remembered that Royal Arch Masonry was the branch whose secrets William Morgan threatened to reveal.) In addition, some elements of the Endowment as originally conceived by Smith are suspiciously similar to celestial ascent and medieval theurgic practices, including passwords to be given to the angels who guard various levels of heaven.

To discuss the Mormon temple properly, one needs to examine the endowment ceremonies in more detail, since the two are inextricably linked. In June 1831, the first Endowment took place as the first male Mormons were ordained to the priesthood of Melchizedek. In December of 1832, Smith had a vision in which he learned he was to build a temple after the example of Solomon. This he managed to complete in 1836, in Kirtland, Ohio. The ceremonies performed by the men that accompanied the dedication of the Kirtland Temple included washing of their bodies and anointing of their heads with oil, after the Old Testament examples. On March 30, 1836, a special ceremony included the men washing each other's feet, a rite that had been part of the ritual among the Wissahickon, Pennsylvania, mystics almost 150 years earlier.

Eventually, Smith had to abandon Kirtland and move farther west, to Nauvoo, Illinois. The "Second Endowment" took place there, and this is where the use of ritual garments was introduced. During these new endowment ceremonies, the idea of ordination is expanded with a theme of initiation. Washing and anointing still takes place, but now the initiate receives a special garment of snow-white cloth, and a new name that becomes the initiate's key word or password. From that point on, the newly initiated Mormon must wear this special garment under his clothes.

Then there is a ritual reenactment of Adam and Eve in the Garden, during which time various secret gestures are taught and oaths are taken. The initiate is then quizzed as to his knowledge of the gestures and the key words.

Obviously, this is the ritual of a secret society, complete with passwords, awkward-looking gestures, special garments, and ceremonial initiation, all taking place in a secret temple that no outsiders are permitted to enter; nor are they permitted to observe the rites in anyway. What transpires inside the temple must be kept secret from everyone, including the member's wife, and must never be discussed with anyone except within the temple itself. Although women may be accepted into the Endowment, they are not ordained; that is reserved for the male priesthood.

The first Mormons initiated in this fashion on May 4, 1842 were themselves all Freemasons. These included Hyrum Smith (Joseph Smith Jr.'s brother), Judge James Adams, Brigham Young (who would take over leadership of the Church upon the death of Smith in 1844), Heber C. Kimball, William Law, Willard Richards, Newel Whitney, George Miller, and William Marks. Smith himself was also, of course, a Freemason, having been initiated six weeks earlier in March. His brother, Hyrum, had been initiated during the height of the anti-Masonic hysteria, in 1827 (the same year Joseph Smith finally obtained the golden plates and the *Book of Mormon*). One cannot help but note that Smith's brother had the same name as the murdered victim in the third-degree Master Mason initiation ritual: Hiram. Ironically, Hyrum Smith would be murdered himself, along with his brother Joseph, at the hands of a mob in Carthage, Illinois, only two years after the Nauvoo Endowment, on June 27, 1844.

Another element in common between the Royal Arch Masons and the Mormon temple endowment ceremony was the fact that originally neither of the two groups wrote down their initiations but passed them down orally. Scottish Rite Masons did copy out the rituals in notebooks; the Royal Arch or York Rite Masons were notorious for not doing so. It was only in 1877 that Brigham Young decided it was prudent to commit the Endowment rituals to writing rather than memory.

But it was the central idea of Royal Arch Masonry of a treasure that had been buried since time immemorial that created the atmosphere in which a seventeen-year old boy approached the sacred Hill Cumorah with trepidation and a seer stone to uncover the golden plates and his own, doomed destiny. Smith would eventually declare his priesthood to be a continuation of that of Enoch, the enigmatic Old Testament personality who lived for 365 years on earth before he left in the company of God. Enoch was the template for centuries of magic, mysticism, and occult ideas, writings, and practices, from the "descenders to the Chariot" of ancient Jewish mysticism to the Enochian magic of the late-nineteenth-century Golden Dawn (and so much in between). It was in 1821 that the recently discovered *Book of Enoch* was published in English translation from the Coptic original, but the mystification around Enoch had begun much earlier when Jewish mystics identified him as a human immortal, the Metatron of the angelic hierarchy who was not an angel and not a man but something in between: a perfected man, a redeemed Adam. That Mormonism began as a cult of restoration is amply documented in Brooke's work. Smith saw himself and his priesthood as restoring the original temple service, restoring the original Freemasonry, returning to that prelapsarian, perfect state that existed before the Fall. Modern Christianity, to Joseph Smith, was apostasy, as was modern Freemasonry. And he was set to remedy that situation.

One of the accomplishments of Mormonism has been subtle, but worth noting. It was what Jon Butler calls the "sacralization" of America.[13] While the first English settlers had come to Massachusetts and claimed the New World to be a New Jerusalem, Smith accomplished that in fact. He saw in the landscape around him a holy land peopled with descendants from ancient Jewish struggles, visited by Jesus, anointed with blood and tears. The burial mounds that are everywhere in the eastern United States were a source of wonder to everyone; to Smith, they were mute evidence of a lost civilization and secret chambers filled with gold, precious documents, and spiritual forces. With a few rocks—magically transformed into seer stones, the Urim and Thummim of his visions—some archaic medieval rituals, and a burning desire to penetrate the Secret Temple, he created a religion that is today the fastest-growing Christian denomination in the world. That he borrowed extensively from Freemasonry (as well as from other hermetic and occult sources) is amply demonstrated by the work of both Brooke and Quinn. That he was, at heart, a ceremonial magician is something that still needs to be understood.

When Joseph Smith Jr. died, a talisman was found on his body. It was a charm straight out of the medieval grimoires that had been his companions since adolescence, when his father was casting circles on the ground and his mother was having visionary dreams. One can find it in Francis Barrett's *The Magus*, available when Smith was a child, and in many other occult works since then. It was the talisman of Jupiter, Smith's ruling planet, and a photograph of it can be seen in Quinn's work.[14]

Unfortunately, it was incorrectly made. Consultation of *The Magus* shows how it should appear. It contains the Hebrew letters for *AL AB*, which means "The Father" and is a holy name of Jupiter. Smith, however, like so many magicians and copyists who have little or no knowledge of Hebrew, copied it badly. It is missing the letter "B." Thus, the meaning is reduced to *ALA*, which means "but," "only," or even "except."

The rest of the talisman is correctly drawn. There are two other words, *ABA* and *YHPYAL* or "Jophiel," the name of the Intelligence of Jupiter (each planet has its "Intelligence," a specific type of spiritual force). Thus, the entire talisman should have read *AL AB ABA YHPYAL*, which could be taken to mean "The Father" across the top, and then "Father Jophiel" for the rest of the seal. Unfortunately, with the missing *B*, the seal now reads "Father but Jophiel" or "Father except Jophiel," a phrase that could be construed as subtracting Jophiel from the talisman, thus negatively changing its nature.

The magic square of Jupiter contains numbers in a grid that, added together, will give one a sum of 136. This is also the number of YHPYAL according to Jewish numerology, in which each letter is also a number. There was, at least, a certain degree of consistency and internal logic in the old grimoires.

Using that same method, *AL AB* plus *YHPYAL* would result in a sum of 174. According to Jewish numerology, this number represents "torches" and "*Splendor ei per circuitum*". Since the *B* is missing, though, the result is only 172. This number is the equivalent of "cut, divided" and "the heel, the end."

This is the talisman that Joseph Smith was carrying at the moment of his death, as he gestured in the Masonic signal of distress hoping that any Freemasons in the area would come to his aid.

None did. He and his brother—the aptly named Hyrum—were murdered by the mob. Martyrs to their religion, and in a sense Masonic martyrs as well, their blood created an empire.

The Masonic temple in Salt Lake City boasts several layers of symbols that are obvious to any Mason. The All-Seeing Eye, which is found in every Masonic temple, is found here. The clasped hands that are so symbolic of the secret handshakes of the brotherhood are carved into the walls at the Mormon Temple, too. The sun, moon, and stars are here, as well as the Big Dipper.[15] Mormons who have done some reading in Freemasonry will recognize their apron, their secret gestures, their passwords and grips, and much of the Endowment rituals in published Masonic lore.

There have been many groups that have called themselves Masonic who were, and are, not recognized by the official Grand Lodges. Many of these are devoted to hermeticism, alchemy, and the occult. The Rites of Memphis and Mizraim would fall into this category, as would Co-Masonry to a certain extent, as well as many others.[16] In a sense, Mormonism is one of these: an unrecognized Masonic Lodge that went its own way and formulated its own rituals, but with a conscious and deliberate nod to its august forebears.

CHAPTER NINE

Princes and Pretenders

[E]very man who becomes a Mason thinks what he pleases to think on all sides of the Masonic subject. . . . It is a perfectly open position, leaving every one rather helpless, but unavoidable in the nature of things.

—A. E. Waite, "Master Building"

AFTER THE MORGAN AFFAIR (see chapter 8), it took a long while for Freemasonry to recover in the United States. Many lodges were dormant for years, some for decades. The Civil War also caused a hiatus in Masonic initiations as the country was convulsed by the conflict. The Masons—who prided themselves on ideas of brotherhood and loyalty to government—now had to contend with a war in which brother fought against brother, and the integrity of government itself was brought into question by force of arms. In addition, the war brought the question of slavery into sharp focus, not only for the people of the United States generally but also for the Masonic fraternity, whose requirements for admission stipulated that one should be freeborn.

Beginning in the eighteenth century, there was a Masonic order for African Americans. Founded by a manumitted slave, Prince Hall, this order grew in size and importance over the centuries and, paradoxically, grew in strength during the period of the Morgan affair, when other lodges were drastically reduced in number. The question of its legality—in terms of the existing Masonic orders that had been chartered by the United Grand Lodge—was a problem more for the regular Masonic bodies than it was for the Prince Hall Masons themselves. Prince Hall brought up the inconsistency between Masonic doctrine and Masonic practice: If all men were equal, why were

African American men not? If all men were brothers, why were African American men not embraced as brothers by the rest of Freemasonry? It was an inconsistency that existed not only in Freemasonry, of course, but in the United States generally. The Civil War was fought to answer that question once and for all.

The schizophrenic attitude of some Freemasons where race and equality were concerned was represented best by one of its most prominent and influential members, the magus of nineteenth-century Masonic ideas, Albert Pike (1809–91). A former officer in the Confederacy, Pike has been accused of helping start the Ku Klux Klan—a tiresome accusation that has no documentation to support it. Pike, however, had made statements concerning the admission of African Americans into Masonic lodges that can only be construed as racist. He resisted "mixing" the African American members in the same lodges as white members and once famously wrote that he would leave Freemasonry rather than have to call an African-American his brother.[1] At the same time, he was a champion of the Native American population and had Indian troops in his command during the Civil War, for which he ran afoul of Jefferson Davis and left the conflict before the war was over. This hideous double standard was, lamentably, common in that era, as anyone with any knowledge of United States history recognizes.

Pike, however, made a significant contribution in another area, that of explaining and amplifying the state of knowledge and understanding of the Masonic degrees. A colleague of the famous Masonic historian Albert Mackey, Pike was raised through all the degrees of the Scottish Rite and asked to use his compendious knowledge of ancient languages and religions to refine the existing rituals and compose a text that could be used by Freemasons as a tool of instruction. This latter became the celebrated *Morals and Dogma of the Ancient and Accepted Scottish Rite of Freemasonry*.

The influence of this text, and of Pike himself, was considerable. Portly, with a large white beard and long white hair falling over his shoulders, and dressed in his Masonic regalia, Pike looked like the stereotype of a medieval magician, a magus. His *Morals and Dogma* covered everything from ancient Egyptian mysteries to Jewish religious practices, the Greek philosophers, Christian concepts, and the meaning and relevance of a whole host of symbols and emblems. It boasts an index—called a "Digest"— that is more than 200 pages long, covering virtually every noun and concept to be found in the main part of the work (which is itself more than 800 pages long). In the process, Pike managed to refine the existing rituals and make changes that brought them in line with what he perceived as the essential truths of the initiations while keeping them true to the original Masonic rites. Taken together, the revised rituals and *Morals and Dogma* provided both the practice and theory of modern Masonry. For more than thirty years, Pike was the head of the Supreme Council of the Scottish Rite, and was based in Washington, D.C., for most of that time.

There is a bronze statue of Albert Pike in Washington at Third and D Streets Northwest. The old magus is depicted as holding a copy of *Morals and Dogma* in his left hand. The statue has been subject to a great deal of negative attention by groups who believe the KKK rumors and who have, from time to time, defaced it. Whether Pike really was a member or leader of the Klan is a question that may never be answered, but the controversy over Pike only contributed to the atmosphere of suspicion that surrounds many discussions of Freemasonry and its influence in American—and global—politics and culture.

THE ORDER

A quasi-Masonic organization that has given rise to some of the most startling rumors of political interference is, of course, Skull and Bones. Founded in 1832 at Yale University, there has probably been no other secret society—save Masonry itself—that has created such controversy yet at the same time maintained its secrecy intact.

Yale University was, of course, the seventeenth-century domain of Ezra Stiles, the alchemist and occultist who served as its president, so the institution had an esoteric pedigree from the very beginning of its existence. One of the founders of the Skull and Bones Society was William Huntington Russell (1809–95) who, it has been alleged, spent time in Germany as a student before returning to Yale to get his degree. It was in Germany, so the legend goes, that Russell either was initiated into the parent lodge of Skull and Bones or picked up the idea for the Yale group; he brought it back and, with Alphonso Taft (future father of American president William Howard Taft), founded the order.

The problem with the history of what is internally referred to as "The Order" is that so much is undocumented and speculative. I have been unable to determine with any degree of satisfaction where Russell attended school in Germany; this would be a critical factor for understanding whom Russell met and what other influences might have been. Many conspiracy theorists have put forward the idea that Russell was initiated into the Illuminati in Germany; Weishaupt was dead by the time Russell arrived on the continent and, in any case, the Illuminati had been suppressed decades earlier. While it is still possible that Illuminati cells continued to exist and initiate, what is not so credible is why they would have exposed themselves to a young American college student.

Of course, the Illuminati were not the only initiates in Germany at the time. There were dozens of Masonic bodies—regular and irregular—as well as Rosicrucian orders and other groups. There does seem to be sufficient evidence to prove that Russell obtained his ideas from Germany due to copies of order publications and illustrations which are accompanied by German mottos and slogans. In addition, Skull and Bones was not created until Russell returned from that country. It would be helpful if more information was available on Russell's German period, but at the time of publication this was so far unavailable.

The importance of Skull and Bones lies in its proximity to power in the United States. Only fifteen persons are initiated into the order every year; this means that only fifteen hundred members have been initiated over the course of the past one hundred years. Yet, the influence of "Bonesmen" over American finances, politics, and culture during that time has been disproportionate to their numbers. A very short list of Bonesmen would include Henry Luce (of *Time* magazine fortune); William F. Buckley Jr.; Harold Stanley, the cofounder of Morgan Stanley; blue-blood American dynasties such as the Whitneys, Vanderbilts, and Phelps; and the Bush dynasty: Prescott Bush, George H. W. Bush, and George W. Bush. Presidential candidate John

F. Kerry was also a Bonesman; and his wife, Teresa Heinz, had been previously married to man whose father was also a member.

This raises one very important question, which has yet to be addressed anywhere but which has serious implications for a nation that prides itself on democratic as well as republican ideals: If only fifteen Bonesmen are initiated every year, for a grand total of 1,500 members in any one *century*, how is it possible that two initiates (John Kerry and George W. Bush) could be running for president in 2004? Assuming a total United States population of 300 million with—for the sake of argument—one thousand Bonesmen alive at one time, the odds against two Bonesmen at the heads of their respective parties running for president against each other at the same time are truly astronomical. When conspiracy theorists insisted that the United States government is in the hands of a powerful few individuals and groups, the 2004 presidential election campaign threw gasoline onto the burning embers of that particular fire.

According to one observer, Skull and Bones was founded as a kind of anti-Masonry.[2] Indeed, the attitudes of its members and the type of power and influence they seem to wield would argue strongly for that claim. It was created during the anti-Masonic hysteria generated by the Morgan affair, at a time when the very idea of a secret society was odious to many Americans. It might have appealed to the sense of humor of a twenty-three-year-old college student to create an anti-Masonic society; one could have all that was attractive to a young man about Freemasonry (the secrecy, the rituals, the oaths) while maintaining a pious anti-Masonic stance. Whatever the rationale, however, or purity of intention of its founders and members, the Skull and Bones Society at Yale University is arguably the single most influential order in the United States today.[3]

THE FREEMASONRY MUSEUM

While Skull and Bones may have its origins in an unknown German society, Germany itself went through a period when all occult orders and secret societies were banned and its members arrested and thrown into prison. This was during the Third Reich, when the Nazi Party gained total control over the country, its population, and its resources. Freemasonry in particular was singled out for destruction.

Prompted by the notorious literary hoax the *Protocols of the Learned Elders of Zion*, the idea that there was an international conspiracy of Freemasons and Jews to take over the world became so ingrained in the general population that even Winston Churchill subscribed to the belief. Created in 1895 and "leaked" to the press as early as 1897, the *Protocols* has served as a rationale for every kind of evil. Believed to have been signed by a number of Jewish "Elders" with the thirty-third-degree notation after their names (thus indicating they were Scottish Rite Masons?), the *Protocols* outlined a comprehensive plan for world domination. The theme behind it is that the Jews had infiltrated Masonic lodges all over the world with the purpose of furthering their own sinister agenda, which included the creation of Bolshevism and communism. By the time Adolf Hitler came to power, the anti-Semitic ravings of *Mein Kampf* had been a bestseller for years and even such an American icon as Henry Ford subscribed to the Judeo-Masonic conspiracy theory.

In order to insure that the Third Reich did not have a potential fifth column within its ranks, Freemasonry was banned along with many other occult orders. As early as May 26, 1934, an order from the reich war minister specifically forbade any member of the Wehrmacht from membership in the Freemasons.[4] Master Masons—considered "distinct enemies of National Socialism"[5]—were singled out for special attention and were forbidden from any but the lowest forms of labor. That same year, Adolf Eichmann—soon to become the architect of the "Final Solution"—was working for the Freemasonry Museum of the SS under the notorious SS-Standartenfuehrer Dr. Gregor Schwartz-Bostunitsch, a Freemasonry "expert" and author of anti-Masonic tracts. The Freemasonry Museum was an archive of captured Masonic records, books, ledgers, and other documents, as well as Masonic artifacts such as ritual tools and garments. There was a "St. John's Temple" set up in one room, and a "St. Andrew's Temple" set up in another. Eichmann's ability to organize and index this material eventually led to his being transferred to the Judenamt, the Jewish Division.

By 1939, Freemasons were once again specifically and categorically banned and their members thrown into the camps. This was especially true of Master Masons and anyone who had held an office in the lodge. Other secret societies were also banned, such as the Golden Dawn and the Ordo Templi Orientis. All were considered "fellow travelers" of Freemasonry. After the flight of Rudolf Hess to England—believed to have been instigated by astrological advice— even astrologers and fortune tellers were arrested, their shops closed, and their books confiscated.

With the defeat of the Third Reich in 1945, however, Freemasonry and its "fellow travelers" gradually returned to the Continent. Brothers came out of hiding and rebuilt what they could, where they could. New alliances were formed, and new temples were built all over the world.

THE P2 AFFAIR

Then, in the 1970s, another scandal involving Masons on both sides of the Atlantic threatened to resurrect ideas of a global Masonic conspiracy. This was the P2 affair, and it was, if anything, worse than the Morgan affair of the previous century. Involving organized crime, the Catholic Church, international banking, right-wing fanatics, assassinations, and global conspiracies—all within a Masonic context—the P2 scandal showed what a secret society with sinister attentions could accomplish.[6]

The origins of Propaganda Due (P2) are to be found in the Grand Orient of Italy, which chartered the lodge in 1877. It is important to realize that Freemasonry had a high-profile pedigree in Italy. The great statesman Giuseppe Garibaldi had served as Grand Master in Italy. This inspired many powerful and rich Italians—and those who merely aspired to that status—to become Freemasons. In that atmosphere, P2 was merely one among many lodges of important and influential men. Originally called Propaganda Massonica, its name was changed to Propaganda Due (or Propaganda 2) when the Grand Orient began numbering its lodges after World War II. Headquartered in the famously esoteric city of Turin in the Piedmont of northern Italy—Nostradamus is said to have lived there briefly, as well as Friedrich Wilhelm Nietzsche and a host of occultists and magicians over the years who gravitated around the area close to a Turin landmark church—Propaganda Massonica was a favorite of the politicians, the wealthy, and the nobility. By the time Licio Gelli became involved in Freemasonry in the 1960s, the lodge was virtually moribund. Yet, when the Vatican banking scandal hit the newspapers in 1981, the P2 membership lists included forty-three members of the Italian parliament, three cabinet ministers, the head of every branch of the military, the intelligence chiefs, the top bankers and financiers in the country, and the most influential media tycoons. It was like an even more ambitious version of the American Skull and Bones society.

The complete membership list totaled more than one thousand in Italy alone; that does not count the number of members in other countries where P2 continues to exist. Those countries include many Latin American countries, France, and Portugal. There are even members in the United States.[7]

Licio Gelli had served in Spain, fighting for Francisco Franco with support from Benito Mussolini. During World War II, Gelli was a Nazi and became an SS *Oberleutnant* in Italy. At the same time, he was also known to have cultivated friends on the Left. No one really knew what Gelli's sympathies really were or, indeed, if he had any at all. After the war, he seems to have been involved with the "rat lines," underground routes through which Nazi war criminals could escape to North America, South America, and other places.

He joined the Masons in 1963, and was so popular and successful that he was given a lodge of his own. This was a "covered" lodge, which meant that its membership lists would be a secret that only Gelli and the Grand Master of Italian Freemasonry would know; this was Propaganda Due.

In fifteen years, P2 had grown from a sleepy lodge with few members and only occasional meetings into a Masonic powerhouse. By 1974, the Grand Orient wanted to expel Gelli and close the lodge completely, but Gelli's influence and financial resources made it hard to enforce either his ousting or a closure. While the P2 lodge appeared closed on the books of the Grand Orient, it continued to operate quite aggressively. It attracted the heads of major corporations as well as the political and military leadership of Italy. Closing it down would have been virtually impossible.

Gelli's ultimate aim—as represented by documents found in his home during the 1981 investigation—was to rewrite the Italian constitution and reform the government entirely. His goals seemed similar to those of Adam Weishaupt centuries earlier. A devoted anticommunist (at least by this time), Gelli became involved in plots and intrigues both in Europe and in South America. Membership in P2 included Argentine right-wing politicians and military officers such as Jose Lopez Rega of the infamous death squads. (Italy and Argentina have a long and close relationship, going back to waves of Italian immigrants who came to that country in the nineteenth century.) Gelli was also involved with right-wing terror groups in Bolivia and other Latin American countries in the fight against communism. Even the 1980 bombing of the train station in Bologna, Italy, was linked to Gelli through Stefano della Chiaie, a famous terrorist and assassin with right-wing credentials who was instrumental in many of the anti–Salvador Allende operations conducted in Chile in the 1970s and in Operation Condor, the broad anticommunist project that involved the dictators of several Latin American countries and conducted assassinations of political opponents throughout the region.

In order to understand this degree of influence, one only has to remember the turbulent political situation in Italy during the Cold War, and the determination of both Italian and other Western intelligence services to prevent Italy from having a communist government. That CIA would have collaborated with Gelli's P2 is a theory that has been advanced and makes perfect sense to anyone who has studied how CIA operated in Italy.[8] An organization with the connections and the network of P2 would have had to have some contact with American intelligence, especially as so many intelligence chiefs were members (both in Italy and abroad). And with P2's reach into the right-wing circles of Latin America at a time when the United States was deeply concerned about the rise of communism there, it made perfect sense for CIA to establish liason with P2.

This, of course, is the raw material of conspiracy theory. The important thing to remember is that—especially during the Cold War—politics made strange bedfellows. The difficulty always rests with the greed and the arrogance of charismatic individuals whose reach exceeds their grasp. P2 was no longer a Masonic society in any normal sense. It had become Licio Gelli's private apparatus, a criminal enterprise with tentacles reaching inside Vatican City itself.

The P2 lodge began to unravel with revelations concerning the Vatican banking scandal and the murder of Roberto Calvi, who was found hanging from a bridge in London; the hanging was said to have a Masonic connection. Much was made of the murder from a Masonic perspective, as journalists tried to show that the style and locus of the crime had Masonic overtones. The banking scandal involved not only the Italian financial institution Banco Ambrosiano—the bank at the center of the story—but also the collapse of Franklin National Bank in the United States and the arrest of Michele Sindona (the "Vatican banker"), another member of P2.

Understandably, Italian Freemasonry denied any connection to P2, calling it an illegal lodge and claiming it had been officially closed in the 1970s. This is a sensitive issue and perhaps the truth will never be known, but the mere fact that P2 involved so many important persons in the Italian government and the Italian financial and cultural communities implies that the Grand Orient had to have known of its existence and merely looked away, deciding it was better not to confront either Gelli or the lodge. The damage was done, however; the newspapers were full of stories implicating Freemasonry in everything from money laundering to terrorism to intelligence operations and assassinations.

CONSPIRACY THEORY

Perhaps it was no wonder, then, that new life was given to the old Judeo-Masonic conspiracy theories of the early twentieth century. By the 1990s, one could find copies of the *Protocols* and Henry Ford's *The International Jew* throughout the Arab and Muslim worlds and in newsstands in Latin American airports. Suspicion about Freemasonry grew exponentially in the developing world. The theories put forward were simply warmed-over copies of what had been published for a hundred years in the American and European media, but now with updated "information" connected to current events.

I myself was introduced to this phenomenon many times over the past decade as I traveled from the United States to South America and Southeast Asia. In 2007, I was surprised to learn that I would meet Abu Bakr Basyir, the man many believe to have been the spiritual author of the Bali bombings of 2002 and who was briefly imprisoned in Indonesia for charges in connection with the event.

That meeting with the Islamic fundamentalist leader was similar to others I have had with right-wing ideologues. It was with a group of mostly foreigners who wanted to hear from his own lips the reasons behind terrorist acts. Abu Bakr Basyir—or "ABB," as he is referred to colloquially—is a man who knows that what he will say will be shocking, or offensive, or both. He was an unapologetic promoter of the Judeo-Masonic conspiracy theory, and believed that America—due to its support of the state of Israel—is a voluntary member of that conspiracy, which has as its aim the destruction of Islam. From him I heard slogans and ideas that would have been quite at home in Germany in the 1930s or, indeed, almost anywhere in Europe and even—it must be said—in America. This was not a man interested in a careful presentation of a political case, but an ideologue who sees the world in a comfortable duality of "us" and "them." The fact that the last time I had heard these statements uttered was from an American born in New York City did not give me much comfort.

In the Indonesian bookstores there are dozens of very popular books—best-sellers—on this very theme. One—*Musa Vs Fir'aun* (Moses versus the Pharaoh)—even has a foreword by Abu Bakr Basyir.[9] Opening any of these books, one is immediately surprised to see the staples of American conspiracy theory: the pictures of the Great Seal on the U.S. dollar bill and interpretations as to its occult significance; charts showing the interrelationships among various political and military leaders; timelines, suggestive photographs and "PhotoShopped" artwork. Of course, the events of September 11, 2001, and its aftermath in the invasions of Afghanistan and Iraq have contributed to the embattled mind-set of the Muslim conspiracy theorists. Jews and Masons are responsible for the world situation, so the narrative states, and the proof is in the conspiratorial pudding.

I am uncomfortable with the term *conspiracy theory* to the extent that it devalues serious criticism of official stories and of what the intelligence community refers to as disinformation and "legends"— that is, false information disseminated as truth. It has become a pejorative term that is used to immediately discredit a competing view of political events. The fact that conspiracies are a commonplace in politics in the rest of the world seems to argue against the existence of conspiracies in the United States. This is a strange conclusion, and one that may say more about American self-image than it does about events taking place in the "real" world. A conspiracy theory, by some definitions, is one that ignores data it finds incompatible or uses data of questionable sources in order to promote a paranoid perspective. It stipulates the existence of groups of individuals who conspire secretly to control events. Since the Masons are a "secret society," or at the very least a "society with secrets," Freemasonry is ideal as a place on which to hang any number of conspiracies. Since outsiders do not know what transpires in a Masonic lodge, it becomes a blackboard on which anything can be written since no one has written anything else—that is, no one can prove otherwise.

However, the essential fact of Freemasonry is the one that is ignored by most theorists who see a sinister plot in the Lodge: initiation.

Any group of individuals who meet in secret can hatch political conspiracies. One does not need to be a Freemason in order to do this. A Masonic lodge is built around the inescapable elements of the three basic degrees: Entered Apprentice, Fellow Craft, and Master Mason. For any conspiracy theory concerning the Masons to be valid, it would have to take into consideration the initiations, their respective degrees, and what they mean—what effect they have on the initiate. This is not done, because Masonic conspiracy theorists are generally not initiates of Masonic lodges. The experience of initiation is not understood or recognized by them.

The P2 was a group of men who came together to cement political alliances, organized by a political activist and right-wing extremist. Like Adam Weishaupt before him, Licio Gelli saw that the Masonic structure could be used to great benefit. Skull and Bones, on the other hand, was created specifically to organize an elitist cabal. William H. Russell saw in the Masonic example a template for his own organization. These were men who used Freemasonry for their own purposes, comfortable in the knowledge that—due to the aura of secrecy and mystery that inherently surrounds Freemasonry—they could avoid scrutiny and use the charismatic nature of a secret society to attract ambitious and powerful men who would maintain the group's secrecy in order to extend that charisma to themselves. And that is the crux of the problem.

In spite of the insistence of Freemasons that they are merely a fraternal order—a kind of Boy Scouts for adults—there are a number of characteristics of the group that bring that professed innocence into question. Foremost among these, of course, is the aura of secrecy that has been a part of the order since its formal inception in 1717 and which also can be detected in its earlier manifestations. This idea of secrecy is not so benign as it first may appear to those who study the Masons, for secrecy implies either guilty actions or a desire to keep certain information privileged (i.e., available only to an elite). Of course, there is another alternative and it is the one that the Masons prefer: that secrecy is a necessary psychological condition for the mental state they wish to achieve. In other words, by wrapping the lodge in a shroud of secrecy the importance of the rituals is enhanced and the impression it makes on the mind and heart of the initiate is thereby more profound.

Since this may be as close to the truth as we will get, we should examine this idea further.

In previous work I have looked at the close connection that exists between ideas of brainwashing and ideas of spiritual initiation.[10] Quite often, the popular media will refer to a specific religious organization as a "brainwashing cult." The impression one has of "brainwashing cult" is of a charismatic leader who uses behavior modification techniques—up to and including torture—to create an army of mindless robots; and all of this activity is generally conducted within a religious milieu, which reduces the resistance of the followers and enhances the credibility of the leader. Unfortunately, genuine models of spiritual initiation follow what appears to be identical methods of behavior modification. How do we discriminate between what is a brainwashing cult and a genuine initiatory order? Is this discrimination nothing more sophisticated than a value judgment imposed on the former by adherents of the latter?

One could propose that a society with the spiritual well-being of its followers foremost in its agenda would ensure that each individual member had freedom of choice at every level of involvement. In other words, that one could leave—easily—with no adverse conditions being imposed. This is true of Freemasonry. It may not be true of Skull and Bones, for instance, where one is told that "once a Bonesman, always a Bonesman," or of P2, where leaving could be construed in harsh light, like attempting to leave an organized crime syndicate.

Another test would be the goals that the organization pursues and how it pursues them. In the case of P2, its agenda was nakedly political. It existed to increase the power of Licio Gelli and his closest associates. It had no humanitarian ideals, unless one considers the crimes it committed in pursuit of anticommunism acceptable practice. In the case of Skull and Bones, Alexandra Robbins has described it as one big "superiority complex." [11]

Another test would be membership practices. To become a Mason, one merely has to ask to join. There are requirements, but these are usually not so strenuous as to exclude most or even many applicants. The cost is not excessive, and there are Masonic temples virtually everywhere in the United States and throughout the world.

Joining Skull and Bones is next to impossible. It is only for Yale University seniors, and one cannot ask to join. One must be "tapped"—i.e., preselected and invited. And there is that restriction on the number of initiates each year. If you are number sixteen on the list and all others have accepted you are no longer eligible for membership. Ever.

A similar arrangement existed (and still exists) for P2. It was from its very beginning with Gelli a secret and "covered" society. No one knew its membership lists except Gelli and possibly the head of Italian Freemasonry (at least until 1974; after that, it is credible that only Gelli himself knew who the members were). Since you did not know it existed, you could not ask to join, and only the rich and powerful were invited anyway.

So, although the rules of secrecy create an existential problem for Freemasonry in that it will never be completely accepted as a benign institution no matter how hard it tries or even in spite of its attempts to appear "cuddly," the incorporation of secret rituals, handshakes, and passwords does not automatically characterize it as sinister. Many sublime things are secret: the correct pronounciation of the Hebrew word for God, for instance, or the formula for making the Philosopher's Stone.

In this age of wholesale assaults on personal privacy—by governments, corporations, insurance companies, employers, computer hackers, and identity thieves—the kind of secrecy inherent in Freemasonry may represent a remedy, or at least a useful example.

Conclusions

Masonry, like all the Religions, all the Mysteries, Hermeticism and Alchemy,
conceals its secrets from all except the Adepts and Sages, or the Elect, and uses
false explanations and misrepresentations of its symbols to mislead those who
deserve only to be misled. . . .

—Albert Pike, *Morals and Dogma of the Ancient and*
Accepted Scottish Rite of Freemasonry

As its author, I undertook this study without prejudice. For someone who has for decades studied secret societies—
their rituals, politics, and even their crimes—there was no automatic
assumption of guilt. Hysteria and paranoia often conjure demons
where there are none. After all, the Nazis had banned the Freemasons, as had various European governments and the Catholic
Church. That did not indicate they deserved the excessive attention.
The Jews had also suffered the same treatment, and much worse; so
did homosexuals, Gypsies, and communists.

The intense hatred of so many powerful groups toward this fraternity demonstrates more about those groups than it does the
Freemasons. Different worldviews are always deemed dangerous—to
the status quo, to those who oppose those worldviews, and to those
who might hold them—as increasingly our world becomes the arena
of what the Germans have called *Weltangschauungskrieg*, or worldview warfare.

The difficulty of conducting research into a society that openly
proclaims itself in possession of secrets that it deems unlawful to
share provides its own set of frustrations, however. Some authors
have written that the Freemasons—since they are under oath to protect their secrets—will dissemble and practice that famous art of disinformation in order to preserve the integrity of the sanctuary. This

means, basically, that no one can trust what they have written, especially when they insist that what they are saying is the truth. Others have claimed, equally seriously, that the Freemasons themselves have no clue as to what their real secrets may be, and this means, once again, that their writings cannot be trusted.

Still others claim that there is an esoteric group of initiates behind the exoteric Masonry that we can see, and this means that the Masons you know might not be lying, but they might not be telling the truth, either. For example, Manly P. Hall notes that "Freemasonry is a fraternity within a fraternity—an outer organization concealing an inner brotherhood of the elect. Before it is possible to intelligently discuss the origin of the Craft, it is necessary, therefore, to establish the existence of these two separate yet interdependent orders, the one visible and the other invisible."[1] And, as Albert Pike writes, "The Blue Degrees are but the outer court or portico of the Temple. Part of the symbols are displayed there to the Initiate, *but he is intentionally misled by false interpretations. It is not intended that he shall understand them, but it is intended that he shall imagine he understands them.* Their true explanation is reserved for the Adepts, the Princes of Masonry."[2] (emphasis added)

With so many options, so many possible ways to look at Freemasonry, I decided to simply adhere to the documents that were available and then analyze them from the point of view of other disciplines (and a basic understanding of history and human nature) to determine where the truth might be. It is a strategy that has worked well when studying government agencies, after all. But the secrets being protected by governments are usually quite predictable and mundane. The secrets being protected by Masonic societies are of a different sort altogether. They claim to have the keys to the secrets of creation, of the universe, of divine wisdom, and that is quite different from the secrets of the payoffs, lies, and corruption of various kinds that one finds among the tedious air-tels and the intelligence agencies' declassified files of their long-concluded operations.

The influence of Freemasonry on the creation of the United States, however, is something that is easier to trace. Yes, many of the founding fathers were Freemasons, but certainly not all of them. It wasn't necessary that all the signers of the Declaration of Independence be Masons, or that every U.S. president be a Mason. The influence of Freemasonry was the influence of the European Enlightenment and, in that sense, all of the signers were Masons. And not only the signers. One could say that Voltaire signed the Declaration. And John Locke. And Jean-Jacques Rousseau, Francis Bacon, and Thomas Paine. But the ideals that contributed to the formation of the country were also those of the Masonic lodge and temple. The Masonic orders made it possible for like-minded individuals to meet "on the level" and understand—with a visceral understanding that did not need discussion—that all were created equal, that each person had the right to ascend the three degrees of initiation, that the doors of the temple were open to everyone who had the will, the desire, and the humility. That kind of thinking—so common among the best of Americans today—was revolutionary for its time. While Voltaire and Locke were writing about it in theory, the Freemasons were living it. They were putting into practice an idea of the voluntary guild that transcends any and all occupations. America had become, in the hands of these Masons and their brothers, a universal guild in which every citizen was an equal member, an initiate into the mysteries of Liberty.

Of course, it did not happen right away. The deeply immoral situation of slavery kept America from experiencing full brotherhood, and Masonry has been too slow to remedy that situation within its own ranks and thus has not provided the kind of moral leadership that Enlightenment principles demanded. There is also a concern about physical deformity that makes it impossible for many otherwise sincere and intelligent individuals to become Masons; due to the rather rigorous physical demands of the initiations themselves (which involve assuming exaggerated postures for long periods of time) as well as the ceremonial "murder" at the third degree initiation, some of this resistance is understandable and has a certain pedigree. (According to the old canon law of the Catholic Church, men who were physically infirm, deformed, or "eunuchs" could not become bishops, for example.) In addition, normative Masonry's refusal to initiate women is another obstacle. From this point of view—the bias against slaves and women, particularly—Freemasonry struggles with a pre-Enlightenment mind-set. Ironically, the forms of

Freemasonry not universally recognized—such as Prince Hall Masonry and Co-Masonry—may well represent the future of the larger order.

Like America itself, Freemasonry is a work in progress, an experiment in the alchemical mixing of spiritual enlightenment and initiation with social progress and civic responsibility. Sometimes, as in the laboratory of the "puffers"—the amateur alchemists who tried to make gold, mistaking elemental gold for spiritual wealth—there would be an explosion. At other times, and almost by accident, a nugget of true gold would be produced.

The Secret Temple is, as Albert Pike and so many other Masonic writers insist, human consciousness itself. Each individual is a rough stone, waiting to be polished into the cornerstone of his or her own destiny. From the prototype of King Solomon's Temple—an edifice that transcends time and space and provides a link between a people's ancient history and its future utopia—to the "virtual" temples of the mystics and magicians of succeeding generations, Freemasonry has recognized that everyone has the right to enter the Holy of Holies, to speak to God; the right, but not the automatic privilege.

For citizens of the United States, the capitol building in Washington, D.C., is the earthly manifestation of this secret temple. In attempting to decode the grids of Washington's city streets to divine secret arrangements of avenues and boulevards one can easily miss the forest for the trees. The city *is* the temple. And, like the Temple in the eras of Jesus, the Zealots, the Hasmoneans, the Romans, or the Hellenizers, there are both money changers and charlatans clogging its pathways. The great national experiment that was begun in 1776 has not yet been completed. The initiation that was begun with the American Revolution culminated in the Civil War, as one type of liberty gave rise to another, one level of initiation to another. America is now on the winding staircase of its second degree in search of its third, and final, initiation.

Adam Weishaupt wanted to create the "new man," and believed the ends justified the means. So did Adolf Hitler. Instead of trying to create supermen, Freemasonry tries to find the real men hidden within blocks of stone. It is the struggle to become human—with all that this implies—that is at the heart of the Secret Temple. Of course, it is not the only path, not the only method of initiation that is available. Freemasonry's organization is flawed, its policies inconsistent at times with its goals. But it does give us an idea of what is possible, of what *could* be accomplished and for that—by combining ideas of initiation with civic responsibility—Freemasonry is a valuable avenue of study for anyone who believes that human organization (and thereby the world itself) can be improved.

Edgar Allen Poe's "A Cask of Amontillado"

"You are not of the masons."

"Yes, yes," I said; "yes, yes."

"You? Impossible! A mason?"

"A mason," I replied.

"A sign," he said, "a sign."

"It is this," I answered, producing from beneath the folds of my roquelaire a trowel.

—Edgar Allen Poe, "A Cask of Amontillado"

IN 1846, A MAGAZINE—*Godey's Lady's Book*—published one of Edgar Allen Poe's most memorable short stories. It involved the character Montresor (a man with a grudge) and his archenemy Fortunato. Montresor, for reasons that are never fully described, has planned the murder of Fortunato during Carnival. Fortunato shows up dressed as a harlequin, and Montresor takes him to his family's ancestral vaults under the pretense of tasting some Amontillado he has just purchased. As they descend deeper and deeper underground, past skeletons spilling out of their coffins and niter dripping from the walls, Fortunato asks Montresor for proof that he is a Mason. Montresor replies by pulling out a trowel.

It is the trowel that Montresor will use to wall up Fortunato alive in his vaults.

The story is a tightly written description of one man's insane, murderous jealousy of another. The fact that it contains a reference to Freemasonry is usually glossed over without much attention given to it; it is, after all, merely an excuse for Montresor to pull out his trowel. There are, however, deeper elements at work in the story and they reveal something about how Freemasonry was understood in the mid-nineteenth century in America.

At one point in the story, Fortunato asks Montresor how his family's coat of arms is designed. Montresor replies that it shows a man's foot stamping on a serpent, and the serpent biting the man on the heel. The Latin motto is *Nemo me impune lacessit,* which means "No one provokes me with impunity," a clear reference to the motive for Fortunato's murder. However, this motto has an intriguing pedigree, as does the heraldic device that accompanies it.

We find the motto on the arms of the Order of the Thistle, a Scottish chivalric order of knighthood established by King James II of England (James VII of the Scots). This is relevant because the followers of James—known as Jacobites—were prominent in many intrigues against the British crown that involved secret societies and, among them, the Masons. James had enjoyed a tumultuous career as monarch throughout his life, and ended it in exile in France; efforts to reinstate him resulted in failure and in the establishment of Hanoverian rule.

The device involving a serpent hearkens back to the famous Gadsden flag and emblem. Used as a patriotic ensign by the American colonists, it depicts a coiled serpent (in this case a rattlesnake) with the legend "Don't Tread on Me." The motto *Nemo me impune lacessit* actually appears above this design on a twenty-dollar bill printed by the state of Georgia in 1778, during the American Revolution. Thus, Poe may have been making an allusion to this design in his short story. Indeed, it was used by America's very first admiral, the Rhode Island native Commodore Esek Hopkins, who was a Mason. The rattlesnake design itself was championed by Benjamin Franklin, who was himself also a Mason.

Further we read, for instance, that Montresor is writing this tale "a half of a century" after the murder. If we posit that the story takes place in 1846, the year the tale was published, then fifty years earlier would have been 1796. That year finds us in the middle of the French Revolution and its Revolutionary Wars involving the young Napoleon Bonaparte. The references in Poe's story are French and

Italian: Montresor is a French name (and the name of a French chateau near Tours), but Fortunato and Luchresi (the name of another character, who appears on the sidelines) are obviously Italian; and Montresor makes references to his palazzo although he claims the design of his family's vaults are common to Parisian catacombs. (Napoleon's French forces invaded and captured Milan during the French revolutionary campaigns.)

Aside from these details, however, the larger story compels us to look for Masonic significance, since the introduction of the Masonic trowel and other references seems to tease us in that direction.

The fact that Fortunato is a Mason, and is dressed as a harlequin, seems significant. In fact, there was a play by R. Charles Dibdin titled *Harlequin Freemason*, billed as a Masonic pantomime, that was performed in 1780 in London. Characterized as a "circumspectly reverential burlesque" on Masonry by David Worrall, it included Masonic references that were already popularly known.

The murder of Fortunato takes place in a crypt. The burial place is a central theme of the third-degree Masonic initiation, and tracing boards for that degree normally show a coffin surmounted by a skull and crossbones, and other mortuary devices. To that degree, the tale of Hiram Abiff's murder is retold and the initiate is made to identify with the master. He is ceremonially slain, and laid in a symbolic representation of a grave before he is raised again and brought into the community of Master Masons.

In Poe's story, the entire journey of Fortunato and Montresor takes place in the burial vaults. After descending a "winding staircase" they come to the catacombs and proceed through room after room of the dead. Three walls of the vault are intact, piled high with coffins and their skeletal remains. The fourth wall has crumbled, and skeletons spill out. Beneath the rubble are the building materials that Montresor has hidden, directly in front of a small niche between two "colossal supports" big enough for a man.

The winding staircase is a Masonic emblem of the second degree, that of the Fellow Craft. It represents the midway point between the lower chamber and the upper chamber of King Solomon's Temple. Instead of going up the staircase, however, which is the route taken in the second-degree initiation, Fortunato is made to go down the staircase. He is then brought before a small chamber between two pillars, where he will be walled in, still alive, by the mason's (Montresor's) trowel.

What Poe has done is create an anti-Masonic allegory. He has reversed the normal initiatory process by taking the Mason—Fortunato, in this case—*down* a winding staircase instead of up, and through a catacomb to face two pillars, the twin pillars of the first-degree ritual. He is walled up between the pillars: Montresor employs the "operative" form of Masonry to this task, laying brick upon brick for a total of eleven layers. The harlequin is chained inside, and dies of asphyxiation. In a final sadistic gesture, Montresor throws his burning torch into the walled enclosure with Fortunato before sealing him up with the final brick: this will cause the air in the small chamber to be used up much more quickly. Instead of the symbolic resurrection of Hiram Abiff in the third-degree ritual, we have the rather more permanent demise of Fortunato the Mason, surrounded on all sides by the coffins and skeletons that are emblematic of that initiation. Montresor kills Fortunato using Masonic symbolism. Seen from this perspective, "The Cask of Amontillado" becomes a clever anti-Masonic tract.

Ironically, the name Fortunato means "happy" or "lucky" in Italian, even "successful"; and Montresor means, simply, "my treasure" in French. Treasure thus trumps success in this tale of revenge. Literary critics have identified the motivation for this story as Poe's revenge on a rival author, the Democratic congressman Thomas Dunn English (1819–1902), who had ridiculed him in print in one of his own stories and with whom Poe had had a fistfight and a notorious feud. English was more successful than Poe in the material sense, serving in the U.S. Congress and enjoying a certain level of literary acclaim. Poe's argument against English was that the congressman had an inferior education when it came to literature and yet presumed to lecture others on it. English savaged Poe in a story that contained references to secret societies, which is possibly where Poe got the inspiration for the Masonic trowel and other motifs in his own short story. Poe clearly identified with "treasure" and condemned "success" to a slow death by way of revenge; we must interpret "treasure" in this case as being something other than filthy lucre.

The central image of this story is the cask of Amontillado itself, a cask that actually appears in the tale. Amontillado, of course, is a form of sherry that originates from a region in Spain. Fortunato arrives at Montresor's villa already drunk; Montresor plies him with more wine as they proceed through the catacombs toward the twin pillars. Wine is an important element in Masonic ritual. Corn, wine, and oil are used to consecrate Masonic temples as well as to anoint cornerstones of Masonic buildings and those of other buildings to which Masons are invited during the ceremony. A drunken Mason chained to a wall between Jachin and Boaz might be seen as the Masonic equivalent of a Black Mass.

While the anti-Masonic furor had died down by the time Poe's story was published, it was still fresh on everyone's mind. In 1846, Masonic lodges all across the country were still having a hard time finding members and holding initiations. In some cases lodges simply disappeared or went inactive for decades. In "The Cask of Amontillado" Poe sealed up not only Fortunato and his rival English behind a wall but also pre–Civil War American Freemasonry itself. It would not be until Reconstruction that Freemasonry would begin to revive from its losses stemming from the William Morgan affair and the concentrated efforts to destroy it by John Quincy Adams and others of the Anti-Masonic Party.

Notes

Chapter one

1. Malcolm C. Duncan, *Duncan's Masonic Ritual and Monitor* (New York: Dick and Fitzgerald, 1866); Robert Lomas, *Turning the Hiram Key: Rituals of Freemasonry Revealed* (Gloucester, MA: Tradewinds Press, 2005). By a popular writer on Masonic and Templar themes, Lomas's book is valuable for the personal perspective it gives of someone undergoing the degree rituals.

2. See, for instance, Samuel Prichard, *Masonry Dissected* (London, 1730); and William Finch, Masonic Treatise (Canterbury, England, 1802).

3. Albert Pike, *Morals and Dogma of the Ancient and Accepted Scottish Rite of Freemasonry* (Richmond, L. H. Jenkins, 1947 [1871]), 7.

4. J. S. M. Ward, *An Interpretation of Our Masonic Symbols*, reprint ed. (Whitefish, MT: Kessinger, 1993), 6.

5 One of the more impressive Masonic temples in America is that of the Grand Lodge of Pennsylvania, in Philadelphia, which boasts seven halls, each designed around a different theme: an Egyptian Hall, a Corinthian Hall, a Renaissance Hall, an Oriental Hall, etc., but they all contain the same basic appointments of the three pillars and the kneeler and pedestal/altar between them, as well as the throne for the Worshipful Master in the east.

6. See Mark 12:10; Matthew 21:42; Luke 20:17; Acts 4:11; 1 Peter 2:7.

7. Peter Levenda, *Stairway to Heaven: Chinese Alchemists, Jewish Kabbalists, and the Art of Spiritual Transformation* (New York: Continuum, 2007), 109–31.

8. See 1 Kings 7:13, 7:40, 7:45.

9. See 1 Kings 6:7; and Josephus, *Antiquities of the Jews*, 8.3.

10. Josephus, *Antiquities of the Jews*, 8.146.

11. Israel Regardie, *The Golden Dawn* (St. Paul, MN: Llewellyn, 2005), 272.

12. The Adeptus Minor initiation ritual in the Golden Dawn is in the form of a crucifixion of the initiate, who is then raised from the dead. See Levenda, *Stairway to Heaven*, 169, for an exploration of this idea in terms of Kabbalah and specifically celestial ascent practices.

Chapter two

1. J. S. M. Ward, *An Interpretation of our Masonic Symbols*, reprint ed. (Whitefish, MT: Kessinger, 1993), 1–7.

2. Frances A. Yates, *The Occult Philosophy in the Elizabethan Age* (London: Routledge and Kegan Paul, 1979).

3. I am indebted to Dr. Oren Stier for pointing this out to me.

4. See Peter Levenda, *Stairway to Heaven: Chinese Alchemists, Jewish Kabbalists, and the Art of Spiritual Transformation* (New York: Continuum, 2008), for a complete analysis of this theme.

Chapter three

1. This allegation appears as recently as Paul Naudon, *The Secret History of Freemasonry* (Rochester, VT: Inner Traditions, 2005), 63. The allegation seems to have been taken directly from a book by Abbe Henri Gregoire, *Histoire des Sectes Religieuses* (Paris, 1828) and repeated extensively in the years since then; see, for example, Sharon Turner, *The History of England during the Middle Ages* (London: Longman, Brown, Green, and Longmans, 1853), 1:583–87; and an unsigned review of Gregoire's book in *The Monthly Review* (London) 11 (1829): 395–403. It should be noted that Naudon himself is a Scottish Rite Freemason. The name Theocletes is problematic since it is Greek, and the Mandaeans—by this time in exile in the south of Muslim Iraq—spoke their own language among themselves but also used Aramaic and presumably Arabic with others. To claim that a Hellenized group of Mandaeans existed in Jerusalem in 1118 is by itself a bold assertion requiring additional evidence.

2. Hugh Schonfield, *Essene Odyssey* (Rockport, MA: Element, 1998), 164. In this book, published a few years before his death, the eminent Dead Sea Scrolls scholar and Nobel Prize nominee linked the Mandaeans with the Essenes and from there to the Cathars and the Knights Templar, based not only on his own researches in early Christianity and the Qumran sect but also—surprisingly—on information brought to his attention by *The Holy Blood and the Holy Grail*. It is indeed strange that someone of Schonfield's reputation can be found giving credence to some of Freemasonry's more speculative claims.

We soon will find both of these themes—baptism and sophia—represented in the practices and beliefs of the first Rosicrucians to come to America in the seventeenth century, the Pietist sects of Johannes Kelpius and Conrad Beissel, thus suggesting an inner, secret tradition that may have its origins with the Templars and a possible Mandaean influence.

3. Known as the *Leviticon*, this document contains both a liturgy of the Templars as well as an abbreviated form of the Gospel of St. John. Its provenance is uncertain.

4. Malcolm Barber, *The Cathars: Dualistic Heretics in Languedoc in the High Middle Ages* (Harlow, England: Longman, 2000), 83–86.

5. Sidney Painter, *French Chivalry: Chivalric Ideals and Practices in Mediaeval France* (Ithaca, NY: Cornell University Press, 1965), 153.

6. Ibid., p. 74.

7. The most accessible sources for a brief overview of Lull's influence on generations of Christian Kabbalists are Frances A. Yates, *The Art of Memory* (Chicago: University of Chicago Press, 1966) and Frances A. Yates, *The Occult Philosophy in the Elizabethan Age* (London: Routledge and Kegan Paul, 1979).

8. The last attempted crusade was that of King Ferdinand of Spain in 1492, which floundered in Italy on the way to the Holy Land.

9. Bernard Lewis, *The Assassins: A Radical Sect in Islam* (New York: Oxford University Press, 1967), is one of the standard works for a general audience. Farhad Daftary, *The Assassin Legends: Myths of the Isma'ilis* (New York: I. B. Tauris, 1995), is one of the later studies by a specialist in Isma'ili doctrine that questions many of the assumptions made by Western scholars, including Lewis.

10. Barbara Frale, "The Chinon Chart: Papal absolution to the last Templar, Master Jacques de Molay," *Journal of Medieval History* 30 (2004): 109–34.

11. Peter Levenda, *Unholy Alliance: A History of Nazi Involvement with the Occult* (New York: Continuum, 2002).

12. Barber, *The Cathars*, 10.

13. See Levenda, *Unholy Alliance*, 280–353. The SS—Heinrich Himmler's famous Schutzstaffel—was designated a criminal organization by the Allied Forces. Anyone who had been a member of the SS was subject to arrest and criminal prosecution. The irony of this is that the SS was just as mystical as the Templars were supposed to have been; their leader, Himmler, had renovated Wewelsburg Castle in Germany after the model of King Arthur and the Round Table in order to provide a spiritual sanctuary for his highest-ranking SS officers as well as a resting place for their ashes—and for the Holy Grail itself should it ever be found. It is disconcerting, to say the least, that the SS was as close to a modern-day Templar order as could be desired; it is further upsetting to a generation of spiritual seekers raised on Michael Baigent, Richard Leigh, and Henry Lincoln's *The Holy Blood and the Holy Grail*, as well as Dan Brown's more recent *The DaVinci Code*, to realize that the spiritual inspiration for much of what would become Nazi ideology came from the Order of New Templars created by Lanz von Liebenfels, a former monk who edited a racist magazine and whose most faithful reader was a young Adolf Hitler. We will examine more of this in chapter 9.

14. See, for instance, Karen Ralls, *The Templars and the Grail: Knights of the Quest* (Wheaton, IL: Quest Books, 2003), 110–15; and Karen Ralls, *Knights Templar Encyclopedia* (Franklin Lakes, NJ: Career Press, 2007), 188–90.

15. See especially David Stevenson, *The Origins of Freemasonry: Scotland's Century 1590–1710* (Cambridge: Cambridge University Press, 1988).

16. Ibid., 136–65.

17. Ibid., 136.

18. Ibid.

Chapter four

1. Information on the Templars' building campaigns can be found in Edward Burman, *The Templars: Knights of God* (Rochester, VT: Destiny Books, 1986), esp. chap. 7; and Malcolm Barber, *The New Knighthood: A History of the Order of the Temple* (Cambridge: Cambridge University Press, 2005), 160–68.

2. See Helen Nicholson and David Nicolle, *God's Warriors: Knights Templar, Saracens, and the Battle for Jerusalem* (New York: Osprey, 2005), 203–5, for some information on existing Templar castles in Europe, the Middle East, and the Balkans.

3. Henry Adams, *Mont-Saint-Michel and Chartes* (New York: Houghton Mifflin, 1933), 92.

4. John James, *Chartres: The Masons Who Built a Legend* (London: Routledge and Kegan Paul, 1985), 122.

5. Ibid., 40.

6. Ibid., 37.

7. Ibid., 164–65.

8. Ibid., 165.

9. David Ovason, *The Secret Architecture of Our Nation's Capital* (New York: HarperCollins, 2000).

10. Christopher Hodapp, *Solomon's Builders: Freemasons, Founding Fathers and the Secrets of Washington D.C.* (Berkeley, CA: Ulysses, 2007), 163–65. Hodapp's dismissal of Ovason's work is cavalier and abrupt and based primarily on the fact that L'Enfant was not a Mason and neither was Ovason, so anyone looking for a reasoned approach to the material will be disappointed.

11. Peter Levenda, *Stairway to Heaven: Chinese Alchemists, Jewish Kabbalists, and the Art of Spiritual Transformation* (New York: Continuum, 2008).

12. In ancient Egypt, Seshat was the goddess in charge of measurement and writing, as well as architecture, and she was also known as "Mistress of the House of Books," or librarian. Her spouse was the god of magic, alchemy, and wisdom, Thoth. Seshat was invoked at the "stretching of the cord" ritual, when the pharaoh would mark the dimensions of a new temple or palace. The implements associated with this ritual would be familiar to present-day speculative Masons: the cord, the mallet, and a sighting on a star in the north.

Chapter five

1. Julius F. Sachse, *The German Pietists of Provincial Pennsylvania* (Philadelphia: privately published, 1895), 115.

2. Ibid., 235.

3. Some diagrams from Secret Symbols were lifted from the monumental work by Georg von Welling, *Opus Mago-Cabbalisticum et Theosophicum*, published in Homburg in 1735 but completed by Welling in 1721. This complex and arcane work was influential in Pietist circles as well as among Masonic and Rosicrucian groups in Europe. J. W. von Goethe is known to have read it, and used it as the model for the books of magic consulted by his fictional character Faust. Until recently (a Weiser Books edition published in 2006, translated by Joseph McVeigh), no complete English translation existed, so estimates of its importance were largely ignored by the English-speaking public. It was, however, of singular interest to the Gold und Rosenkreuzer society, founded in 1777, which is discussed later in this chapter.

4. David Ovason, *The Secret Architecture of Our Nation's Capital* (New York: HarperCollins, 2002). Ovason's thesis is that the constellation Virgo and especially the star Spica have special relevance for the United States and for American Freemasonry generally, and elements of this concept were incorporated

into the design of Washington, D.C. Although his work has a foreword by a high-ranking Mason who is impressed with Ovason's research and who admits of its plausibility, Ovason's thesis has been challenged by another Freemason and author, Christopher Hodapp, in *Solomon's Builders: Freemasons, Founding Fathers and the Secrets of Washington D.C.* (Berkeley, CA: Ulysses Press, 2007), 162–65.

5. Sachse, *The German Pietists*, 34.

6. Ibid., 130–31; the original spelling and grammar is retained. Note the use of terms such as *Judgment, Victory, Justice,* and *Mercy,* which may be referring to spheres on the Kabbalistic Tree of Life, and the image of imperfect metals changing into gold, a gold that is refined seven times (a perfect alchemical image).

7. See Jeff Bach, *Voices of the Turtledoves* (University Park: Pennsylvania State University Press, 2003), for a comprehensive critique of Sachse's claims of a Rosicrucian element in the Wissahickon and Ephrata communities.

8. John L. Brooke, *The Refiner's Fire: The Making of Mormon Cosmology, 1644–1844* (New York: Cambridge University Press, 1994); D. Michael Quinn, *Early Mormonism and the Magic World View* (Salt Lake City, UT: Signature Books, 1998).

9. Brooke, *The Refiner's Fire,* 36, 80; Quinn, *Early Mormonism,* 10.

10. Quinn, *Early Mormonism,* 10.

11. Julius F. Sachse, *The German Sectarians of Pennsylvania,* vol. 1 (Philadelphia: privately published, 1899), 39.

12. Frances A. Yates, *The Occult Philosophy in the Elizabethan Age* (London: Routledge and Kegan Paul, 1979); Frances A. Yates, *The Rosicrucian Enlightenment* (London: Routledge and Kegan Paul, 1972).

13. Sachse, *The German Sectarians,* 393–95.

14. Ibid., 354.

15. Mark A. Tabbert, *American Freemasons: Three Centuries of Building Communities* (New York: New York University Press, 2006), 35.

16. Sachse, *The German Sectarians,* 357.

17. David Stevenson, *The Origins of Freemasonry: Scotland's Century 1590–1710* (Cambridge: Cambridge University Press, 1988), 144.

18. William S. Webb and Charles E. Snow, *The Adena People* (Knoxville: University of Tennessee Press, 1981), 81.

19. Thomas McAdory Owen, *History of Alabama and Dictionary of Alabama Biography,* vol. 1 (Chicago: S. J. Clarke, 1921), 669.

20. Sachse, *The German Sectarians,* 359.

21. Ibid., 359.

22. Ibid., 360–61.

23. Ibid.

24. Ibid.

25. Ibid. p. 361.

26. Astonishingly, as the present work was being prepared for publication, I came across a biography of the Italian count and Mason Alessandro di Cagliostro—published in 1910—that contains precisely this complete regimen down to the smallest detail! Titled "The Secret of Regeneration or Physical Perfection by which one can attain to the spirituality of 5557 years (Insurance Office of the Great Cagliostro)," it is cited in W. R. H. Trowbridge, *Cagliostro* (London: Chapman and Hill, 1910), 122–23, where it is identified as a joke, written by the Marquis de Luchet as a satire on Cagliostro's work. However, as Trowbridge points out, Cagliostro himself did not deny he wrote the tract. That leaves us with the question, where did Sachse get this data in such complete detail, and what was his purpose in attributing the practice to the Ephrata commune? Sachse does state that the Zionitic Brotherhood was somehow connected to the Masonic Rite of Strict Observance or the "Egyptian cult of Freemasonry," but the Zionitic Brotherhood predated Cagliostro's Egyptian Masonry by decades. This is a conundrum, which may say more about Sachse than Ephrata.

27. See Mircea Eliade, *Shamanism: Archaic Techniques of Ecstasy* (London: Arkana, 1989), especially chap. 2, "Initiatory Sicknesses and Dreams."

28. Mircea Eliade, *The Forge and the Crucible: The Origins and Structure of Alchemy* (Chicago: University of Chicago Press, 1978).

29. Bro. R. I. Clegg, "How to Study Freemasonry," *Builder*, July 1915, 154.

30. Sachse, *The German Sectarians*, 362–64.

31. Jan Stryz, "The Alchemy of the Voice at Ephrata Cloister," retrieved June 14, 2008 from www.esoteric.msu.edu/Alchemy.html.

32. Ibid.

Chapter six

1. In spite of this bloody history, the American Carolinas were named after him.

2. Often confused with Jacobins, the name of the revolutionary association that gave rise to the French Revolution.

3. Tobias Churton, *The Magus of Freemasonry* (Rochester, VT): Inner Traditions, 2004), 206–7, citing C. H. Josten, *Elias Ashmole (1617–1692)* (Oxford: Oxford University Press, 1966), 1364.

4. Ibid., 197. This design was not used, however.

5. See the Royal Society, "Brief History of the Society," retrieved June 30, 2008, from http://royalsociety.org/page.asp?id=2176.

6. Graeme Paton, "Intelligent People 'Less Likely to Believe in God'" *Daily Telegraph* (London), June 12, 2008.

7. Thomas Kuhn, *The Structure of Scientific Revolutions* (Chicago: University of Chicago Press, 1962).

8. Benjamin Franklin, quoted in Mark A. Tabbert, *American Freemasons* (New York: New York University Press, 2006), 11.

9. Emile Durkheim, *The Elementary Forms of Religious Life* (New York: Free Press, 1995).

10. W. Watts Miller, "Secularism and the Sacred: Is There Really Something Called 'Secular Religion?'" in *Reappraising Durkheim for the Study and Teaching of Religion Today*, edited by Thomas A. Idinopulos & Brian C. Wilson (Boston: Brill, 2002), 27.

11. This is not hyperbole; as we will see, as late as the Third Reich, Masons were rounded up and sent to detention camps along with communists, religious activists, homosexuals, gypsies, and, of course, Jews.

12. For a detailed look at the Nine Sisters Lodge, see R. William Weisberger, "Parisian Masonry, the Lodge of the Nine Sisters, and the French Enlightenment," *Heredom*, 10 (2002): 155–202.

13. Ibid., 175.

14. Ibid., 171.

15. One of the most entertaining of the popular books with an Illuminati theme is the *Illuminatus!* trilogy by Robert Anton Wilson and Robert J. Shea (New York: Dell, 1975). It had an enormous influence over the occult renaissance in the United States during the 1970s and 1980s, even as it merrily conflated many conspiracy theories and occult ideas with concepts borrowed from among others, LSD guru Timothy Leary. To make matters more interesting, the first novel of the trilogy was dedicated to Kerry Thornley (1938–98), a minor figure in the assassination of John F. Kennedy, and Gregory Hill (1941–2000), a friend of Thornley's who wrote an antiestablishment manifesto called the *Principia Discordia*.

16. In a letter of Thomas Jefferson to James Madison, dated January 31, 1800, he writes: "Wishaupt [sic] believes that to promote this perfection of the human character was the object of Jesus Christ. That his intention was simply to reinstate natural religion, & by diffusing the light of his morality, to teach us to govern ourselves. ... He believes the Free masons were originally possessed of the true principles & objects of Christianity, & have still preserved some of them by tradition, but much disfigured." From *The Thomas Jefferson Papers* at the Library of Congress.

17. A letter of George Washington to George Washington Snyder, October 24, 1798, states, "It was not my intention to doubt that the doctrines of the Illuminati, and principles of Jacobinism had not spread in the United States. On the contrary, no one is more truly satisfied of this fact than I am. The idea that I meant to convey, was, that I did not believe that the Lodges of Free Masons in this Country had, as Societies, endeavoured to propagate the diabolical tenets of the first, or pernicious principles of the latter. . . ." Library of Congress, George Washington Papers.

18. Winston Churchill, "Zionism versus Bolshevism: A Struggle for the Soul of the Jewish People," *Illustrated Sunday Herald*, February 8, 1920.

19. The earlier date comes from Charles William Heckethorn, *The Secret Societies of All Ages and Countries* (London: George Redway, 1897), 1:231. Heckethorn is not necessarily the most reliable of chroniclers, however, so the date is questionable.

20. Peter Levenda, *Stairway to Heaven: Chinese Alchemists, Jewish Kabbalists, and the Art of Spiritual Transformation* (New York: Continuum, 2007), 180–90.

21. Gershom Scholem, *Sabbatai Sevi: The Mystical Messiah*, Bollingen Series 93 (Princeton, NJ:, Princeton University Press, 1973.

22. Heckethorn, *The Secret Societies*, 231–35.

23. For a fuller discussion of this theme, see the Levenda, *Stairway to Heaven*, 180–90.

24. See the suspiciously favorable biography by W. R. H. Trowbridge, *Cagliostro* (London: Chapman and Hall, 1910), for details of Cagliostro's life and a quite thorough bibliography. For a hostile summary of Cagliostro's life and works, see Albert G. Mackey, *An Encyclopedia of Freemasonry and Its Kindred Sciences* (Philadelphia: Moss, 1879), 138–43.

25. For more background on this phenomenon, see Ellic Howe, *The Magicians of the Golden Dawn: A Documentary History of a Magical Order 1887–1923* (New York: Samuel Weiser, 1978); and Jocelyn Godwin, *The Theosophical Enlightenment* (Albany: State University of New York Press, 1994).

Chapter seven

1. Bernard Bailyn, *The Ideological Origins of the American Revolution* (Cambridge, MA: Belknap Press of Harvard University Press, 1967), 150–51.

2. Ibid., 26–30.

3. I use the term *men* deliberately, for women still are not allowed to become Freemasons nor were they even to vote in the United States until the twentieth century.

4. The Benjamin Franklin Lodge #719 of Hamilton, Ohio, states it will have a float on July 4, 2008, designed after the Boston Tea Party, "where many Masonic Brothers Participated." From their Web site http://www.benjaminfranklin719.org last accessed June 8, 2008.

5. This and other data in this section confirming Masonic membership, including dates of initiations, comes from Mark A. Tabbert, *American Freemasons: Three Centuries of Building Communities* (New York: New York University Press, 2006). Tabbert is director of collections at the George Washington Masonic National Memorial, and thus can be considered authoritative where "official" Masonic sources are concerned in this context.

6. See http://memory.loc.gov/ammem/gwhtml (retrieved June 2008), from which these excerpts are taken.

7. Lord Mahon, *History of England* (Boston: Little, Brown, 1853), 5:13.

8. Retrieved June 8, 2008, from http://grandlodge.blogspot.com/2008/03/benjamin-franklin-english-freemason.

9. Steven C. Bullock, *Revolutionary Brotherhood*, Chapel Hill: University of North Carolina Press, 1996, 95.

10. Ibid., 92–93.

11. Tabbert, *American Freemasons*, 34, 41.

Chapter eight

1. Joseph Smith Sr.'s brother, Hyrum, had been a member of the Mount Moriah Lodge at Palmyra, New York, and Heber C. Kimball of the Milner Lodge. See

John L. Brooke, *The Refiner's Fire: The Making of Mormon Cosmology, 1644–1844* (Cambridge: Cambridge University Press, 1994), 157.

2. Ibid., 158.

3. Ibid., 152–53.

4 Ibid., 158.

5. See Charles C. McClenechan, *Book of the Ancient and Accepted Scottish Rite of Freemasonry*, reprint ed. (Whitefish, MT: Kessinger, 2003), 139–48, and Thomas C. Webb, *The Freemason's Monitor, Or, Illustrations of Masonry* (Salem, MA): Cushing and Appleton, 1818), 17–21, for the Masonic lecture concerning this degree and the roles of Moses, Noah, and Enoch and the subterranean vaults, buried treasure, and the like.

6. Christopher Hodapp, *Solomon's Builders: Freemasons, Founding Fathers and the Secrets of Washington D.C.* (Berkeley, CA: Ulysses Press, 2007), 231–32.

7. C. Brent Morris, "The Royal Secret in America before 1801," retrieved June 30, 2008, from http://www.morningstarconsistory.com/PDF/The-Royal-Secret-in-America-Before-1801.pdf.

8. Brooke, *The Refiner's Fire*, 167.

9. Steven C. Bullock, *Revolutionary Brotherhood: Freemasonry and the Transformation of the American Social Order, 1730–1840* (Chapel Hill: University of North Carolina Press, 1996), 277–78.

10. Mark A. Tabbert, *American Freemasons: Three Centuries of Building Communities* (New York: New York University Press, 2006), 58.

11. Brooke, *The Refiner's Fire*, 168.

12. Jerald and Sandra Tanner, *The Mormon Kingdom*, vol. 1 (Salt Lake City, UT: Utah Lighthouse Ministry, 1969, 155).

13. Jon Butler, *Awash in a Sea of Faith: Christianizing the American People* (Cambridge, MA: Harvard University Press, 1990), 242.

14. See D. Michael Quinn, *Early Mormonism and the Magic World View* (Salt Lake City, UT: Signature Books, 1998), fig. 28A.

15. See the author's own *Stairway to Heaven*, New York: Continuum, 2008 for a full discussion of the significance of this asterism to western—and eastern—occult and mystical practices and concepts. The use of the Dipper here is consistent with the themes explored in that work.

16. We can add the Societas Rosicruciana In Anglia, the Societas Rosicruciana in America, the Ordos Temple Orients, the Golden Dawn, etc., all dating to the late nineteenth and early twentieth centuries.

Chapter nine

1. Albert Pike to Josh Campbell, September 13, 1875, reprinted in William H. Upton, *Negro Masonry* (Boston: The MW Prince Hall Grand Lodge of Massachusetts, 1902), 214–15.

2. "'Bonesmen' for President," interview with Skull and Bones researcher and author Alexandra Robbins, March 10, 2004, on MSNBC's *Countdown with Keith Olbermann*; from http://www.msnbc.msn.com/id/4500423.

3. I state this while acknowledging that the Freemasons have produced at least fourteen U.S. presidents and that—during the 1948 presidential election—all four candidates were Freemasons, thus prefiguring the 2004 election when both candidates were Bonesmen. However, the sheer number of Freemasons in the United States versus the tiny number of living Bonesmen indicates that Skull and Bones is influential out of all proportion to its—or the country's—numbers. Additionally, there is virtually no information available on Skull and Bones, while there is a great deal available on Freemasonry for anyone who wishes to look. On Skull and Bones, see Kris Millegan, ed., *Fleshing Out Skull and Bones* (Walterville, OR: Trine Day, 2003); and Antony C. Sutton, *America's Secret Establishment* (Walterville, OR: Trine Day, 2002. These books are useful primarily for their reproduction of important Skull and Bones documents, such as photographs, membership lists, and the like. There is no definitive history of the order available anywhere aside from these texts.

4. Peter Levenda, *Unholy Alliance: A History of Nazi Involvement with the Occult* (New York: Continuum, 2002), 147–51.

5. Ibid., 149.

6. The story is told in several places. Readers can consult Larry Gurwin, *The Calvi Affair* (London: Pan Books, 1984; and Levenda, *Unholy Alliance*, 306–8.

7. David Yallop, *In God's Name* (London: Corgi Books, 1996), 171–82.

8. Ibid.

9. Shalahuddin Abu Arafah and Abu Fatiah al-Adnani, *Musa Vs Fir'aun* (Solo, Indonesia: Granada Mediatama, 2007.

10. Peter Levenda, *Sinister Forces: A Grimoire of American Political Witchcraft*, vol. 3, *The Manson Secret.* (Walterville, OR: Trine Day, 2005).

11. "'Bonesmen' for President" (see note 2, above).

Conclusions

1. Manly P. Hall, *Lectures on Ancient Philosophy and Introduction to the Study and Application of Rational Procedure*, 397.

2. Albert Pike, *Morals and Dogma of the Ancient and Accepted Scottish Rite of Freemasonry* (Richmond, VA: L. H. Jenkins, 1947), 819; emphasis added.

Appendix

1. David Worrall, *Theatric Revolution: Drama, Censorship and Romantic Period Subcultures 1773–1832* (Oxford: Oxford University Press, 2006), 138.

Bibliography

A note on sources

Where possible, I have tried to use primary sources; however, there are not many when it comes to early—that is, pre-1717—Freemasonry, and even after 1717 many lodges kept poor records or the records were lost due to war, suppression, and the like. Primary sources would include the *Regius Manuscript* and the *Cooke Manuscript*, which are available in several versions but do not offer much in the way of understanding Masonry's modern forms. Many Masonic texts and rituals were published almost immediately after the creation of the London Grand Lodge in the eighteenth century by a variety of Masons and anti-Masons. In every case, during the composition of this study, a conscious effort was made to determine the provenance of these texts and the prejudice of the author(s).

Speculative histories, such as that by Michael Baigent, Richard Leigh, and Henry Lincoln, have not been relied upon for primary data; their value has largely been that of representing some of the more popular beliefs and conceptions concerning Masonry's origins. However, that said, I agree that much of the information contained in these histories is of value to the interested reader and contains a great deal of historical context that might otherwise have been overlooked. I do not necessarily subscribe to the conclusions presented in them, but in every case I have attempted to keep an open mind.

Web sites

A great source of ongoing Masonic research is to be found on a handful of Web sites representing Masonic lodges that specialize in such studies. The most useful to date have are listed herein.

Ars Quatuor Coronatorum, http://www.quatuorcoronati.com. This is the godfather of all Masonic research lodges and represents a wealth of documentation on Freemasonry by serious scholars and academics as well as informed laypersons. It is highly recommended.

The Grand Lodge of British Columbia and Yukon, http://freemasonry.bcy.ca. A useful resource that attempts to cover every aspect of Freemasonry—regular and irregular—and a good place to start for cameos of famous Masonic personalities. Copies of the *Regius Manuscript* and the *Cooke Manuscript* may also be accessed here.

The Library of Congress, http://memory.loc.gov. An excellent resource for online scans of the letters of George Washington, Thomas Jefferson, and many other founding fathers; heaven-sent for those who, only a few years ago, would have had to make the trip to Washington, D.C., to view the material directly.

Northern California Research Lodge, http://www.calodges.org/ncrl. A good resource on Latin American Freemasonry as well as some mystical aspects of the order.

The Royal Society, http://royalsociety.org.

Written sources

Abu Arafah, Shalahuddin, and Abu Fatiah al-Adnani. *Musa Vs Fir'aun*. Solo, Indonesia: Granada Mediatama, 2007.

Adams, Henry. *Mont-Saint-Michel and Chartres*. New York: Houghton Mifflin, 1933 [1912].

Allen, Paul M. *A Christian Rosenkreutz Anthology*. Blauvelt, NY: Rudolf Steiner Publications, 1968.

Arola, Raimon. *Simbolismo del Templo*. Barcelona: Ediciones Obelisco, 2001 [1965].

Bach, Jeff. *Voices of the Turtledoves: The Sacred World of Ephrata*. University Park: University of Pennsylvania Press, 2002.

Baigent, Michael, Richard Leigh and Henry Lincoln, *The Holy Blood and the Holy Grail*. London: Jonathan Cape, 1982.

Bailyn, Bernard. *The Ideological Origins of the American Revolution*. Cambridge, MA: Belknap Press of Harvard University Press, 1967.

Barber, Malcom. *The Cathars: Dualistic Heretics in Languedoc in the High Middle Ages*. Harlow, England: Longman, 2000.

———. *The New Knighthood: A History of the Order of the Temple*. Cambridge: Cambridge University Press, 2005 [1994].

Bogdan, Henrik. *Western Esotericism and Rituals of Initiation*. Albany: State University of New York Press, 2007.

Brooke, John L. *The Refiner's Fire: The Making of Mormon Cosmology, 1644–1844*. Cambridge: Cambridge University Press, 1994.

Bullock, Steven C. *Revolutionary Brotherhood: Freemasonry and the Transformation of the American Social Order, 1730–1840*. Chapel Hill: University of North Carolina Press, 1996.

Burman, Edward. *The Templars: Knights of God*. Rochester, VT: Destiny Books, 1986.

Butler, Jon. *Awash in a Sea of Faith*. Cambridge, MA: Harvard University Press, 1990.

Caro y Rodriguez, Francisco. *The Mystery of Freemasonry Unveiled*. Palmdale, CA: Christian Book Club of America, 2006 [1927].

Charpentier, Louis. *The Mysteries of Chartres Cathedral*. London: Research Into Lost Knowledge Organisation, 1972.

Churchill, Winston. "Zionism versus Bolshevism: A Struggle for the Soul of the Jewish People." *Illustrated Sunday Herald,* February 8, 1920.

Churton, Tobias. *The Magus of Freemasonry.* Rochester, VT: Inner Traditions, 2006.

Clegg, R. I. "How to Study Freemasonry." *The Builder,* July 1915.

Clerval, A. *Chartres: Its Cathedral and Monuments.* Chartres, France: Librairie Paul Renier, n.d.

Czmara, Jean-Claude. Sur *les traces des Templiers.* Association Hugues de Payns, n.d.

Daftary, Farhad. *The Assassin Legends: Myths of the Isma 'ilis.* London: I. B. Tauris, 1995.

Dedopulos, Tim. *The Brotherhood: Inside the Secret World of the Freemasons.* New York: Thunder's Mouth Press, 2004.

Duncan, Malcom. *Duncan's Masonic Ritual and Monitor.* New York: Dick and Fitzgerald, 1866.

Durkheim, Emile. *The Elementary Forms of Religious Life.* New York: Free Press, 1995.

Eliade, Mircea. *The Forge and the Crucible: The Origins and Structure of Alchemy.* Chicago: University of Chicago Press, 1978.

―――. *Shamanism: Archaic Techniques of Ecstacy.* London: Arkana, 1989 [1964].

Elior, Rachel. *The Three Temples: On the Emergence of Jewish Mysiticism.* Portland, OR: Littman Library of Jewish Civilization, 2005.

Finch, William. *Masonic Treatise.* Canterbury, England: n.p., 1802.

Frale, Barbara. "The Chinon Chart: Papal Absolution to the Last Templar, Jacques de Molay." *Journal of Medieval History* 30 (2004), 109–34.

Gardiner, Samuel Rawson. *The First Two Stuarts and the Puritan Revolution 1603–1660.* New York: Thomas Y. Crowell, 1970.

Godbeer, Richard. *The Devil's Dominion: Magic and Religion in Early New England.* New York: Cambridge University Press, 1994.

Godwin, Jocelyn. *The Theosophical Enlightenment.* Albany: State University of New York Press, 1994.

Godwin, Jocelyn, Christian Chanel, and John P. Deveny. *The Hermetic Brotherhood of Luxor.* York Beach, ME: Weiser, 1995.

Gould, Robert Freke. *History of Freemasonry.* Vol. 1. New York: n.p., 1884.

Gurwin, Larry. *The Calvi Affair: Death of a Banker.* London: Pan Books, 1993.

Hall, Manley P. *Lectures on Ancient Philosophy and Introduction to the Study and Application of Rational Procedure.* Los Angeles: Hall, 1929.

Heckethorn, Charles William. *The Secret Societies of All Ages and Countries.* London: George Redway, 1897.

Hodapp, Christopher. *Solomon's Builders: Freemasons, Founding Fathers and the Secrets of Washington D.C.* Berkeley, CA: Ulysses Press, 2007.

Howe, Ellic. *The Magicians of the Golden Dawn: A Documentary History of a Magical Order 1887–1923.* New York: Samuel Weiser, 1978.

James, John. *Chartres: The Masons Who Built a Legend.* London: Routledge and Kegan Paul, 1985.

Josephus. *Antiquities of the Jews.*

Knight, Stephen. *The Brotherhood: The Secret World of the Freemasons.* New York: Dorset Press, 1986.

Kuhn, Thomas. *The Structure of Scientific Revolutions.* Chicago: University of Chicago Press, 1962.

Landon, H. C. Robbins. *Mozart and the Masons: New Light on the Lodge "Crowned Hope".* London: Thames and Hudson, 1991.

Lawlor, Robert. *Sacred Geometry: Philosophy and Practice.* London: Thames and Hudson, 1982.

Leadbeater, C. W. *Freemasonry and Its Ancient Mystic Rites.* New York: Gramercy Books, 1998.

Levenda, Peter. *Sinister Forces: A Grimoire of American Political Witchcraft. Vol. 3, The Manson Secret.* Walterville, OR: Trine Day, 2005.

———. *Stairway to Heaven: Chinese Alchemists, Jewish Kabbalists, and the Art of Spiritual Transformation.* New York: Continuum, 2007.

———. *Unholy Alliance: A History of Nazi Involvement with the Occult.* New York: Continuum, 2002.

Lewis, Bernard. *The Assassins: A Radical Sect in Islam.* New York: Oxford University Press, 1967.

Lindsay, Jack. *The Origins of Alchemy in Graeco-Roman Egypt.* New York: Barnes and Noble, 1970.

Lomas, Robert. *Turning the Hiram Key: Rituals of Freemasonry Revealed.* Gloucester, MA: Fair Winds Press, 2005.

Lundquist, John M. *The Temple: Meeting Place of Heaven and Earth.* London: Thames and Hudson, 1993.

Mackey, Albert G. *An Encyclopedia of Freemasonry and its Kindred Sciences.* Philadelphia: Moss, 1879.

Mahon, Lord. *History of England.* Boston: Little, Brown, 1853.

McClenechan, Charles C. *Book of the Ancient and Accepted Scottish Rite of Freemasonry.* Reprint ed. Whitefish, MT: Kessinger, 2003 [1884].

Meyer, Marvin W., ed. *The Ancient Mysteries.* New York: HarperCollins, 1987.

Millegan, Kris, ed. *Fleshing Out Skull & Bones: Investigations into America's Most Powerful Secret Society.* Walterville, OR: Trine Day, 2003.

Miller, W. Watts. "Secularism and the Sacred: Is There Really Something Called 'Secular Religion'?" In *Reappraising Durkheim for the Study and Teaching of*

Religion Today. Edited by Thomas A. Idinopulos and Brian C. Wilson. Boston: Brill, 2002.

Morris, C. Brent. "The Royal Secret in America Before 1801" Retrieved June 30, 2008, from http://www.morningstarconsistory.com/PDF/The-Royal-Secret-in-America-Before-1801.pdf.

Naudon, Paul. *The Secret History of Freemasonry.* Rochester, VT: Inner Traditions, 2005.

Newton, Joseph Fort. *The Builders.* Cedar Rapids, IA: Torch Press, 1914.

Nicholson, Helen, and David Nicolle. *God's Warriors: Knights Templar, Saracens, and the Battle for Jerusalem.* New York: Osprey, 2005.

Oldenbourg, Zoe. *Massacre at Montsegur: A History of the Albigensian Crusade.* New York: Dorset Press, 1990.

Ovason, David. *The Secret Architecture of Our Nation's Capital.* New York: HarperCollins, 2002.

Owen, Thomas McAdory. *History of Alabama and Dictionary of Alabama Biography.* Vol. 1. Chicago: S. J. Clarke, 1921.

Painter, Sidney. *French Chivalry: Chivalric Ideals and Practices in Mediaeval France.* Ithaca, NY: Cornell University Press, 1965.

Paton, Graeme. "Intelligent People 'Less Likely to Believe in God.'" *Daily Telegraph* (London), June 12, 2008.

Pickthall, Muhammad Marmaduke. *The Meaning of the Glorious Qur'an.* Singapore: Omar Brothers, n.d.

Pike, Albert. *Morals and Dogma of the Ancient and Accepted Scottish Rite of Freemasonry.* Richmond, VA: L. H. Jenkins, 1947 [1871].

Poe, Edgar Allen, "A Cask of Amontillado." *Godey's Lady's Book*, 1846.

Prichard, Samuel. *Masonry Dissected.* London, n.p., 1730.

Quinn, D. Michael. *Early Mormonism and the Magic World View.* Salt Lake City, UT: Signature Books, 1998.

Ralls, Karen. *Knights Templar Encyclopedia.* Franklin Lakes, NJ: Career Press, 2007.

———. *The Templars and the Grail: Knights of the Quest.* Wheaton, IL: Quest Books, 2003.

Redford, Donald B., ed. *The Ancient Gods Speak: A Guide to Egyptian Religion.* New York: Oxford University Press, 2002.

Regardie, Israel. *The Golden Dawn.* St. Paul, MN: Llewellyn, 2005.

Robin, Jean. *Operacion Orth: El increible misterio de Rennes-le-Chateau.* Madrid: Heptada Ediciones, 1990.

Robinson, John J. *Born in Blood: The Lost Secrets of Freemasonry.* New York: M. Evans, 1989.

Sachse, Julius F. "Beginnings of American Freemasonry." *American Freemason,* June 1911.

————. *The German Pietists of Provincial Pennsylvania.* Philadelphia: privately published, 1895.

————. *The German Sectarians of Pennsylvania.* Vol. 1. Philadelphia: privately published, 1899.

Scholem, Gershom. *Sabbatai Sevi: The Mystical Messiah.* Bollingen Series 93. Princeton, NJ: Princeton University Press, 1973.

Schonfield, Hugh. The *Essene Odyssey: The Mystery of the True Teacher and Essene Impact on the Shaping of Human Destiny.* Dorset, England: Element, 1998 [1984].

Schulz, Regine, and Matthias Seidel, eds. *Egypt: The World of the Pharaohs.* Koenigswinter, Germany: H. F. Ullmann, 2007.

Schwaller de Lubicz, R. A. *Sacred Science: The King of Pharaonic Theocracy.* Rochester, VT: Inner Traditions, 1982.

————. *The Temple in Man.* Rochester, VT: Inner Traditions, 1977.

Sede, Gerard de. *El misterio de Rennes-le-Chateau.* Barcelona: Ediciones Martinez Roca, 1991.

Shelley, Mary Woolstonecroft. *Frankenstein, or, the Modern Prometheus.* New York: Bantam, 1981 [1818].

Simson, Otto von. *The Gothic Cathedral.* New York: Harper Torchbooks, 1964.

Stevenson, David. *The Origins of Freemasonry: Scotland's Century.* Cambridge: Cambridge University Press, 2000.

Stryz, Jan. "The Alchemy of the Voice at Ephrata Cloister," retrieved June 14, 2008, from http://www.esoteric.msu.edu/alchemy.html.

Sutton, Antony C. *America's Secret Establishment,* Walterville, OR: Trine Day, 2002 [1983].

Tabbert, Mark A. *American Freemasons: Three Centuries of Building Communities.* New York: New York University Press, 2006.

Tanner, Jerald, and Sandra Tanner. *The Mormon Kingdom.* Vol.1. Salt Lake City, UT: Utah Lighthouse Ministry, n.d.

Trowbridge, W. R. H. *Cagliostro.* London: Chapman and Hall, 1910.

Troyes, Chrétien de. *Erec et Enide.* Project Gutenberg. Retrieved October 30, 2008 from http://www.gutenberg.org/etext/831.

Turner, Sharon. *The History of England during the Middle Ages.* London: Longman, Brown, Green, and Longmans, 1853.

Upton, William H. *Negro Masonry.* Boston: MW Prince Hall Grand Lodge of Massachusetts, 1902.

Waite, A. E. "Master Building," *The Builder,* October 1915.

————. *The Real History of the Rosicrucians.* London: Redway, 1887.

————. ed. *The Works of Thomas Vaughan: Mystic and Alchemist.* New York: University Books, 1968.

Wallace-Murphy, Tim. *The Enigma of the Freemasons.* New York: Ivy Press, 2006.

Ward, J. S. M. *An Interpretation of Our Masonic Symbols.* Reprint ed. Whitefish, MT: Kessinger, 1993.

Wathen, James F., *Is The Order of St. John Masonic?* Rockford, IL: Tan Books, 1973.

Webb, Thomas C. *The Freemason's Monitor, or, Illustrations of Masonry.* Salem, MA: Cushing and Appleton, 1818.

Webb, William S., and Charles E. Snow. *The Adena People.* Knoxville: University of Tennessee Press, 1981.

Weisberger, R. William. "Parisian Masonry, the Lodge of Nine Sisters, and the French Enlightenment." *Heredom* 10 (2002): 155–202.

Welling, George von. *Opus Mago-Cabbalisticum et Theosophicum.* York Beach, ME: Weiser, 2006.

White, Michael. *Isaac Newton: The Last Sorcerer.* London: Fourth Estate, 1998.

Wilmshurst, W. L. *The Meaning of Masonry.* New York: Barnes and Noble, 1999 [1922].

Wilson, Robert Anton, and Robert Shea. *Illuminatus!* New York: Dell, 1975.

Worrall, David. *Theatric Revolution: Drama, Censorship and Romantic Period Subcultures 1773–1832.* Oxford: Oxford University Press, 2006.

Yallop, David. *In God's Name.* London: Corgi Books, 1996.

Yarker, John. *The Secret High Degree Rituals of the Masonic Rite of Memphis.* Whitefish, MT: Kessinger, n.d.

———. *The Secret Rituals of the Adoptive Rite of Freemasonry.* Whitefish, MT: Kessinger, n.d.

Yates, Frances A. *The Art of Memory.* Chicago: University of Chicago Press, 1966.

———. *The Occult Philosophy in the Elizabethan Age.* London: Routledge and Kegan Paul, 1979.

———. *The Rosicrucian Enlightenment.* London: Routledge and Kegan Paul, 1972.

Index